The Age of Unproductive Capital

The Age of Unproductive Capital:

New Architectures of Power

By

Ladislau Dowbor

Cambridge Scholars
Publishing

The Age of Unproductive Capital: New Architectures of Power

By Ladislau Dowbor

This book first published 2019

Cambridge Scholars Publishing

Lady Stephenson Library, Newcastle upon Tyne, NE6 2PA, UK

British Library Cataloguing in Publication Data
A catalogue record for this book is available from the British Library

ISBN (10): 1-5275-2129-X
ISBN (13): 978-1-5275-2129-2

Dedicated to ex-president Lula, who took millions out of poverty, and is paying for it in jail.

"Nowhere are these connections between finance, inequality and poverty more apparent than in the provision of banking services to the poor and to families in financial difficulties"

Roosevelt Institute, Epstein and Montecino, 2016

"Brazil has long had some of the highest interest rates in the world. There is a vast body of literature seeking to understand the reasons for such high interest rates."

World Bank, 2016, pg.67

"The national financial system will be structured in a way to promote the balanced development of the country and to serve the collective interest"

Article 192°, Constitution of the Federal Republic of Brazil

CONTENTS

PREFACE TO THE ENGLISH EDITION

Whatever happened to Brazil? How could a hugely successful administration, with results widely publicized throughout the world that include 20 million new jobs, 50 million taken out of poverty, removal from the FAO world hunger map, and impressive growth in both economic and social terms, have so suddenly been thrown into political and economic turmoil? A thinly disguised parliamentary coup, deep recession, and the whole process's emblematic personality, ex-president Lula, sent to jail on the basis of accusations which, according to the *New York Times*, would not have been received by any civilized judiciary system. This is a complete reversal of the period of democratic government between 2003–2013, which was termed "The Golden Decade of Brazil" by the World Bank.

Brazil is not only important for Brazilians. It is the 8th economic world power, it has 210 million inhabitants, and it has managed to raise hopes in so many other countries that share the common complaints of dramatic inequality, poverty, and subservient international relations. Infant mortality has been halved and life expectancy at birth has grown from 65 to 75 years, which has raised comments that Brazilians have 10 more years to complain about their government. A broad spectrum of international south-south relations has generated a new political climate of regained sovereignty and mutual respect, particularly within Latin America but also in Africa and other regions.

Yet the backlash was absolutely overwhelming, with the oligarchy and the upper middle-class denouncing that the pro-poor policy was unsustainable, that the government was financially broken, and that a gang of corrupt leftists had taken over politics and state enterprises. Banks, the huge Globo media group, the militant judiciary, Congress (elected by corporate money, legal at the time) and the upper middle class joined forces to bring down not only President Dilma, but also all the policies that had permitted the poor to have access to better living conditions. Their final victory was to jail Lula, in order to prevent him from participating in the national elections in October 2018. We no longer need generals to mess things up; judges are quite up to the job. As it turned out, an openly fascist ex-captain, Bolsonaro, in impressively skewed elections, with massive fake-news and financial support, was elected president for the next four years. Barbara Tuchman would call it The March of Folly.

Brazil is not an island. Similar crises are hitting a number of countries, it seems that democracy has no place in this new economic and financial set-up. Therefore, unveiling the Brazilian drama has led us to understand the new power architecture of global finance. We have adopted a long-standing rule: follow the money. This includes the banking system, the new ways finance can control both business and governments, and the emergence of unproductive capital. All this political theatre is not about corruption, of course. It is about power. This is not a book full of economic theory, with equations and mysterious "laws" as, instead, it is a down-to-earth, plain-language analysis of how things work. While my analysis centers on Brazil, its application extends well beyond these parameters.

INTRODUCTION

We all have our favorite crises. These are crises of values, pandemics, demography, economics, energy, financial speculation, education, cultural pasteurization, identities, the banalization of life, the misery that explodes in the world, and the shortage of water that already affects over one billion people. The issue is no longer choosing the crisis that seems most threatening. The real threat comes from an impressive convergence of critical trends and from the synergy of a range of behaviors that, although understandable, are deeply irresponsible, often criminal, and plague our small spacecraft.

The overall purpose here is not to be a wailing wall or to create an array of our misfortunes. Nowadays, human beings are not significantly better or worse than previous generations. The central issue is that the institutions that govern us and the ground rules of society can lead us to extremely positive dynamics—such as the social democracy phase between 1945 and 1975 in so-called developed countries—and it can throw us into absurd and destructive conflicts, irrespective of how much technology, knowledge, or wealth we have.

The chaos that progressively spreads in the world is directly tied to a set of institutions that no longer meet our requirements for productive and civilized living. A wide gap has been created between our technological advances, which have been, and continue to be, spectacular and our civilized conviviality that has become stagnant and may even be regressing. It is a systemic dysrhythmia; a mismatch in times. This challenge has been correctly conceptualized as a civilizing crisis.

Part of this civilization crisis is also centered on a mismatch in spaces. The economy has become globalized, with transnational corporations and financial giants operating on a world scale, while governments continue to be largely national and powerless in the face of prevailing economic flows. The political regulatory instruments remain fragmented in the 200 countries that constitute our real political planet. With the resulting disorganization, insecure populations seek solutions by migrating or supporting reactionary movements.

The world is clearly ripe for a planetary governance, in order to achieve a minimum of coherence between the spaces of economics and those of politics. The fragments of global governance that have emerged with the UN, the World Bank, the IMF, the WTO and similar, or *ad hoc* meetings, such as G8, G20 or BRICS, clearly signal the need to rethink spaces and to create a different system of governance.

Since politics is what it is, the most general tendency is to seek the culprits, be they right or left. The media that today penetrate almost every home on the planet will know how to manipulate the hatred that has been generated. To support prejudices yields more audience points than to clarify matters. This leads us to take problems personally, instead of understanding dynamics. A little bit of common sense suggests that we need a better understanding of both what has gone wrong and the ground rules of the game, which will allow us to make the planet work.

First of all, we need to use common sense to pay closer attention to poor judgment within politics. In general, politics has more to do with emotions, hopes, and fears than with rationality. Was Hitler a psychopath? It is much more important to understand how large economic groups supported him, how more than half of German doctors joined the Nazi party, and how the population finally voted and elected him. The election of Donald Trump worries me just as it worries Democrats all over the planet. More troubling than the person, is the fact that the United States—a wealthy nation with so many universities and a booming culture—elected him. People have been sensitive towards his arguments that were not arguments at all, but emotional expressions, insecurities, and hatreds with which they could identify.

Functioning governance is not built on hatred, it requires a rational overview of what might work and it is important to even consider irrationalities. Are we going to solve the drama of inequality and migration by building a wall? A fenced-in condominium called the USA? The truth is that the inherited system, so-called neoliberalism, no longer fits the modern world. The modern world needs to reinvent its ways.

This book articulates several aspects of the research that I have developed in the last years, herein expanded and grouped under a systemic overview. The common denominator or guiding axis for these separate strands is the quest for governance and for a decision-making process that works. Data from previous studies has been updated. Current research, studies, and discussions have been added. We will characterize the systemic challenges, delineate the new architecture of power on the stage of global capitalism, analyze the actions that brought about financialization, and finally present how this process has been manifested in the most recent Brazilian crisis.

First, a remark on the reliability of our analysis. Today in the economic field—which is so closely linked with politics and also deeply rooted in our emotions, family heritage, corporate hatred or whatever—scientific information is often rejected *en bloc* for the simple conviction that it is unfriendly information. This tribal treatment of scientific analysis allows that, for instance, in the United States, Democrats consider the climate issue as real while Republicans consider it an unsupported invention: why would Republicans be less scientific? How can science be filtered in such way by political emotions and by clan identifications? Indeed, it is so easy to consider something as rational and scientific when it endorses our prejudices. We are not naturally objective and I worry about this.

Two precautions: first, I have taken care in this work to point out, as strictly as possible, the primary sources of information. That is, I do not work with comments from a newspaper that favors my opinion, but with the primary source of the institution that has compiled the statistics and, therefore, has to answer to other research institutions. In addition, each piece of information is presented along with the link; this allows the reader to verify the accuracy of the mentioned data. Some time ago I organized a course entitled the *Primary Sources of Economic Information* at PUC-SP, in order to try to strengthen the ability of future economists to work with data rather than opinions. To think, as we all know, is laborious. Many would rather have an opinion.

Second, to the greatest extent possible, I seek objectivity. This is slippery because, like all of us, I tend to find something objective when it convinces me or reinforces my standpoint. Over the years, I have learned the importance of paying attention to data that is not in tune with my point of view and, clearly, this is something that needs to be checked. Perhaps the most brilliant reading in this area is Gunnar Myrdal's little book, *Objectivity in Social Research*. Old, but excellent. Basically, it shows that rather than wanting to present "just the facts", it is better to state right from the start the convictions and values, because this gives the reader a general view of the situation. This old book is easily available in our emergency library, *Estante Virtual*.

What are my convictions? The force that moves me is a deep indignation. Today, 800 million people are starving, which is not due to their own fault but because of a system of resource allocation over which they have no influence. The impotence of not being able to provide food for your child is a terrible feeling. Millions of children die every year; this is about five times the number of New York's Twin Tower victims every day. Such an evident injustice as well as the conceit of the wealthy who show off their success without seeing the misfortunes they reproduce, frankly, pisses me off. Therefore, my most powerful motivation is to understand the "why": the mechanisms and the alternatives. This is because simply being pissed off will not solve much.

It is relatively easy to point out the culprits and expect them to disappear. However, they will not disappear because the problem is not restricted to people and their lies, instead, in the system: in the form of social organization, in the decision-making process prevalent in society, and in the so-called governance. It is my conviction that the way forward is to build a more enlightened society, with governments and companies legally obliged to operate in a more transparent manner and with more decentralized management systems and participatory communities. In short, more democratic societies. For those who have read the previous books that I have written, such as A *Reprodução Social* (Social Reproduction) *The Broken Mosaic, Economic Democracy* or *O Pão Nosso de Cada Dia* (Our Daily Bread), my propositive standpoint will be obvious. Shouting and hate speech will be of little use, we have to think in an organized way about how decisions are taken in the current system and what alternatives are opening in this age of so much technology and so much misused wealth.

The last item of this introduction is concerned with my career. Working in my early twenties during the 1960s at "Jornal do Comércio" in Recife, I was overwhelmed by the level of wealth and opulence on the one hand, and misery and truculence on the other. There is no science, no religion, and no ethics to justify that. I decided to study economics as an endeavor to understand how barbarism and primitivism could be sustained and, at the same time, be presented as if it were natural. From then on, my problems began. I fought against the 1964–1985 military dictatorship because I believed—and I still believe—that fighting a dictatorship is not only legitimate, it is a duty. Exiled, I got my master's degree and my doctorate in socialist Poland, the land of my parents. There I realized the nonsense that was written about socialism. In a way, I stopped believing in the "isms" of any genre and started to look for what works.

I taught development economics and public finance at the University of Coimbra, then worked for seven years in various African countries within the United Nations: a professional link that also allowed me to understand economic and social situations in Asia and in several countries in Latin America. I now believe in "isms" even less and seek, more and more, to find what actually works: a sort of civilized pragmatism, with the conviction that if it only works for the elites it is not sufficient because certain things must be available for everyone.

Economic analysis is strongly tainted by ideologies, and whenever people are in trouble and need to refute arguments, the tendency is to refute the person instead. It is easier. Frankly, I could say that this is not my problem, but since I know that there will be no solution until the number of people who understand what is happening increases significantly, I stubbornly continue to organize and disseminate information as clearly as possible and as honestly as I can. Back in the 1990s, when the then-First Lady and anthropologist Ruth Cardoso asked me to help with the Solidarity Community, I helped for four years, for free. People of the left criticized me, saying that I was "sleeping with the enemy". Today, it is evident that the redistributive and inclusion policies of the Lula governments, which I strongly supported, make up an important pathway, albeit with structural limitations, which I present in the text below. People of the right criticized me, calling me "Petista" (a follower of Lula's Partido dos Trabalhadores), which is apparently easier than to face the arguments and reason over our real challenges.

I beg you to spare me, as I am only a Corinthian, which is not always easy. I am three-quarters of a century old, I have managed ministries of economics in several countries, I have been a consultant to the UN Secretary General, and I have written more than forty books. My problem is not to wave an ideological banner or to beat pans that only echo misinformation. I just do my homework: I read, study, teach, and write. Enjoy it.

1– THE DIMENSION OF CHALLENGES

In this first subject, I want to outline the articulation of the three dynamics that structurally unbalance the development and quality of life in the world. Simply stated, we are destroying the planet for the benefit of a minority while the resources necessary for sustainable and balanced development are sterilized by the global financial system.

The environmental dynamics

Our small planet is clearly suffering from a viral attack called *homo sapiens*. Sometimes from the window of the plane, looking down from the top at the urban clusters that multiply on the surface of the earth, gray over green, I have the impression of a disease spreading like spots that may appear on our skin. The vast deforested areas and the numerous columns of smoke that rise in the distance as a result of forest fires only heighten this impression. In fact, the least we can say is that we are not taking good care of our home.

The chart below presents a summary of megatrends, in the historical period from 1750 to date. The scales have been made compatible and some of the lines represent processes for which we have only more recent figures; however, overall the chart allows us to join areas traditionally studied separately: such as demography, climate, car production, paper consumption, water contamination, extinction of sea life, and others. The synergy of the process is obvious, as well as the dimension of the environmental challenges.[1]

---

[1] *New Scientist*, October 18, 2008, p. 40: to access the chart online see http://dowbor.org/ar/ns.doc; the whole file may be consulted in www.newscientist.com/opinion; the support graphs and primary sources can be seen in http://dowbor.org/ar/08_ns_overconsumption.pdf; Tim Jackson, David Suzuki, Jo Marchant, Herman Daly, Gus Speth, Liz Else, Andrew Simms, Suzan George, and Kate Soper contributed to the graph.

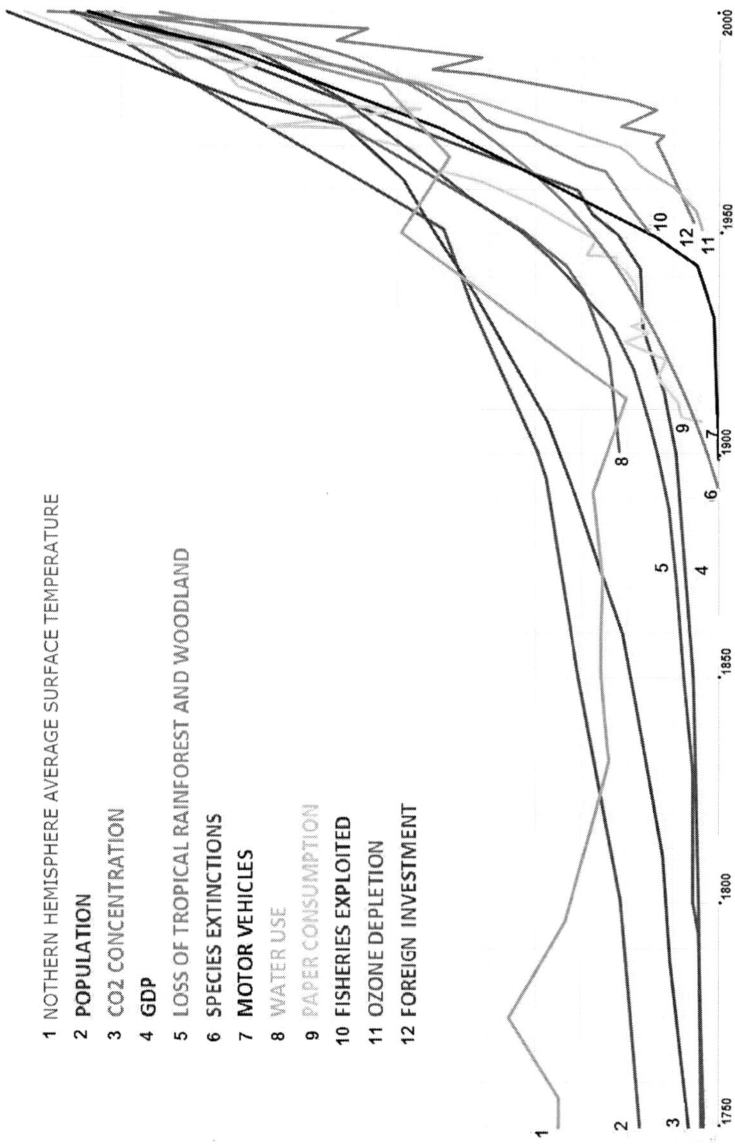

Source: *New Scientist* (October 18, 2008 p. 40).

It does not matter that the graph is from 2008, since these are megatrends that cover the period from 1750 to the present, which equals two and a half centuries in the broad overview of the Anthropocene. It is important to note the dramatically rising curve after 1850, which worsens in the most recent period. The population curve (2) in the above graph is sufficiently explicit. I understand it by thinking of my father. When he was born in 1900, there were 1.5 billion people on the planet and today, in 2018, there are 7.5 billion. I am talking about my father, not prehistory. The population grows at a lower rate, but on a much larger basis: we increase by 80 million each year. Everyone wants to consume more, all corporations want to extract and sell more, and increasingly powerful technologies allow this process to expand. Or course, from a systemic and long-term outlook this does not make sense.

The *New Scientist*'s comment on these megatrends focuses directly on our own concept of economic growth and it is ironic that the chart was presented in the midst of the financial crisis of 2008:

> The science tells us that if we are serious about saving Earth, we must reshape our economy. This, of course, is economic heresy. Growth to most economists is as essential as the air we breathe: it is, they claim, the only force capable of lifting the poor out of poverty, feeding the world's growing population, meeting the costs of rising public spending and stimulating technological development—not to mention funding increasingly expensive lifestyles. They see no limits to that growth, ever. In recent weeks it has become clear just how terrified governments are of anything that threatens growth, as they pour billions worth of public money into a failing financial system. Amid the confusion, any challenge to the growth dogma needs to be looked at very carefully. This one is built on a long-standing question: how do we square Earth's finite resources with the fact that as the economy grows, the amount of natural resources needed to sustain that activity must grow too? It has taken all of human history for the economy to reach its current size. On current form it will take just two decades to double.[2]

The convergence of tensions generated over the planet became evident. We can no longer rejoice over the increase in fishing when we are extinguishing sea life, or the increase in agricultural production when we are extinguishing the aquifers and contaminating the planetary freshwater reserves. This is not to mention the increase in car production and the expansion of other productive chains that also cause climate warming. It is

[2] *New Scientist*, October 18, 2008, p. 40

quite impressive that in 2016 WWF noted that between 1970 and 2010, in just forty years, we have destroyed 52% of the planet's fauna.

Even more striking is the climatic effect of greenhouse gases, which was proven in 1859, while the first broad discussion of this threat occurred in Stockholm in 1972. It took us 20 more years to present a first climate convention in 1992 in Rio de Janeiro. Finally, the Paris Conference in 2015 decided that now we are really going to act. Well, we would have to to convince the new president of the USA. Interestingly, recent research shows that Americans' convictions about climate change do not depend on their level of scientific knowledge, but rather on the party to which they belong. Apparently, the feeling of belonging to "our club" or "our tribe" is more important than research and scientific evidence. The truth is that systemic and long-term threats, even if scientifically proven, have little room in our awareness or daily struggles. Even though they are clearly critical threats.

Today we have strikingly accurate statistics involving ocean overfishing, the destruction of forests, the contamination and overexploitation of water resources, and similar aspects in the most diverse sectors of activity. Solutions must be systemic. A broader awareness might—just might—enable deeper changes by disseminating an understanding of the challenges. Considering the existing awareness and the perplexity brought about by abounding irrationalities, the obvious question arises: What development do we want? And in order to ensure this development, what State and regulatory mechanisms are needed? There is no way to minimize the scale of the challenges. Our planet shows all of its fragility and our irresponsibility, or helplessness. We are all looking for political bases to support governance on the planet, in nations, and even in cities where the majority of the world's population lives today. The decision-making process has to change, and governance needs to become much more competent and drastically reoriented towards sustainability.

The growing inequality

We are not only violating the planet at an environmental level. On the social front, according to the World Bank, poverty has declined by about 1 billion people in recent decades, which is a breakthrough, even though the $1.90 per day criterion is absurdly low. Of this 1 billion, 700 million are

Chinese.[3] It is an improvement, indeed. In general, however, the truth is that we are failing to meet the challenge of balanced and inclusive development and much less the challenge of inequality. The World Economic Forum itself points out in 2017 that "Over the past several years, a worldwide consensus has emerged on the need for a more socially-inclusive approach to generating economic growth. However, inclusive growth and development remain primarily an aspiration. No systemic framework has emerged to guide policy and practice." (WEF, 2017, p. v) Here, in addition to the obvious realization that we are experiencing growth that propagates exclusion, is the acknowledgement that we lack governance for inclusive growth.

There is no objective reason for the social dramas borne by the world. If we round the world GDP to 80 trillion dollars, we reach an average per capita product of 11 thousand dollars. This represents $3,600 per month per family of four: about R$ 11,000 per month. This is also the case in Brazil, which is exactly on the world average in terms of income. There is no objective reason for the gigantic misery in which billions of people live, other than the fact that "No systemic framework has emerged to guide policy and practice"; the system is mismanaged, or rather poorly governed, and there are no prospects on the horizon.

As a matter of fact, inequality has reached obscene levels. When 8 people own more wealth than half of the world's population, while 850 million people go hungry (a figure that is rising again), to believe that the system works signals, frankly, advanced mental blindness. Did those eight fortune-owners produce all that? Or have they simply set up a system of wealth appropriation through papers? And how is that possible? They own financial papers which produce little product, but much rent.

The fog surrounding the most recent financial mechanisms of growing inequality has been dissipating in recent decades. From the 1980s on, capitalism enters the stage of domination by the financial intermediaries over the productive processes—"the tail is wagging the dog" as the American saying goes—and this deepens inequality. However, it was only after the crisis of 2008, with the impact of panic, that research on both the new mechanisms of speculative gains and the creation of inequality was undertaken on a new and global scale.

---

[3] "For four decades, China, while increasingly integrating its economy with the global economy, grew at double-digit rates and lifted more than 700 million people out of poverty. This successful track record of economic growth is well known." The World Bank, *World Development Report 2017*, p. 2 e 3

An extensive World Bank study, *Voices of the Poor*, was a major contribution that basically showed that poor people remain poor and only those who have been wellborn become wealthy. It is the so-called poverty trap, which has also been called structural poverty: put simply, real poverty blocks opportunities to break free from it. How does a child study in a house where there is no electricity? How do you store medicines or food? With Amartya Sen we came to understand poverty as the lack of freedom to choose the life that one wants to live; it is, essentially, a lack of options. ECLAC's excellent, *La Hora de la Igualdad*, has shown that Latin America and the Caribbean have reached a degree of inequality that demands a focus on development strategies to resolve this issue.

The setback in the United States is particularly worrying and unquestionably explains recent political transformations. A short and exceptionally good text provides some shocking statistics:

> Our data shows that the bottom half of the income distribution in the United States has been completely shut off from economic growth since the 1970s. From 1980 to 2014, the average national income per adult grew by 61 percent in the United States, yet the average pre-tax income of the bottom 50 percent of individual income earners stagnated at about $16,000 per adult after adjusting for inflation. In contrast, income skyrocketed at the top of the income distribution, rising 121 percent for the top 10 percent, 205 percent for the top 1 percent, and 636 percent for the top 0.001 percent.

Particularly important, research shows that the increase in wealth at the top is primarily due to income from financial allocation and unproductive capital. The political implications do not escape the authors: "An economy that fails to deliver growth for half of its people for an entire generation is bound to generate discontent with the *status quo* and a rejection of establishment politics."[4]

---

[4] Thomas Piketty, Emmanuel Saez and Gabriel Zucman – *Economic Growth in the United States: a Tale of two Countries* - December 6, 2016 – Washington Center for Economic Growth (3p)
http://equitablegrowth.org/research-analysis/economic-growth-in-the-united-states-a-tale-of-two-countries/

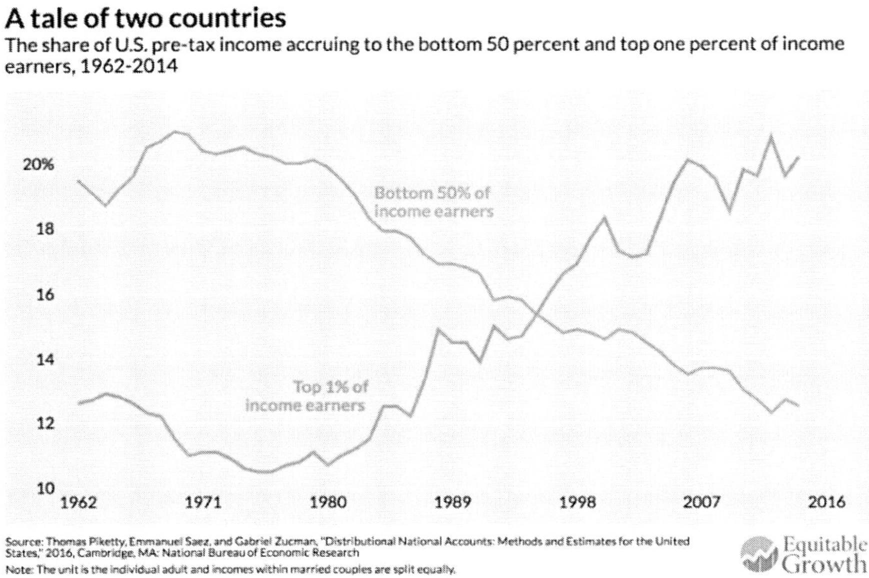

Source: http://equitablegrowth.org/research-analysis/economic-growth-in-the-united-states-a-tale-of-two-countries/. After the 1980s, there was a radical inversion of the appropriation of the 50% who earn less and the 1% who earn more.

The concentration of income is absolutely scandalous and compels us to see not only the ethical problem, the injustice, and the dramas of billions of people, but also the economic problem. Indeed, we are excluding people who could not only be living better, but also contributing more substantially to the productive capacity, thereby boosting economic demand and production. There will be no tranquility on the planet while the economy is only organized for 1/3 of the world's population. How much longer will we blame the poor themselves for their poverty and alleged lack of effort or initiative, which indirectly suggests that the wealth of the rich results from their dedication and merit? Inequality is the result of an institutionalized system whose structural dynamics must be reversed. The rich, on the other hand, have an impressive propensity to think that they are rich because of their own exceptional qualities. There is no shortage of economic discourse to reinforce this thinking.

Today, studies allow us to understand inequality in a much more systemic way. On income inequality—the money that goes into our pocket for private expenses—we have all the information we want; we even know that Brazil is among the 10 most unequal countries on the planet. However, families also depend on accumulated assets, such as home and household goods, which we qualify as wealth or assets. Equally important are the indirect wages constituted by access to public policies such as health, education, security, as well as infrastructure, such as paved streets and street lighting. A Canadian may have a lower salary than an American, but he has universal free access to public goods and services that more than make up for the difference. Finally, families depend on access to common goods such as open beaches, clean air, uncontaminated rivers, and so on. The balance of these various welfare factors is essential to engender governance that makes sense and ensures a decent life.[5]

Inequality in terms of wealth or assets has been widely publicized, especially after the 2008 crisis. It is the net household wealth that shows a radically greater inequality than access to income. The logic is simple: those who receive medium or low salaries pay for food and transportation and those who have high incomes buy houses for rent, stocks, and other financial papers that yield rent, which all leads to a process of wealth accumulation. This is further enhanced when wealth is passed from father to son creating castes of the wealthy. A simple example helps us to understand the cumulative enrichment process: a billionaire who invests 1 billion dollars to make a modest 5% a year is increasing his wealth by $137,000 a day. One cannot spend this amount of earnings in consumption. Re-invested, the 137,000 will further enhance the wealth, generating the so-called *snowball effect* of riches to the rich. The permanent flow of rights over the production of third parties is received without even taking your hands out of your pockets.[6]

---

[5] A clear example is the case of vital access to electric power. The International Energy Agency informs us that in 2016 1.2 billion people had no access to electricity, while 2.7 billion still cooked with biomass and suffer "continued exposure to the smoky indoor environments that are currently linked to 3.5 million premature deaths each year". World Energy Report 2016, IEA 2016 (summary), p.2
http://www.iea.org/publications/freepublications/publication/WorldEnergyOutlook2016ExecutiveSummaryEnglish.pdf

[6] The lack of correspondence between the productive effort and remuneration is at the center of concern in the *UN Report on Human Development 2015*, which states that "without proper policies, work's unequal opportunities and rewards can be divisive, perpetuating inequities in society." The expression "can be divisive" is part of the moderate way the UN presents critical issues.

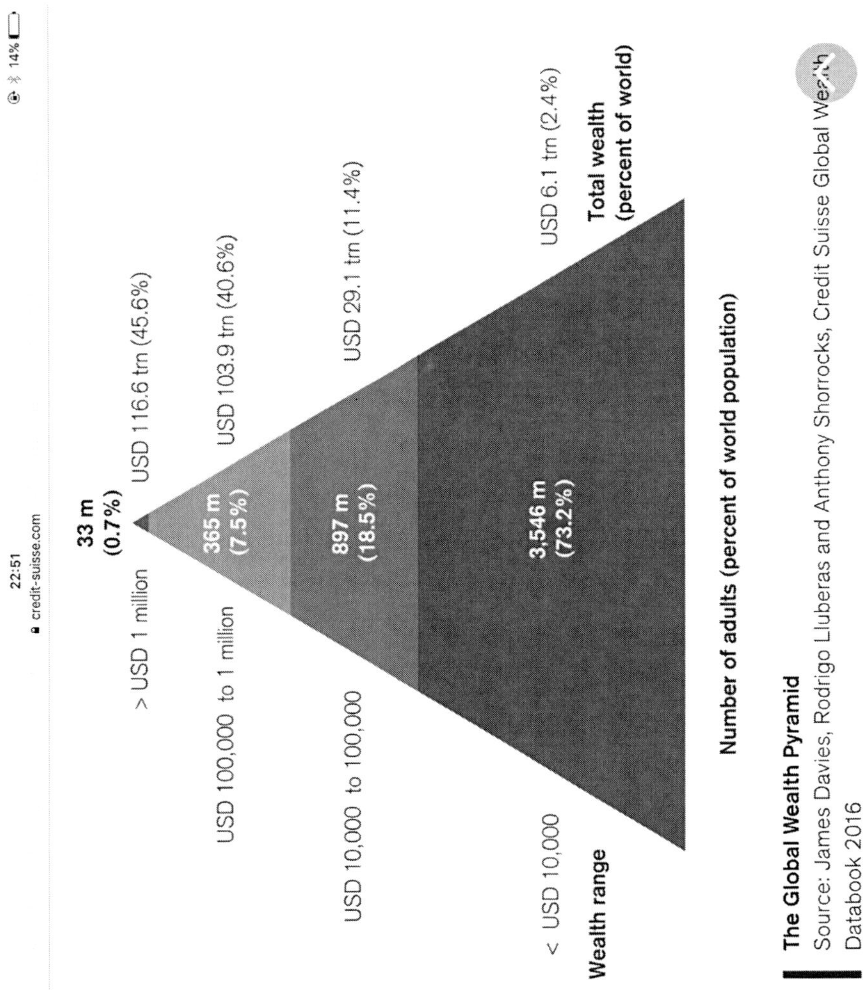

Income inequality has traditionally been measured by means of the Gini coefficient. The higher it is, the greater the inequality. In order of magnitude, the coefficient of income inequality is in the range of 0.25 in Sweden, 0.45 in the USA, 0.50 in Brazil, and is close to 0.60 in South Africa, which was, until recently, subject to apartheid. However, the inequality of wealth is becoming incomparably greater and has reached the absurd level of 0.80: a frightening inequality. The data below is part of a survey by the Swiss financial group *Crédit Suisse*, an institution above any suspicion of antipathy towards the rich.

Reading the pyramid is simple. At the top, adults who have more than one million dollars equals 33 million people, which is equivalent to 0.7% of total adults on the planet. The sum of their available wealth is $116.6 trillion, representing 45.6 percent of the assessed wealth of $256 trillion. One must remember that the great fortunes in this part of the pyramid are not owned by real producers, but are dominated by people who deal with stock, information flows, or commodity intermediation. The top of the pyramid is particularly interesting and consists of so-called ultra-high net worth individuals. If we expand the wealthiest 0.7% to 1%, we find that this 1% has more wealth than the remaining 99% of the planet. Note that a significant part of this great fortune does not appear because it is in tax havens, as detailed by James Henry from the Tax Justice Network.

Oxfam summarizes this worsening inherited situation:

> Despite world leaders signing up to a global goal to reduce inequality, the gap between the rich and the rest has widened. This cannot continue. As President Obama told the UN General Assembly in his departing speech in September 2016, "a world where 1% of humanity controls as much wealth as the bottom 99% will never be stable". Nevertheless, the crisis of global inequality remains unabated:
>
> - Since 2015, the richest 1% has had more wealth than the rest of the planet.
> - Currently, eight individuals hold the same wealth as the poorest half of the world.
> - Over the next 20 years, 500 people will pass on more than $2.1 trillion to their heirs: a sum higher than the GDP of India, which has a population of 1.2 billion.
> - Income of the poorest 10% increased by about $65 between 1988 and 2011, while that of the richest 1% increased by about $11,800, or 182 times more. (Oxfam, 2016, p. 2)

The concentration of income and wealth on the planet is reaching absolutely obscene levels.[7] The financialization of economic processes has

[7] There is already an endless amount of literature providing warnings about this subject. An excellent analysis of the increasing severity of these figures can be found in the *Report on the World Social Situation 2005: The Inequality Predicament,* United Nations, New York 2005. The document from the World Bank, *The Next 4 Billion*, evaluates the 4 billion people who "do not have access to the benefits of globalization" and is equally interesting (IFC). *The Next 4 Billion*, Washington, 2007 reveals that we are talking about two thirds of the world

been feeding for decades on the appropriation of productivity gains, which has been essentially enabled by the technological revolution in a radically unbalanced way. This mechanism is described in a particularly authoritative way by Gar Alperovitz and Lew Daly in their little book, *Unjust deserts: How the Rich Are Taking Our Common Inheritance.* The authors point out that if it were not for the technologies developed during and after World War II, such as the computer, the transistor, and other innovations, Bill Gates would still be playing with cathode ray tubes in his garage. Technological advances are planetary and belong to society at large, but appropriation is concentrated. The authors have developed the concept of "unearned income".[8]

This concentration is not only due to financial speculation, but its contribution is dominant, and it is absurd to divert capital from the obvious planetary priorities. Trying to understand the dimensions of the 2008 crisis, *The Economist* carries an impressive figure with regard to social surplus that has essentially been brought about by technological advances in the production area, but which benefits financial services: "The financial-services industry is condemned to suffer a horrible contraction. In America the industry's share of total corporate profits climbed from 10% in the early 1980s to 40% at its peak in 2007".[9] Calling financial services an industry is obviously self-serving.

There is a clear cleavage between those who bring technological innovations and produce socially useful goods and services—the process engineers, so to speak—and the financial intermediaries who appropriate the surplus and presently have a dominant say over the system. The engineers make important technological breakthroughs, but the use and commercialization of this technology belong to the finance, marketing, and legal affairs departments that dominate business, and then it benefits the shareholders and financial groups that are in control. It is a system that has generated a profound gap between who contributes productively to society and who is paid.

---

population. Since the onset of the financial crisis in 2008, figures have deteriorated even further and now strongly affect even the so-called developed countries, including the United States, thereby causing a widespread feeling of frustration.

[8] Gar Alperovitz and Lew Daly, *Unjust deserts: How the Rich Are Taking Our Common Inheritance* (The New Press, New York, 2008).

[9] *The Economist, A Special Report on the Future of Finance*, January 24th 2009, p. 20

Putting together the two graphs—the one from the *New Scientist*, on the environmental historical megatrends, and the pyramid from the Oxfam report—we come to a pretty obvious conclusion: we are destroying the planet for the benefit of at most 1/3 of the world's population and, in a very particular way, for the benefit of 1%. This basic data guides our future actions: to reverse the march of planet destruction and reverse the cumulative process of generating inequality. In order to achieve this, we must reorient the allocation of financial resources.

The truth is that we do not even measure the quality of resource allocation. Our main measure of progress, GDP, neither measures the environmental disaster nor the social drama. It does not account for *what* is produced, who receives the product, or the decrease of the planet's natural assets but, instead, accounts for the pollution that requires large programs of recovery as growth. In fact, GDP only provides the national average for how intensively the production machine is being used. [10]

A system in which the motivation axis is limited to profit without having to deal with environmental and social impacts remains locked in its own logic. It has everything to gain from the maximum extraction of natural resources and externalization of costs, and nothing to gain by producing for those who have little purchasing power. Short-term profit motivation works both against sustainability and against inclusive development. The deformation is systemic. It is the very concept of corporate governance that must be rethought. The ground rules need to change. The belief that if each one pursues individual advantages then the outcome will be the best possible is no longer acceptable. Adam Smith is a little dated here. The need to rescue the system's governance is unavoidable and the time we have to do it keeps getting shorter.

---

[10] See especially the report by Amartya Sen, Joseph Stiglitz, and Jean Paul Fitoussi, *Report by the Commission on the Measurement of Economic Performance and Social Progress*, available in www.stiglitz-sen-fitoussi.fr.. The environmental disaster created by British Petroleum in the Gulf of Mexico increased the USA's GDP by the volume of activities required to clear the coast and decontaminate a large region. The GDP measures the intensity of resources used, not the usefulness of what is done. See my technical note on this deformed accounting in http://dowbor.org/2009/04/o-debate-sobre-o-pib-estamos-fazendo-a-conta-errada-abr-2.html/.

Sterilization of financial resources

The bottom line is that the cause of the current difficulties is not a lack of financial resources but their appropriation by financial corporations that use them to speculate rather than invest. The financial system presently drains the productive system instead of stimulating it.

The 2008 crisis was a planetary shock. In 2018 we are still suffering from its impact because the essential dynamics that generated it are still present. It could undoubtedly have been a great opportunity to re-regulate the financial system and return economic usefulness to financial resources. The general regulatory framework that has structured finance since the 1929 crisis (the Glass-Steagall Act) was diluted by Reagan and Thatcher in the 1980s, and the finishing touch was its liquidation by Clinton in 1999. Attempts to organize a regulatory system from 2008 on by means of the Dodd-Frank Act simply did not work and the little achieved was lost. The main economic force of the so-called market runs without control.

The crisis was faced, not by decreasing the huge gaps through which resources leak out, but by transferring gigantic sums of public resources to compensate for the leaks. This appropriation of public resources by financial groups was given the friendly name of Quantitative Easing: "easing" here suggesting the feeling of those who loosen their belts with satisfaction after a hefty meal. We can speculate again and say that "the happy days are back", thereby repeating Wall Street and other similar centers' attitude toward this new phase.

As such problems remain unchanged, the gigantic mollusk that was based on fraud and the misappropriation of resources carries on uncontrolled, with the increased disadvantage of having grown to the extent that it can now dictate its own rules. With the election of Donald Trump in the United States, we can now see the dissolution of the final bit of regulation that the Obama administration had tried to implement. However, the academic community, research centers, and even governments decided that it was time to find out something about how the financial system actually works.

We have already seen from the *Crédit Suisse* data that the richest 1% possess more resources than the remaining 99% of the planet. The dimension of these fortunes does not allow them to be transformed into demand, notwithstanding the endless luxury consumption, because, instead, these fortunes are reinvested in other financial products. The truth is that financial allocations yield more than productive investment. The world GDP has grown between 1% and 2.5% over the years. Financial allocations earn 7% to 9% and often much more. Thus, a dynamic of transformation of productive capital into financial assets was generated and the real economy was swallowed by planetary financialization.[11]

We will later address details of this transformation, which are essential to understanding the political and economic planetary woes as well as the crisis in Brazil. However, for the time being we are interested in knowing that such resources exist, but that their productivity is sterilized by a generalized system of speculation which drains the real economy. Equally important is that public resources, our taxes, are also fueling this machine today through public debt.

The order of magnitude is impressive. For comparative purposes, let us remember that the huge global effort to tackle climate change, outlined in the Paris Agreement in 2015, set the ambitious goal of raising $100 billion annually to finance sustainability initiatives in the developing world. Such a sum of resources seems important. However, surveys of the Tax Justice Network and other groups since the 2008 crisis have shown that we have between 21 and $32 trillion in undeclared resources placed in tax havens; these are resources that, in addition to not being invested, do not even pay due taxes. *The Economist* rounds this up to 20 trillion and the figures may vary slightly. The fact is that what runs in the speculative paralegal world of the havens represents 200 times more than the ambitious goal of the Paris world summit. And, if we compare the stock of resources in tax havens with the world GDP of about $80 trillion, we are bound to see the mismatch between the means and the ends.

Sustainable Development Goals (SDGs) approved in New York in 2015, are certainly a breakthrough and we have today, with 17 goals, milestones to guide our steps up to 2030. But goals 16 and 17, which deal with the means to attain a minimum of sustainability, represent only dreams and the wishful thinking that so well characterizes desire without teeth.

Less well-known than the SDG is the action plan entitled Addis Ababa 2015 Action Agenda. Legally, this is an integral part of the SDG agreement, but has, however, focused specifically on how to finance sustainable development. With due caution in the expressions used, the

[11] For more details see the excellent *How Money Works: the facts visually explained,* published in 2017 by Penguin Random House. Senior editor Kathryn Hennessy.

conference noted that "Regulatory gaps and misaligned incentives continue to pose risks to financial stability, including risks of spillover effects of financial crises to developing countries, which suggests a need to pursue further reforms of the international financial and monetary system."[12] Translated, it means that international financial chaos does not allow resources to be "aligned", and that solutions require financial and monetary system reforms. At this stage, we are not going forward but backwards.

In its report on the world economic situation and outlook for 2017, the UN notes that "international capital remains volatile, and net flows to developing countries are expected to remain negative for at least 2017, underscoring the challenges of financing sustainable development in the long term" (p. viii). "Negative net flows" mean that the poor are financing the rich: i.e., the financial system drains. When our wallet is stolen, it usually qualifies as a negative net flow. The language of the UN is unrivalled.[13]

More importantly, it is a system that does not even reinvest productively the resources it drains: "In addition, productive investment in many developing countries has slowed in recent years, with much of the accumulated debt channeled into financial sector and real estate assets (see discussion in box III.1), escalating risks of assets bubbles, rather than boosting overall productivity" (p. 33). The same analysis is presented for corporate debt, which "has not been used to finance productive activities, but has instead been channeled mostly into very few sectors with an, at best, ambiguous impact on long-term productivity and transformational investment" (p. 89). Such an assessment of the main UN economic report helps to justify the focus of the present study: the financial system not only does not finance production but also drains its capacity. What we want to assert here is that it is not a lack of resources that plagues the world but their uncontrolled use or, arguably, the fact that they are only controlled by those who have no interest in making them socially and economically useful.

***

We have outlined the kind of Bermuda triangle formed by environmental drama, social tragedy, and financial chaos. Our dilemmas are not

---

[12].https://sustainabledevelopment.un.org/frameworks/addisababaactionagenda (105)
[13] UN – *World Economic Situation and Prospects 2017* – New York, 2017 http://www.un.org/en/development/desa/policy/wesp/

mysterious. We are managing the planet for a minority, through a production and consumption model that is destroying our natural resources and transforming the inequality/environment binomial into a slow-motion catastrophe. Meanwhile, the resources to finance the necessary policies are spinning within the circles of financial intermediaries, in the hands of a few hundred groups that cannot even manage the great amount of money they control with a minimum of competence.

The challenge is to redirect resources to finance social policies aimed at bringing about an inclusive economy and to also aid the reconversion of production and consumption processes that would revert environmental destruction. Obviously, we would have to convince the 1% that control this financial universe directly through banks and other institutions and, more and more, indirectly through the appropriation of political processes and legislation. People do not understand what a billionaire is. That challenge is not part of our daily lives and the volume of their financial earnings is such that only a small part of it results in consumption, even of luxury goods. Most of the earnings are reinvested and the fortune turns into a snowball, generating the super-rich, who literally do not know what to do with their money. Obviously, there is no shortage of advisors, accountants, and counseling institutions to help them: such as, for example, *Crédit Suisse*.

An important mechanism results from the difference between the economic behavior of the rich and the poor, as well as the ones who are just getting by. Actually, those who earn little purchase clothes for their children, pay rent, and spend a large part of their income on food and transportation. Those who earn little do not buy beautiful houses, farms, yachts, or high-yield financial papers. The poor spend; the rich accumulate. The poor's spending generates demand and stronger economic dynamics, while the accumulation of financial papers only drains demand and productive investment capacity. In short, without redistributive processes, environmental, social and economic dramas become worse. It is not just a matter of justice and moral decency; it is common sense that will benefit the system.

The main challenge is to generate a new governance that allows society's resources to be productive again: for our savings to generate cheap credit that favors the consumption of families and the expansion of demand, for medium and long-term credit to favor business investments, and for resources allocated to public debt service to be invested in infrastructure and social policies. We need financial resources to be productive again.

The analysis that lies ahead is centered on the governance of the system. Whatever the "ism" that attracts us, a system that remunerates the economic agents in a profoundly disproportionate way in relation to their productive contribution is dysfunctional: we are rewarding unproductive capital, and making life more difficult for those who make a productive contribution. The reward system is twisted. We are facing a new power architecture and we must understand how it works.

2 - THE GLOBAL CORPORATE CONTROL NETWORK

For decades, we have been following the news about large companies buying one another, in order to form larger and larger groups, so that they can become more competitive in an increasingly aggressive market environment. But, of course, this process has limits. In general, in the main productive chains, the race ends when there are few companies that, instead of fighting, discover that it is more convenient to articulate and work together for their own and their shareholders' benefit. Not necessarily, of course, for the wellbeing of society.

Controlling a productive chain in a structured and hierarchical way naturally generates a great economic, political, and cultural power. Through the huge flow of resources, it has an economic power greater than the GDP of many countries. Its political power is through the appropriation of much of the State apparatus. Its cultural power is due to the culture of consumption and behavioral dynamics created by the global mass media through very heavy advertising campaigns, which generates many of the problems our world faces.

A basic feature of corporate power is how little is known about it. The United Nations had a department, the United Nations Center for Transnational Corporations (UNCTC), which published excellent reports on transnational corporations in the 1990s. In 1995, with the advent of the World Trade Organization (WTO), they simply closed the UNCTC down and discontinued the publications. Therefore, what is probably the planet's main organized power nucleus—corporate power—is no longer studied, except by specific research dispersed in academic institutions and fragmented in many countries or sectors.

The most publicized document on corporations is the excellent documentary *The Corporation*. A first-rate scientific study that, in two hours and twelve chapters, shows how corporations operate, how they are organized, and what impacts they generate. Another excellent documentary, *Inside Job*, which received an Oscar in 2011, shows how the financial segment of corporate power works, but focuses, instead, on the generation of the financial crisis. We also have the 2012 British documentary on the banking system, *The Four Horsemen*, which has excellent interviews on and analysis of financial power. There are also films such as *The Capital* (*Le Capital*), where only the characters are fictional, because often resorting to fiction is the only way to approach reality. Works of this type allow us to understand the logic of the system, bringing about the basis of available knowledge. However, we are badly lacking systematic research into and the publication of empirical data on how corporations function, how decisions are made, who takes them, and with what legitimacy. The fact is that we know very little about corporations, which serve as the main vectors of world power.

It is natural and healthy that we take great care to not invent diabolic conspiracies and malicious machinations. However, in all the main sectors the activities are concentrated at the top of the pyramid, this means that with the fact that we have only a few extremely powerful companies, we begin to understand that it is a matter of power in the broad sense. Acting in a planetary space, in the absence of world government, and faced with the fragility of the multilateral political system, corporations wield great power without any significant counterweight.

Research using concrete data by the ETH (Swiss Federal Institute for Technological Research), in 2011, was the first to bring light to the global system on this scale. It is worth presenting it in some detail. The title of the survey is "The Network of Global Corporate Control" [14] and the citations below all refer to the same document.

The methodology is very clear. They selected the 43,000 most important corporations in the Orbis 2007 database, which is made up of 30 million companies, and began to study how they relate, the economic weight of each, its network of connections, the financial flows, and which companies have interests that allow indirect control. In statistical terms, a "bow tie" system results, where we have a group of corporations at the knot of the tie and branches to one side that point to the corporations that the knot

[14] S. Vitali, J.B Glattfelder e S. Battiston – *The Network of Global Corporate Control* - Chair of Systems Design, ETH Zurich – corresponding author sbattiston@ethz.ch – The full text has been made available in arXiv in pre-publication, and published by PloS One on October 26, 2011.
http://www.plosone.org/article/related/info%3Adoi%2F10.1371%2Fjournal.pone.0025995;jsessionid=31396C5427EB79733EE5C27DAFBFCD97.ambra02
The extensive international discussion generated, with responses by the authors of the research, can be found at
http://j-ode.blogspot.com/2011/10/network-of-global-corporate-control.html

controls with ramifications to the other side that point to companies that participate in the knot.

The innovation is that ETH research has carried out this work for all major corporations on the planet in order to chart the global control map, including the steps on a power ladder that sometimes smaller corporations hold by controlling a small group of companies that, in turn, control a number of other companies and so on. What we have is exactly the title of the survey: "The network of global corporate control".

Ideologically, the study is above suspicion. ETH Zurich is part of the best technological research on the planet, roughly equivalent to MIT in the United States. Its researchers hold 31 Nobel Prizes, beginning with Albert Einstein. The team that worked on the article knows everything about network mapping and the resulting architecture. The research paper introduction, with 10 pages, short for research of this size, is accompanied by 26 pages of methodology to make all procedures transparent. At no point do they draw hasty political conclusions; they merely expose in a very systematic way the map of corporate power and discuss the implications.

Although perhaps a somewhat difficult read for lay people, this research allows us to understand how the corporate power of the planet is organized. What emerges from the research is clear:

> The structure of the control network of transnational corporations affects global market competition and financial stability. So far, only small national samples were studied and there was no appropriate methodology to assess control globally. We present the first investigation of the architecture of the international ownership network, along with the computation of the control held by each global player. We find that transnational corporations form a giant bow-tie structure and that a large portion of control flows to a small tightly-knit core of financial institutions. This core can be seen as an economic “superentity” that raises new important issues both for researchers and policy makers. (p.1)

Corporate control is defined as the participation of economic actors in corporations, which correspond to "the chances of seeing one’s own interest prevailing in the business strategy of the firm". When designing the web of participations, one reaches the concept of network control. This concept defines the total amount of economic value over which an agent has influence. We will later see the pyramid of power that this system allows.

This model analyzes the operational income and economic value of corporations, details the mutual cross-shareholdings, and identifies the strongest connected units within the network.

> This kind of structure, only observed so far in small samples, has explanations such as anti-takeover strategies, reduction of transaction costs, risk sharing, increasing trust and groups of interest. No matter its origin, however, it weakens market competition [...] As a result, about 3/4 of the ownership of firms in the core remains in the hands of firms of the core itself. In other words, this is a tightly-knit group of corporations that cumulatively hold the majority share of each other. (p. 5)

This mapping leads, in turn, to control concentration analysis. At first, as they are open-market companies, one imagines a relatively distributed degree of power and control. The study looked at "how much this control is concentrated and who are the top control holders." This is an innovation compared to the numerous previous studies that have measured the concentration of wealth and income.

According to the authors, there are no previous quantitative estimates on the control. The calculation consisted of identifying which fraction of actors at the top control more than 80% of the entire network. The results are strong: "we find that only 737 top holders accumulate 80% of the control over the value of all TNCs (transnational corporations). This means that network control is distributed much more unequally than wealth. In particular, the top ranked actors hold a control ten times larger than what could be expected based on their wealth" (p. 6). This latter data is of great importance for the very concept of the architecture of power.

Below is an example of some international financial connections. In red, European groups; in blue, North American; and other countries in green. The dominance of the first two is evident and closely linked to the current global financial crisis. Only a small number of these links is shown here:

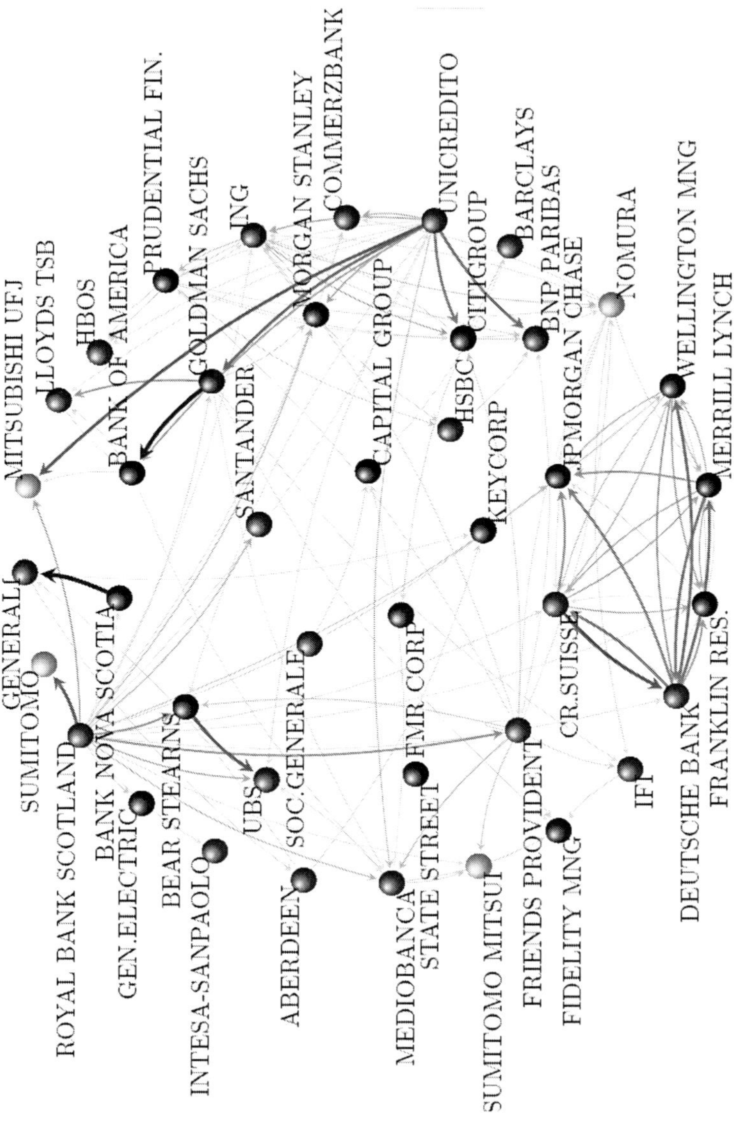

Source Vitali, Glattfelder and Fattiston,
http://j-node.blogspot.com/2011/10/network-of-global-corporate-control.html

By combining the top ranked players control of power with their interconnections,

> we find that, despite its small size, the core holds collectively a large fraction of the total network control. In detail, nearly 4/10 of the control over the economic value of TNCs in the world is held, via a complicated web of ownership relations, by a group of 147 TNCs in the core, which has almost full control over itself. The top holders within the core can thus be thought of as an economic "superentity" in the global network of corporations. A relevant additional fact at this point is that 3/4 of the core are financial intermediaries.

The numbers are very impressive and they have had an impact on the scientific world, as well as, inevitably, repercussions on the political world. The data not only confirms but also aggravates the complaints of protest movements; this refers to the 1% who play with the resources of the other 99%. The *New Scientist* (2011) reproduces a comment by Glattfelder, one of the researchers, who sums up the issue thus: "In effect, less than 1 per cent of the companies were able to control 40 per cent of the entire network." Most are made up of financial institutions such as Barclays Bank, JPMorgan Chase & Co, Goldman Sachs, and the like.[15]

Andy Haldane, executive director of financial stability at the Bank of England in London, mentions that the ETH study "gave us a tantalizing glimpse of a brave new world for finance. Analysis such as that on 'the network that runs the world' is welcome because it represents a leap forward. A key ingredient for success elsewhere has been a common language and shared access to data. At present, finance has neither."

Haldane also comments on the huge scale of the problem: "The growth in certain financial markets and instruments has far outstripped Moore's Law of a doubling of computer power every 18 months. The stock of outstanding financial contracts is now around 14 times annual global GDP" (*NS*, 2012, p. 9).[16]

---

[15] New Scientist - http://www.newscientist.com/article/mg21228354.500-revealed--the-capitalist-network-that-runs-the-world.html?DCMP=OTC-rss&nsref=online-news

[16] Andy Haldane, *The Money Forecast, New Scientist*, December 10, 2012; the fact that this "paper market" that revolves around the chaotic and unregulated system attains this volume is simply frightening. On the derivative markets, see the excellent text *The Mechanics of the Derivatives Markets*. This last study brings a clear definition of financial speculation: "Speculators use derivatives to seek profits by betting on the future direction of market prices of the underlying asset.

Some implications are quite evident. Although in the opinion of a few analysts, quoted by the *New Scientist*, companies buy each other for business reasons and not to dominate the world, to ignore the connection between this concentration of economic power and political power is naive or demonstrates an evident lack of realism.

Since the Reagan and Thatcher years, many countries reduced taxes on the wealthy, which laid the foundations for the recent worsening of planetary inequality; however, there is still no doubt about the political power behind the initiatives. The law passed in the United States in 2010 that permitted the financing of election campaigns by corporations has equally obvious implications. The dismantling of laws requiring financial institutions to provide information and regulating their activities has clear origins.[17]

Another important conclusion of the ETH survey is the systemic frailty we generate in the world economy. When there are thousands of companies, there is real competition. No one can "make" the market or dictate prices, much less dictate the use of public resources. With large numbers of small and medium-sized enterprises, power imbalances adjust with several timely changes, ensuring a certain systemic resilience. With the current climb of corporate power, the oscillations acquire another dimension and therefore become structural. As such, the volatility of oil prices, which has a dramatic effect on the organization of economic policies in many countries, is directly connected to these power structures.[18]

Hedge funds, financial institutions, commodity trading advisors, commodity pool operators, associate brokers, introducing brokers, floor brokers and traders are all considered to be speculators" – IEA – p. 9 file:///C:/Users/Ladislau%20Dowbor/Downloads/The_Mechanics_of_the_Derivatives_Markets.pdf April 2011. The BIS of Basel presents an order of 540 trillion dollars of derivatives issued (situation in February 2017) for a world GDP of about 75 trillion; this is 7.5 times greater.

[17] Hazel Henderson comments on this impact for American democracy with an imposing article: The best congress money can buy, www.ipsnews.net/columns.asp?idnews=50338 Paul Krugman and Robin Wells, in turn, recall that "it is difficult to find a sense in the growing ability of bankers to get rules to be rewritten in their favor, if they do not mention the role of money in politics and how this has expanded like a cancer in the last 30 years." Paul Krugman and Robin Wells, Por qué las caídas son cada vez mayores? Nueva Sociedad N. 236, Nov–Dec. 2011, www.nuso.orgs

[18] The increased systematic risk in large integrated systems is studied by Stiglitz in *Risk and Global Economic Architecture,* 2010, http://www.nber.org/papers/w15718.pdf

The authors also mention the implications for the control of trusts, as cartel control policies operate only nationally: "Antitrust institutions around the world closely monitor complex ownership structures within their national borders. The fact that international data sets as well as methods to handle large networks became available only very recently, may explain how this finding could go unnoticed for so long" (p. 7) In other words, these corporations operate around the world, while regulatory bodies are fragmented in 200 countries. Add the impact of disorganization brought about by tax havens, and regulation becomes fictitious.

Another implication is the systemic financial instability generated. We normally say that large financial groups are too big to fail. Seeing how they are interconnected, the image changes; the system is too big and too powerful not to coerce us into maintaining its privileges. However, "recent works have shown that when a financial network is very densely connected it is prone to systemic risk. Indeed, while in good times the network is seemingly robust, in bad times firms go into distress simultaneously. This knife-edge property was witnessed during the recent financial turmoil"(p. 7).

A key point here is that the authors stress the power effect of the financial system on other corporate areas: "According to some theoretical arguments, in general, financial institutions do not invest in equity shares in order to exert control. However, there is also empirical evidence of the opposite. Our results show that, globally, top holders are at least in the position to exert considerable control, either formally (e.g., voting in shareholder and board meetings) or via informal negotiations" (p. 8).

Finally, the authors address the obvious issue of the super-rich club: "From an empirical point of view, a bow-tie structure with a very small and influential core is a new observation in the study of complex networks. We conjecture that it may be present in other types of networks where 'rich-get-richer' mechanisms are at work. However, the fact that the core is so densely connected could be seen as a generalization of the 'rich-club phenomenon'" (p. 8).

The overwhelming presence of European and American groups in this universe undoubtedly also helps articulations and accentuates imbalances. Obviously, it is a club of the rich—and very rich—that appropriates resources produced by society in entirely inconsistent proportions to what they contribute. They are also people who control the investment of gigantic resources, far beyond their capacity for management and rational investment.

A further effect is the tendency towards dominance of speculative systems over productive systems. Companies that effectively produce goods and services useful to society would be very interested in contributing to a better system of resource allocation because they are largely indirect victims of the process. In this sense, the ETH research points to a structural deformation of the system that must eventually be faced.[19]

The crucial fact that stands out from ETH's research is that no conspiracy is necessary. When there is a network with such a small number of people at the top, there is nothing that cannot be solved over the weekend on the golf course. This network of personal contacts is of enormous relevance. But, above all, whenever interests converge, no conspiracy is needed for the members of this "rich club" to jointly battle their interests. There is no lack of examples, such as the already mentioned battle to reduce the taxes paid by the very rich, to avoid taxation on financial transactions, or to avoid control of tax havens.

The outcome is a double dynamic of organized intervention for the protection of systemic interests, resulting in powerful corporatism, and the competitive chaos that blocks any rational systemic organization. The corporate giant that embraces far more resources than its management capacity is too dominant to be regulated by market mechanisms, and too powerful to be regulated by elected governments. It is equally unable to manage the gigantic volumes of resources it controls, as will be seen later. This shows that the world financial system spins freely, playing with values that represent many times the global GDP.[20]

---

[19] Krugman and Wells sum up well the central issue of diversion of resources needed to foster the economy for speculative activities: "Apesar de ciertas reivindicaciones académicas (originadas en su mayoría en las escuelas de negocios), las enormes sumas de dinero canalizadas a través de Wall Street no produjeron una mejora en la capacidad productiva de EEUU mediante la 'asignación eficiente de capital para su mejor aprovechamiento'. Por el contrario, la productividad del país disminuyó al dejar el capital librado a la argucia financiera, los paquetes de compensación absurdos y las valuaciones bursátiles infectadas por la burbuja" – Paul Krugman and Robin Wells, *Por qué las caídas son cada vez mayores*, Nueva Sociedad N. 236, Nov/Dec. 2011, p. 212 – www.nuso.org

[20] Haldane, in the article quoted above, reinforces well this lack of systemic organization of the financial world: "Historically, finance has not thought of itself

During the global panic brought about by the financial crisis in 2008, austerity policies, public debts, and irresponsibility of governments were discussed; however, the leading actor—financial intermediation institutions—was kept out of sight. At the beginning of the crisis, *Finance & Development*, an IMF publication, printed the question, "Who's in charge?", on its cover, which implied that no one was coordinating anything. For better or for worse, this question is answered.

Below are the names of the first 50 corporations listed. Note that in the classification by sector (NACE Code), numbers beginning with 65, 66, and 67 correspond to financial institutions. Lehman Brothers, which went bankrupt in 2008, is entitled to a side note from the authors. Remember that money is intangible—today only magnetic signals—and that connectivity is planetary, so that the territory ceases to exist as a limit to action. To use their expression, “space is dead”.

This study of the global corporate control network, even if it is from 2011, shows the main overview of this new economic animal that we inherited from decades of economic concentration and the expansion of global financial power. It is an essential contribution that helps us to understand the new architecture of power. Since then research has been carried out on how this gigantic mollusk works with its numerous and confusing tentacles. There are recent and reliable surveys that allow us to better understand how so-called corporate governance works.

---

as a system. Instead, financial theory, regulation and data-collection have tended to focus on individual firms. Joining the dots was in no one’s job description. Economics has always been desperate to burnish its scientific credentials and this meant grounding it in the decisions of individual people. By itself, that was not the mistake. The mistake came in thinking the behavior of the system was just an aggregated version of the behavior of the individual. Almost by definition, complex systems do not behave like this. Interactions between agents are what matters."- Andy Haldane, The Money Forecast, *New Scientist* December 10, 2011, p. 28 - Chaotic in the quest for profit maximization, but with a powerful systemic reaction to any attempt at external regulation or taxation, it is a new and dangerous economic agent.

Rank	Economic actor name	Country	NACE code
1	BARCLAYS PLC	GB	6512
2	CAPITAL GROUP COMPANIES INC, THE	US	6713
3	FMR CORP	US	6713
4	AXA	FR	6712
5	STATE STREET CORPORATION	US	6713
6	JPMORGAN CHASE & CO.	US	6512
7	LEGAL & GENERAL GROUP PLC	GB	6603
8	VANGUARD GROUP, INC., THE	US	7415
9	UBS AG	CH	6512
10	MERRILL LYNCH & CO., INC.	US	6712
11	WELLINGTON MANAGEMENT CO. L.L.P.	US	6713
12	DEUTSCHE BANK AG	DE	6512
13	FRANKLIN RESOURCES, INC.	US	6512
14	CREDIT SUISSE GROUP	CH	6512
15	WALTON ENTERPRISES LLC	US	2923
16	BANK OF NEW YORK MELLON CORP.	US	6512
17	NATIXIS	FR	6512
18	GOLDMAN SACHS GROUP, INC., THE	US	6712
19	T. ROWE PRICE GROUP, INC.	US	6713
20	LEGG MASON, INC.	US	6712
21	MORGAN STANLEY	US	6712
22	MITSUBISHI UFJ FINANCIAL GROUP, INC.	JP	6512
23	NORTHERN TRUST CORPORATION	US	6512
24	SOCIÉTÉ GÉNÉRALE	FR	6512
25	BANK OF AMERICA CORPORATION	US	6512
26	LLOYDS TSB GROUP PLC	GB	6512
27	INVESCO PLC	GB	6523
28	ALLIANZ SE	DE	7415
29	TIAA	US	6601
30	OLD MUTUAL PUBLIC LIMITED COMPANY	GB	6601
31	AVIVA PLC	GB	6601
32	SCHRODERS PLC	GB	6712
33	DODGE & COX	US	7415
34	LEHMAN BROTHERS HOLDINGS, INC.	US	6712
35	SUN LIFE FINANCIAL, INC.	CA	6601
36	STANDARD LIFE PLC	GB	6601
37	CNCE	FR	6512
38	NOMURA HOLDINGS, INC.	JP	6512
39	THE DEPOSITORY TRUST COMPANY	US	6512
40	MASSACHUSETTS MUTUAL LIFE INSUR.	US	6601
41	ING GROEP N.V.	NL	6603
42	BRANDES INVESTMENT PARTNERS, L.P.	US	6713
43	UNICREDITO ITALIANO SPA	IT	6512
44	DEPOSIT INSURANCE CORPORATION OF JP	JP	6511
45	VERENIGING AEGON	NL	6512
46	BNP PARIBAS	FR	6512
47	AFFILIATED MANAGERS GROUP, INC.	US	6713
48	RESONA HOLDINGS, INC.	JP	6512
49	CAPITAL GROUP INTERNATIONAL, INC.	US	7414
50	CHINA PETROCHEMICAL GROUP CO.	CN	6511

Source: S. Vitali, J.B Glattfelder and S. Battiston, The Network, of Global Corporate Control

3 - CORPORATE GOVERNANCE

We are slowly beginning to understand the complexity of the corporate system, which today, for better or for worse, rules us. On the one hand, at the *intra*-corporate level, gigantism leads to inextricable bureaucracies that generate chaotic behavior and systemic risks. On the other hand, the same giants are providing for *inter*-corporate structures of articulation, which is quite similar to governments in the sense of its practice of direct political power. What we perceive is a doubly concerning articulation: both *intra*- and *inter*-corporate. Understanding this world of giants is now vital. They comprise the most powerful structuring dynamics of modern global society.

When the name of the BlackRock corporation appears on the cover of *The Economist*, with its revenue of 14 trillion dollars (almost equivalent to the GDP of the United States), we have to adjust our concept. Is it, indeed, the State who has become an uncontrolled giant? What changes when corporations become more gigantic than States themselves? At the close of the year 2015, *The Observer* notes that "takeovers, mainly originating from the USA or the Far East, broke records in terms of values of the business deals carried out, reaching a total of US $4.6 trillion in early December. According to *Dealogic* data, in 2015, there were nine business deals of over US $50 billion each, five more than in 2014 " (*Observer*, December 28, 2015).

The merger of Bayer and Monsanto in 2016, to give an example, generated immense power without a counterweight in the universe of world agriculture. With so many years of corporate concentration, through mergers and acquisitions, giants were created with a great power of control; however, due to gigantism itself, this was mostly uncontrolled. The post-2008 regulatory measures such as the Dodd-Frank Law have brought about almost nothing new and the Trump government is destabilizing the little already achieved.

The worldwide impact of the 2008 crisis encouraged a series of studies on these dynamics. We are beginning to understand the mechanisms and the operational logic of corporate giants and of the new geopolitical and geo-economic configuration. The research by the Swiss Federal Institute of

Technological Research, as shown above, identified the 147 groups—75% of them banks—that control 40% of the global corporate system. We now have a clearer picture of the traders: 16 groups that control nearly all the commodity trade on the planet. With few exceptions, they are based in Switzerland and are responsible for the dramatic commodity price variations of essential products in the entire world economy: such as grains, metallic and non-metallic minerals, and energy. In other words, the blood of planetary economics.

We should also remember that *Crédit Suisse*'s data for 2016 shows that 8 families hold assets equal to those of the poorest half of the world population; this is a direct result of financial mechanisms. Also, the wealthiest 1% controls more than half the world's wealth; that is, 1% of the population has more assets than 99% of the ordinary mortals. The extremely concentrated power of large corporate groups, the power of the financial system in the center, and the extreme concentration of wealth on the planet are part of an articulated dynamic. It unquestionably works for the 1%, as never before in history, but it does not work for the planet, neither on an environmental level nor on a social one, and much less on a political level. Worse yet, it does not even work on an economic level.

Many theoretical studies have already outlined these disturbing dynamics. Among them is the forerunning work on this new generation of studies by David Korten, *When Corporations Rule the World* of 1995, which presents, in a very clear way, the new structural design of capitalism at the turn of the millennium.[21] The work of Thomas Piketty, *Capital in the 21st Century*, which had a great impact not only because of its literary and scientific quality but also because it unravels the wheels of the organized chaos that rule us, thereby showing that we are facing a new political, economic, and cultural logic. Equally essential are the works of François Chesnais, particularly on financial capital.

Here, we are interested in the research, *The Intrafirm Complexity of Systemically Important Financial Institutions*, which was coordinated by R. L. Lumsdaine (and others) that involved various institutions such as Oxford University. The study offered a fascinating view on how these corporate giants work; a dynamic that has little to do with what we

[21] More recently in 2009, and therefore in the midst of the crisis, Korten published an encompassing little study, *An Agenda for a New Economy*; see review in Portuguese at http://dowbor.org/2009/02/agenda-for-a-new-economy-2.html/.
Equally interesting is his book *Post-corporate Capitalism*, 2001, reviewed in http://dowbor.org/2000/05/o-mundo-pos-corporativo-2.html/

imagine as the traditional productive entrepreneur: the *homo faber* as presented to us by business magazines. We are getting closer to understanding, not only the general theory of financialization, but also the wheels of its functions, names, and values.

Now a word on the concept of *Systemically Important Financial Institutions*, SIFIs. These are the 28 leading global financial institutions and the "core of the core" in relation to the 147 corporations above that were studied by the Swiss ETH. They were individualized by the weight they bear on the world economy. What happens to them and the initiatives they take affects the entire world economic system. These are institutions "whose disorderly failure, because of their size, complexity and systemic interconnectedness, would cause significant disruption to the wider financial system and economic activity." Researchers have essentially focused on the internal decision-making process of these economic galaxies, in particular the hierarchy of control: "The control hierarchy is a network representation of the institution and its subsidiaries" (Lumsdaine, p. 1). Regarding the graph with "little bubbles" we saw above (on p. 22) which shows the relations between corporations, now the "little bubbles" are being opened up in order to study their internal complexity.

The survey shows the extremely complex universe that each corporation is in itself, insofar that a food company can, for example, buy a mining company and dozens of other companies from a variety of sectors simply because they are a source of profit without having any particular expertise in the activities in which it invests. This brings us to the concept of *Intraconnectedness of a firm*, which another key concept in the methodology adopted (Lumsdaine, p. 2). "Ours is a novel approach that uses the innate network structure of the control hierarchy. In doing so, we therefore highlight the importance of considering *intr*a-firm complexity in addition to the more commonly-studied *inter*-firm complexity" (Lumsdaine, p. 3).

The 28 financial corporations classified in SIFI (Systemically Important Financial Institutions) each work with average consolidated assets in the order of $1.82 trillion for banks and $0.61 trillion for the insurance companies analyzed (p. 11). For the sake of comparison, let us remember that the USA GDP is in the order of $17 trillion; the GDP of Brazil, the 8th world power, is $1.7 trillion. It is even more important to remember that, according to Jens Martens's data, the United Nations system has 40 billion dollars a year for all its activities[22] (GPF, 2015).

In the absence of a world government, and with the national government's capacity fragmented into 200 nations, any regulation or planning of what is taking place on the planet seems to be out of our reach. This allows for a global free-for-all. There are trillions of dollars in the hands of private groups whose field of action is the planet, while the capabilities of global regulation barely crawl. The global power that really exists is largely in the hands of giants that no one elected, and over which there is less and less control. Of course, with modern technologies, world-scale management has become much more accessible, connectivity ensures instant contact and real-time tracking, and the power of dealing with information processing by algorithms has created a new corporate management context, for better or for worse.

How these institutions are administered is of enormous importance. Together, they handle something like $50 trillion: the equivalent of the total public debts of the planet and three quarters of the world GDP. The dimension, complexity, and lack of transparency make it an opaque universe, so the research we summarize here gains significance. Indeed, not even a minimal transaction fee that allows mapping flows is accepted. But we also find, in this research, the extent to which people at the top of the corporate pyramids have a limited understanding of what is happening in their own house, due to gigantism, territorial dispersion, and diversity of activities.

The image of the tree below helps to understand the logic of the research:

[22] Barbara Adams and Jens Martens – *Fit for whose purpose?* – Global Policy Forum, New York, Sept. 2015 – https://www.globalpolicy.org/images/pdfs/images/pdfs/Fit_for_whose_purpose_online.pdf

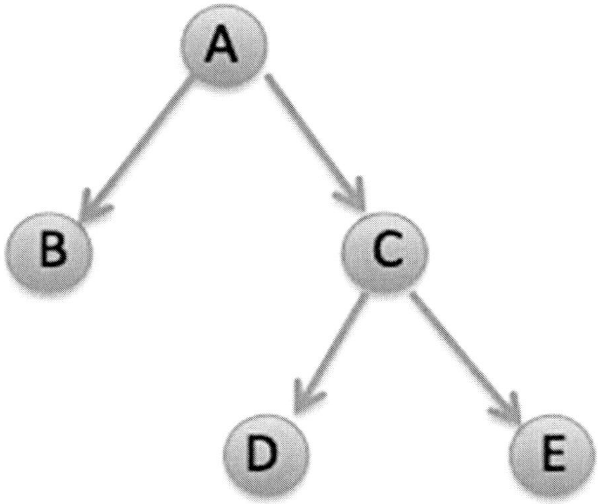

In a given corporation, the company marked as A represents the root of the group that controls two subsidiaries B and C, while the subsidiary C controls the subsidiaries D and E. These two, as they do not control other companies, are called "leaves" and are on the outer edge of the tree. Subsidiaries B and C are called "children" in relation to A, which is the "parent" company. This structure is regular, with each unit controlling two others, and has a depth of "two", the distance from A to nodes B and C. Therefore, we can have a structure with more or less depth, more or less dispersed "leaves", and more or less cross-over or overlapping controls, which is very common (Lumsdaine, p. 27).

This is highly complex because "The number of nodes in a tree ranges from 330 to 12,752 while the number of distinct countries and SIC (Standard Industrial Classification) codes ranges from 23 to 86 and 27 to 164, respectively" (Lumsdaine, p.10). That is, these are corporations that control thousands of companies, in dozens of countries, and often surpassing a hundred sectors of economic activity. They are galaxies with extremely limited capacity for internal monitoring; therefore, the financial result is the only criterion followed by, for example, the parent company located in the United States or Switzerland.

These corporations face problems of governance, fraud, corruption, and disorganization worse than any other public sector. Evidence of this is that virtually all of them are paying billions of dollars in fines for illegal large-scale activities. Many of the commanding officers of these corporations say they "did not know" about their fraud, which might well be excuses, but if this is the case then it is frightening that they quite possibly do not really know what is going on inside the giant that they, in theory, command.

We, therefore, have the full burden of bureaucratic gigantism without the slightest political control over these corporations; this would be allowed by a democracy. We will return to this subject later when analyzing the capture of political power by corporations.

Among the 28 large systemically meaningful institutions, we are talking about a depth of more than seven hierarchical levels: "In addition, 11 firms now have more than seven levels while just two years earlier, none did. Across all firms in the sample, by 2013 roughly 25% of the nodes were deeper than the third level. Thus, from the perspective of consolidated supervision, the challenges associated with assessing these firms increased dramatically, with many entities in the organization being much farther removed from the parent" (Lumsdaine, p. 11).

That is to say, corporate financial giants are becoming more centralized and bureaucratic. "The increased degree of depth is an indication of a shift toward a more bureaucratic organizational structure" (Lumsdaine, p. 14).

See the image below for the immense complexity of the corporate governance system.

As customers and mere mortals, we only see the unit at the top, on the credit card we have in our hands, the product we see in a supermarket shelf, or the attendant at the bank branch. The product seems reasonably simple, but we are unaware of the gigantic bureaucratic and uncontrollable tangle that takes place in the whole. Moreover, the number of controlled sectors (manufacturing, mining, trade, healthcare, telephone finance and insurance, public administration, etc.) in just one group, between 27 and 164 as we saw above, is appalling. Consider this pyramid-shaped image of corporate decision-making: "An institution that concentrates its decision-making among only a few senior managers who are then held accountable for large portions of the firm would have a larger proportion of nodes at lower levels of the tree. Such a diffuse tree might also be found among organizations that have experienced significant growth by acquisition, such as many financial institutions in the decade preceding the recent financial crisis, where the tree of an acquired complex organization may

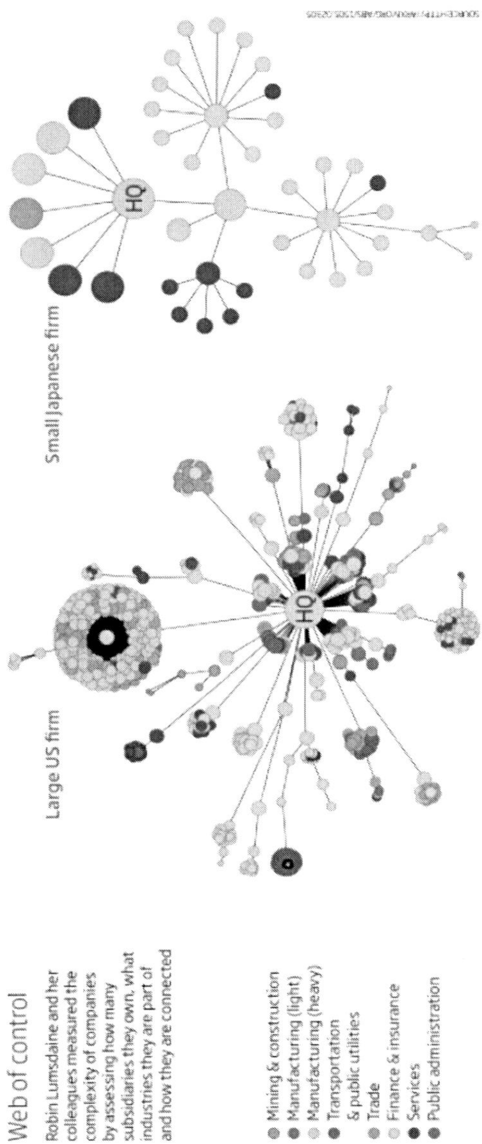

Source: Jacob Aron - Capitalism's hidden web of power, *New Scientist*, May 23, 2015

have been grafted to the tree of the acquiring parent somewhere below the highest level, creating a hierarchical structure of great depth (a “bureaucratic” structure)" (Lumsdaine, p. 10). We are at the heart of the problem of structural bureaucratization that permeates the entire decision-making process within a corporation. Faced by the impossibility of knowing what takes place, corporations resort to algorithmic management, as well as automated and simplified decision-making so that computers optimize narrowly defined results.

When there are scandals like Volkswagen’s, with the systemic deceit of the population and governments, or by Enron, HSBC, GSK, Barclays, Goldman & Sachs, Deutsche Bank, Wells Fargo, or by Big Pharma, we ask ourselves how decisions are made. And what about initiatives with planetary impact, such as the Halliburton battle to spur on the invasion of Iraq? The decades of struggle by tobacco groups to deny the connection with cancer? The way we do not control the widespread use of antibiotics to accelerate fattening in the meat chain, even though we have now proven its connection to the multiplication of resistant bacteria and other digestive dysfunctions?

The list reaches virtually every major corporate group. In 2014, in the article "Corporate America is finding it increasingly difficult to stay on the right side of the law", *The Economist* notes the existence of 2,163 corporate convictions since 2000 and warned: "the number of convictions and the size of the fines have grown impressively over the period" (*The Economist*, August 30, 2014). This is only in the context of federal lawsuits.

By prioritizing the administrative and control complexity of what is taking place, rather than size itself, Lumsdaine's study shows that, in the regulatory frameworks of Basel II, Basel III, and the Dodd-Frank law, "size is usually considered in financial (e.g., dollar) terms, rather than in terms of features of organizational structure," that is, internal complexity and bureaucracy. According to the authors of the research, although the size of the corporation is obviously important, this standpoint is insufficient. "Despite the ease of implementation, a size-based threshold is in many ways unsatisfactory, precisely because it does not take into account the level of complexity of a firm’s business activities" (Lumsdaine, p. 15).

Between the perfect tree, where the corporation operates in one country and one sector (SIC), receiving grade 1, and the total complexity, with grade zero (many sectors, many countries, complex hierarchies), the authors present all the intermediate situations, including firms and the number of levels (depth) of the corporate hierarchy (Lumsdaine, p. 10). This allows for a reasonable quantification of the complexity of a corporation operating in many countries, in many sectors of activity, with numerous dispersed business units, an increasing number of hierarchical levels, and in varied and complex legal frameworks of different countries.

Below we have provided a list of the analyzed corporations. Those that belong to the group of 28 systemically important financial firms (SIFIs) are marked with an asterisk. To make the list more complete, we have included some that were not analyzed in the survey. The classification tables (which we do not present here because of their dimensions) do not identify the firms, thereby preserving their anonymity; however, a specific firm may easily be recognized by the figures.

Banks and Insurance Companies

* Bank of America (US)
Allianz (DE)
* Citigroup (US)
Aviva (GB)
* Goldman Sachs (US)
Axa (FR)
* JP Morgan Chase (US)
Swiss Re (CH)
* Morgan Stanley (US)
Zurich (CH)
* Royal Bank of Canada (CA)
* Barclays PLC (GB)
* HSBC Holdings PLC (GB)
* Royal Bank of Scotland PLC (GB)
* Standard Chartered (GB)
* Credit Suisse AG (CH)
* UBS AG (CH)
* BNP Paribas SA (FR)
* Société Générale SA (FR)
* BBVA (ES)
* Banco Santander SA (ES)
* Mitsubishi UFJ FG (JP)
* Mizuho FG (JP)
* Nomura (JP)

* Sumitomo Mitsui FG (JP)
* Banca Intesa (IT)
* UniCredit (IT)*
* Deutsche Bank AG (DE)
* ING Groep NV (NL)

SIFIs not included in the dataset:
[Wells Fargo (US)*]
[Lloyds (GB)*]
[Banque Populaire (FR)*]
[Crédit Agricole (FR)*]
[Commerzbank (DE)*]
[Dexia (BE)*]
[Bank of China (CN)*]
[Nordea (SW)*]

Corporate gigantism has generated a worrisome internal inefficiency that largely explains why all of them are paying huge fines with convictions ranging from disregard for human rights to systemic fraud in the financial arena, as well as pure deception of clients. This is evident from Deutsche Bank, Wells Fargo, and others that were sentenced in 2016.

Most importantly, in the dozens of completely different sectors of activity in which they participate, in many countries and with thousands of companies controlled, the common denominator is their financial results. A mining company like Samarco, which created the worst environmental catastrophe in Brazil, must be profitable, period. Billiton, in Australia, barely knows where this mining company is located and who the financial associates in Brazil are; all of them follow in detail the profits available for distribution.

These financial groups are at the heart of the dynamics we wish to clarify in the present work: how the traditional way of extracting added value in a productive company by low wages is complemented with more sophisticated processes based upon the financialization that is dominant today. Currently, this appropriation of the social product is carried out through global mechanisms, which are above the regulatory power of States. We shall return later to the discussion of this essential theme, but it is particularly interesting to understand how gigantism causes the erosion of accountability that has become widespread in the corporate world.

4 - The Decision-Making Process and the Dilution of Responsibility

With increasing numbers of hierarchical levels and organizational complexity, at the top of the corporation one imagines that at the base of the company their instructions are complied with. Meanwhile, at the base of the pyramid, in the company that physically produces something, one imagines that at the top, in the financial control headquarters of the conglomerate, someone knows what actually is going on; for example, in terms of social or environmental impacts. However, given their gigantism, there is a very large process of dilution of responsibility: one never knows who was responsible for a particular corporate crime or who warned of a problem.

When Brazil ruled that the fruit juices we buy in supermarkets must have a minimum of 15% of "fruit juice", companies continued to maintain the ridiculous content of fruit and renamed the cartons as "nectar": a term which is not legally categorized. Anyone who complained or wanted them to take responsibility for their actions would enter complex and successive levels of ownership and control of the company. When they finally reached the top, in some distant country, lawyers would say that they are not free to disclose names. We are not just talking about the "poor customers" who hear on the phone that "your call is very important to us", but about government inspection institutions or specialized NGOs.

The main factor of this systemic deformation of corporate giants has much to do with administrative impotence. Managers at the top of the pyramid, who are responsible for thousands of companies, in various sectors of activity and in different countries, simply reduce their objectives to a single criterion: the financial result. Not only because this is the prevailing logic of the company, but because it is the only one they can measure and because it is the main instrument of power. These managers impose the profitability that must be attained on a distant branch, which has been subordinated to a fifth or sixth level of financial holdings, and do not care about the rest.

The criteria for remuneration and the bonuses of the various distant or intermediary boards are directly concerned with profitability. This verticalizes the criterion of maximizing the financial results from the top to the bottom of the pyramid, thereby creating a process that is both coherent and absurd. Banco do Brasil, to give an example, had an innovative and important initiative with Sustainable Regional Development. However, credit managers and branches' scores continued to be defined by the maximization of deposits and the minimization of risk. None of them would endanger their payments with initiatives to help fund small businesses in their municipality, which would have increased the risk. The main goal wins over the others and when this goal belongs to the financial institutions that are, after all, at the top, the rest does not really matter much.

When Volkswagen generated the absurdities brought to light in 2016, by setting up a strategy of planetary trickery and fraudulent testing on pollution emissions from their cars, it became clear that this behavior is only the current practice. This was a fraud that we came to know because the case was particularly publicized. Actually, the fraud was not identified by the company's internal mechanisms, nor by the government control bodies, but by an NGO which was not accountable to anyone. As a matter of fact, the issue is not the fraud itself, but that it is a common and usual practice by well-paid and well-educated people. These are people who perfectly understand the fraud, who practice it, and then create ethical shields to sleep in peace. Many do feel the contradictions of what they do, but they see themselves as impotent within the system.[23]

The Lumsdaine study that we have seen above helps us to better understand this systemic dilution of responsibility by the complexity and fragmentation of the giants. There is, however, a vacuum to be filled in terms of research into corporate governance that this study does not cover: the internal power that oscillates between the technical sphere, people who understand the real product that will reach the consumer, and the business sphere. In practice, it is the finance department who ends up running the corporations, backed by the powerful legal department—an authentic internal ministry—and the marketing department, who is responsible for the image of the company. A fundamental fact is that the criterion of the corporation's contribution to society is not expressed. For this we have

---

[23] Joris Luyendijk, whose work we will see later, provides an excellent analysis of how executives deal with this ethical dualism, of having to present financial results to shareholders pretending to be unaware of illegalities and negative social impacts. Some cannot stand it and resign, others rationalize, others still decide for total cynicism. Suicides are not rare. *Swimming with Sharks*, *The Guardian*, 2015

marketing, public relations, and the image that is sold. The fact that the media rely on this advertising to live also helps and so we rarely find any journalistic investigation or article criticizing corporations. To lambast government is less risky.

Between Samarco's engineer who suggests reinforcing the dam in Mariana (MG) and the demand for profitability by Billiton, Vale, Valepar, and Bradesco, the power balance is radically unequal. What does the manager of Billiton in Australia, a giant that controls innumerable mining companies in the world, know about Samarco and the presently dead "Rio Doce" river, where I used to play as a kid picking Acari from the stones?

Another example is that the sixth-largest pharmaceutical group in the world, GSK, is paying $3 billion in fines for various types of drug fraud. This is a company that is technically very competent in its properly productive dimensions with excellent laboratories and researchers, which have been multiplying as the group buys companies around the world. GSK sold Wellbutrin, a powerful antidepressant, as a weight loss pill, which is criminal. It sold Avandia, hiding the results of a research that pointed to the increased risk of heart disease caused by the drug. It sold Paxil, an antidepressant used for suicidal tendencies which, in fact, had no more pernicious effect than any placebo, with disastrous effects. The conviction of the company only happened because four GSK technicians made a complaint because they understand medicines, while the top of the company only understands business (*Time*, 2012).

How has a health-care company been able to keep up a huge large-scale fraud on multiple products during many years of successive management? After the conviction and following outbursts by deceived users and articles in the media, the company's shares rose, which is contrary to what would have been expected if the company were judged for its contributions to health. With these scams, GSK has made incomparably higher profits than the cost of the court settlement in 2012; in addition, the large institutional investors holding the bulk of the shares have reacted positively to the scandal. In other words, the financial power at the top imposes its profitability criteria on the group and this criteria has been and continues to be replicated across the various levels of the corporate pyramid.

In GSK's advertising, we see photos of laboratories with technicians in white coats, or maybe a mother holding a baby, and receive a message of safety and protection. It is advertising that keeps media alive because it adapts accordingly and reports little, so the circle is closed. In terms of justice and criminal trials, the widespread practice today is that those responsible do not need to acknowledge guilt; this means they resort to the so-called settlement, a judicial agreement, which in this case came to 3 billion dollars. In 2015, a new chairman of the board took over at GSK who was, by chance, the former chairman of the scandalous Royal Bank of Scotland. He does not know anything about pharmacy; he does not need to. That is not the business.

With much more power in the hands of financial giants than in those of the productive companies, financial profitability is demanded, which limits initiatives at the technical level by people who know the productive processes of the real economy and could safeguard a minimum of professional decency and corporate ethics. There is chaos in terms of coherence regarding the interests of economic and social development but, conversely, there is a very oriented and logical chain when it comes to ensuring a greater flow of financial resources towards the top of the hierarchy.

A great distance has been created between the company that actually produces food, for example, and the different levels of holdings to which it belongs. Institutional investors such as pension funds and others, who have little interest in whether there are pesticides or antibiotics in the products sold, track only the revenues from the stock mix of their investment portfolio. With such a degree of concentration, hierarchy, bureaucratization, and gigantism, the so-called "systemically important" economic groups are simply ungovernable in terms of ensuring coherence in activities which are in the interest of society. They stumble from one legal process to the next and from crisis to crisis, with the maximization of financial results as the sole common denominator of rationality. From Joseph Stiglitz's standpoint, they locked themselves into narrow, short-term goals, thereby crippling the economy.

A very important factor of the responsibility crisis is the enclosed environment in which these corporations live. Undoubtedly, they are very present in the media through advertising that aims to create a positive image of the group. At the same time, they block any initiative of the media to publicize what happens within the companies. The strict prohibition of employees to divulge what goes on inside the group, even after they leave; the justification of secrecy about technological processes; the harassment of eventual whistle blowers—employees who report activities harmful to consumers or the environment—all create a closed environment with no external control or transparency. In this context, it is extremely difficult for corporations to improve themselves internally, reduce bureaucracies, and remedy illegalities. There is no decent corporate governance without transparency: self-regulation is a fiction.

This fracture of the responsibility chain profoundly changes the business world. In a company owned by Ermírio de Moraes it was known who was responsible. Today, we face a legal department; this is after facing the public relations department. Additionally, we will then discover that there are numerous hierarchical levels and, finally, only a thin rope to hold and pull. Everything is fluid in these gigantic mollusks where any argument penetrates endless meanders and is lost in the smile of an official who says that it is not his fault because, in reality, the blame is diluted in a shapeless mass: the system.

The basic principle that made the system work was competition. In a way, a company had to gain consumer trust and try to better meet their needs, which leads to a healthy competition. At this level in the hierarchy of the corporate giants, agreements are more profitable than wars. When there is war, it is to impose a single standard—the winner's standard—and strengthen the oligopoly. A giant like BlackRock, with its trillions of dollars invested in speculative processes—including credit, foreign exchanges, and commodities—will have an end-of-the-line impact on its modest consumers. Can anyone have any influence on BlackRock, a company that you have probably never heard of, even though it is taking money out of your pocket through price and interest variations built into the production chain? The financial system, which today strips families and companies more than it serves them, is a good example of the systemic deformation of the whole.[24]

Tensions and wars between corporations are real in their quest, for example, to conquer markets or technological know-how. In this unstable environment, the State could introduce counterweights and regulation mechanisms. However, when it comes to protecting profit, maintaining opacity, reducing or cancelling taxes for financial profit or to regulate tax havens, large corporations react as one body through the institutions and representations that we will see below. In this case, as States are fragmented and limited in their jurisdiction by national borders, they do not have sufficient weight to deal with the attack, as nefarious as it may

[24] A short and entertaining text allows us to stand steady on our feet in terms of what a big financial corporation is: see the example of HSBC in the summary by Vladimir Safatle http://www.cartacapital.com.br/revista/837/quem-nos-governa-9428.html

be, on the policies necessary for the development of the country and its population. Giants that generate chaos in their activities, which unite and growl when their privilege is threatened, corporations have simply created a new political reality. We are getting closer to what David Korten has formulated so clearly: *When Corporations Rule the World*.

5 - FINANCIAL SYSTEMIC OLIGOPOLY

François Morin, former advisor to the Banque de France and author of a dozen books on the organization of financial systems, really knows his subject. He wrote a small book, *L'Hydre Mondiale: l'oligopole banquaire*, which enables us to understand how the oligopoly of the planet's financial giants operate. Extremely clear and didactic, with simple tables, Morin explains the mechanisms of power used by these groups.

In Robin Lumsdaine's research (mentioned above) we saw the gigantism and the issue of the internal articulation of these strange and new financial creatures, who control thousands of companies in the most varied areas from all across the world. They navigate on the planetary connectivity and virtual money that the new technologies offer. Morin's analysis reveals the organization of the *inter*-corporate system: that is, how they relate. "Actors that have acquired a global dimension, these banks became oligopoly in the 1990s because of the dominant positions they occupied in the major money and financial markets. This oligopoly has in turn become a 'systemic oligopoly' when, as from 2005, the banks that constitute it took advantage of their leading positions, multiplying fraudulent agreements. Is it a surprise that under these conditions, in view of this systemic oligopoly, so new and so powerful, the States have become outdated, or even hostages?" (Morin, p. 115)

Through years of mergers and acquisitions, any knowledgeable person could already understand the transition from competitive capitalism to a system of oligopolies in the various production chains. With the control of financial groups over the whole system, often including thousands of productive enterprises, the focus shifts. What is interesting in this study by Morin is that it both gives visibility to and explains the cogwheels of the system; once one notices its functioning, one must realize how dysfunctional a system that thrives on the general instability and drainage of real economy resources to the speculative area can be. It is a system that, at the same time, causes general economic instability and provides political control instruments that prevent any serious form of regulation. Instability is its natural habitat and, as we are well aware in Brazil, economic instability naturally generates political instability.

In Morin's analysis we find JPMorgan Chase, Bank of America, Citigroup, HSBC, Deutsche Bank, Santander, Goldman Sachs, and others, with a balance sheet of more than $50 trillion in 2013, when the world GDP was $73.5 trillion. The relationship between these financial giants and the States is particularly interesting: the world public debt of $51.8 trillion is at the same level as the volume of equity controlled by the 28 financial groups that Morin analyzes, which is also in the order of $50 trillion.

The States, because of its public indebtedness to private giants, became hostages and unable to regulate this financial system in the best interests of society. "In view of debt-weary States, the power of the large private banking players seems scandalous, particularly if we consider that the latter are essentially the source of the financial crisis, and thus a large part of the current excessive indebtedness of the States" (Morin, p. 36).

The table below presents the situation of the States in view of the rupture caused by the crisis of 2007–2008:

The States and systemic oligopoly: the rupture caused by the crisis of 2007–2008 (in trillion dollars)						
	2003	2005	2007	2009	2011	2013
Global GDP	37.8	46.0	56.2	58.4	70.8	73.5
World public debt	23.6	26.4	30.0	37.5	46.3	51.8
Derivative products from systemic banks	197.2	297.7	595.3	603.9	647.8	710.2

Source: Morin, François *L'hydre mondiale: L'oligopole bancaire* 2015, p. 36

If we think that so many countries, including Brazil, have attempted to sacrifice public investments and social policies in order to satisfy this concentrated financial world, then seeing the political dimension that the system has taken on becomes unavoidable. However, the mechanisms must still be explained.

An essential contribution from Morin's study is the analysis of how this group of banks has created, from 1995 on, governance instruments such as the Global Financial Markets Association (GFMA), the Institute of International Finance (IIF), the ISDA (International Swaps and Derivatives Association), the AFME (Association for Financial Markets in Europe), and the CLS Bank (Continuous Linked Settlement System Bank). Morin shows how the largest banks are distributed in these institutions. The IIF, for example, is "the true thinking head of globalized finance and of the largest international banks" and is now a political power. "The president of the IIF has an official status, recognized, that enables him to speak on behalf of the big banks. We could say that the IIF is the parliament of banks, its president has almost the role of head of state. He is one of the great global decision makers" (Morin, p. 61).

Check below the interconnection between banks and these institutions:

Interconnexion entre les banques systémiques:					
	Présence dans les conseils d'administration (CA)				
	GFMA	**IIF**	**ISDA**	**AFME**	**CLS Bank**
Barclays	X	X	X	X	X
BNP Paribas	X	X	X	X*	X
Citigroup	X	X	X	X	X
Crédit Suisse	X	X	X	X	X
Deutsche Bank	X	X	X	X	X
Goldman Sachs	X	X	X	X	X
HSBC	X	X*	X	X	X
JPMorgan Chase	X*	X	X	X	X
Société Générale	X	X	X*	X	X
UBS	X	X	X	X	X
UniCredit	X	X	X	X	X
Bank of America	X		X	X	X
Bank of New York Mellon	X	X		X	
Mitsubishi UFJ FG	X	X			X
Mizuho Bank Ltd	X	X	X		
Morgan Stanley		X	X	X	
Royal Bank of Scotland	X		X	X	
Standard Chartered	X	X	X		
Bank of china	X	X			
BBVA		X		X	
Crédit Agricole	X			X	X

Nordea	X				X
State Street					
ING	X				
Well Fargo	X				
Sumitomo Mitsui					
Nombre de sièges au CA	**22**	**18**	**17**	**17**	**15**
Autres banques	8	16	5	5	9
Total général de sièges au CA	30	34	22	22	24

* Président du conseil d'admistration.
Liens institutionnels (au 10/20/2014
GFMA: Global Financial Markets Association.
IIF: Institute of International Finance.
ISDA: International Swaps and Derivatives Association.
AFME: Association for Financial Markets in Europe.
CLS Bank: Continuous Linked Settlement System Bank.

Source: Morin, François – *L'hydre mondiale: L'oligopole bancaire* – 2015, p. 61

Reading the table above vertically indicates where the systemic banks exist as legal entities on the boards of directors of each of the five institutions of the sector. A horizontal reading shows how some institutions, particularly the larger ones, are more interconnected than the others. China is present with the Bank of China, but almost all are Western private banks, strongly dominated by the USA, as well as a large presence from the main European countries.

There is little doubt about the overall trend: the world's financial giants are endowing themselves with instruments of political control. The volumes of resources are, on the whole, higher than those administered by the public systems and, today, they also control the main news on the media and, therefore, public opinion. Increasingly, they enter the spaces open to them by the legal power, which should, instead, be the last bastion of the protection of equality before the law. We will address this subject further when we discuss the process of capturing power. At this point, what matters is to note that far beyond the erosion of competition, which is natural in a process of oligopolization, we are facing an articulated structure of global financial power.

6 - TAX HAVENS

The planetary financial giants are seeking to transform their financial power into organized political power. At the internal level of a country, such dynamics would be considered illegal, infringing the laws on trusts and cartels. However, this new architecture of power vitally relies on the true legal vacuum in which these groups move. Jurisdictions and central banks move at a national level, while the financial systemic oligopoly moves in planetary space even if having strong national roots. This is particularly the case in the United States and Britain due to their ample extraterritoriality, thanks to the expansion of the tax havens network. This is the subject of Nicholas Shaxson's excellent review: *Treasure Islands: uncovering the damage of offshore banking and tax havens*, considered by Jeffrey Sachs to be "an utterly superb book."

We are used to read complaints about tax havens, but only very recently have we begun to realize the central role they play in the world economy. These are not islands in an economic sense but are, instead, a systemic network of territories that escape national jurisdictions. This allows all major global financial flows to by-pass their fiscal obligations; thereby hiding the origins of resources or masking their destination.

All the major financial groups in the world and the largest economic groups in general now have branches (or headquarters) in tax havens. This offshore resource is a dimension of virtually all the economic activities of corporate giants and forms a kind of large global compensation chamber, where the various financial flows enter a zone of secrecy, zero tax, or equivalent; this means that they are relatively free from any effective control.

In tax havens, resources are channeled into a variety of uses. They are passed on to companies with different names and nationalities, washed and formally clean, and made free from any sin. Everything does not become secret, but with the fragmentation of the financial flow, which appears in other places and with other names, the whole system becomes opaque. This includes countless companies that formally belong to concrete nations. "If you cannot see the whole, you cannot understand it. The activity does not take place in any jurisdiction—it takes place between jurisdictions. ‘Elsewhere’ became 'nowhere': a world without rules" (Shaxson, p. 28).

The volume of resources in tax havens has become better known since the 2008 crisis. With the pressure of successive G20 meetings and the technical work of the TJN (Tax Justice Network), GFI (Global Financial Integrity), ICIJ (International Consortium of Investigative Journalists) and *The Economis*t, in addition to leaks like the most recent in Panama and the Bermudas, as wll as the Paradise Papers, we have $21 to 32 trillion in tax havens for a world GDP of 73.5 trillion (2013). Brazil participates with something like US$520 billion, which is equivalent to 27% of the GDP (accumulated stock, not annual flow).

In 2015 the OECD approved the first program to restrain drains and global financial chaos: BEPS (Base Erosion and Profit Shifting). This was another of the many attempts to create a legal framework to constrain the planetary chaos generated. However, at the base lies a structural problem: the financial system is planetary while the laws are national and there is no world government. Also, the political weight of the financial giants is sufficient to eliminate regulation attempts by specific governments; this extends to playing them against each other or by provoking a race to the bottom.

The system has a direct impact on production processes and macroeconomic policies at a national level. "Keynes understood the basic tension between democracy and free capital flows. If a country tries to reduce interest rates, to stimulate troubled local industries, capital is likely to leak out abroad in the pursuit of higher remuneration, frustrating the intent" (Shaxson, p. 56). Keynesian policies often fail to be functional when the territorial unity between a nation’s macroeconomic policies and the global space of the financial system is broken.

When one can earn more by investing in financial products and, above all, avoid paying taxes, any nation's economic policy becomes unrealistic. Thus "the offshore system has grown like metastases across the globe, and a powerful army of lawyers, accountants and bankers has emerged to make the system work [...] As a matter of fact, the system seldom adds any value, but instead is redistributing the wealth upwards and risks downwards, creating a new global greenhouse for crime" (Shaxson, p. 130).

The tax issue is crucial. The offshore fiscal mechanism presented here is based upon a 2009 IMF report, which deals with "the old trick of transfer pricing: profits are offshore, where they are tax-free, and costs (payment of interest) are onshore, where they are deducted from taxes" (Shaxson, p. 216). The connection to the global financial crisis is direct. "It is no coincidence that so many of those involved in financial deals like Enron or Bernie Madoff's fraudulent empire or Sir Allen Stanford's Stanford Bank or Lehman Brothers or AIG were so deeply entrenched in offshore" (Shaxson, p. 218).

Most of the activities are legal. The great corruption generates its own legality through the control of economic policies; a process that Shaxson qualifies as the "capture of the State". It is not illegal to have a Cayman Islands account, where legality and secrecy are complete in “a place that seeks to attract money by offering politically stable facilities to help people or entities to circumvent rules, laws and regulations of other jurisdictions" (Shaxson, p. 228).

Essentially, this is systemic corruption. "In essence, corruption involves insiders who mistreat the common good, secretly and with impunity, undermining the rules and systems that promote the public interest, and undermining our confidence in these rules and systems. In this process, they aggravate poverty and inequality and entrench the interests involved and an unaccountable power" (Shaxson, p. 229).

The basis of corporate laws, and of corporations, is that the anonymity of ownership and the right to be treated as legal entities, enabled them to declare their legal headquarters where they want, no matter where their activities effectively take place, which would have as counterweight a transparency of accounts. "At the onset corporations had to fulfill a set of obligations with societies where they were located, and, in particular, to be transparent in their business and pay taxes [...] Tax is not a cost to shareholders, to be minimized, but a distribution to the company's stakeholders: a return on the investments that societies and their governments have made in infrastructures, education, safety and other basic requirements of all corporate activity" (Shaxson, p. 228).

Shaxson did not create a pamphlet against tax havens in his research; however, he did dismantle the mechanisms of international finance that support them and proposed a tool to understand the world’s chaos. This mechanism affects us all, both in the injustice of taxes and also in the prosaic day-by-day via product prices and in the opacity of the contents.

"The construction of secret monopolies through offshore lack of control seems to prevail widely in certain sectors and greatly helps to explain why, for example, cell phone bills are so high in certain developing countries" (Shaxson, p. 148).

The impacts are systemic: "Bribes contaminate and corrupt governments, and tax havens contaminate and corrupt the global financial system" (Shaxson, p. 229). The truth is that this established system makes any legal and criminal control of banking very difficult. Virtually all large groups have dozens of convictions for various frauds but almost no case has judicial sequels, such as the personal conviction of those responsible. The system created involves a fine; this is a settlement that exempts the corporation, upon payment, of an avowal of guilt. The company, while acting illegally, must merely make a financial provision to face the probable costs of the legal settlement.

An exercise in systematizing financial felony can be found in the *Corporate Research Project* website, which presents convictions and agreements grouped by company. In general, when convicted and required to pay fines (without acknowledging guilt), corporations perform a major show of changing a few heads at the top of the corporation. Then follows the inevitable announcement that there were errors, but that the company is healthy and that distortions will be redressed. Those responsible not only remain free but in possession of legally applicable bonuses since there was no acknowledgment of guilt. Comparing the convictions with the images from corporate films that recruit youngsters and announce the company's high ethical values and economic vitality with the rooster of corporate crime is a depressing but instructive exercise.

Today corporations have their own legal apparatus, such as the International Center for the Settlement of Investment Disputes (ICSID) and similar institutions in London, Paris, and Hong Kong, amongst others. Typically, they will attack a country for imposing rules concerning the protection of the environment or social rights which they deem unfavorable and the sue them for profits they could have had.

An extensive article, published in *The Guardian*, presents this new expanding field of international relations and discusses how it is transforming the ground rules. The authors describe this trend as "an obscure but increasingly powerful field of international law". The legal dimension is in full evolution because, since the corporations have formed a parallel judiciary that allows them to sue the States, this radically expands their legal instruments of political power. Luís Parada, a lawyer for governments in dispute with global private groups argues that "the ultimate question in this case is whether a foreign investor can force a government to change its laws to please the investor as opposed to the investor complying with the laws they find in the country."[25]

This legal dispute is also an essential dimension of the TTIP Transatlantic Trade and Investment Partnership, which is within the sphere of the Atlantic and TPP Transpacific Partnership. This involves treaties in the Pacific sphere by tying to get countries to adhere to transnational rules in which national States will lose the capacity to regulate environmental, social, and economic issues as well as, moreover, the corporations themselves. Conversely, it will be the corporations who will impose their laws on all of us. With the new political cycle in the United States, the future of this international configuration is uncertain today as Donald Trump intends to reject the instruments of partnership and exercise international power more directly. However, in fact appointments of corporate executives, including Goldman Sachs, to key positions in the USA government, allows us to predict more truculent actions.

The Economist's contribution to tax haven research essentially refers to the location that holds $20 trillion and identifies the major financial centers that manage these resources: the American state of Delaware, Miami, and London. These paradisiacal islands, therefore, provide a legal location and protection in terms of jurisdiction, taxation, and information; however, its management is carried out by the large banks we know as "systemically significant" such as Barclays, HSBC, Goldman Sachs, UBS, and so on.[26]

It is a gigantic drain that allows financial cycles to remain shielded against investigation. An excellent short summary by Kofi Annan on the illegalities practiced by transnational corporations in Africa, particularly transfer mispricing—artificially low made up prices on African raw material exports to pay less taxes—reveals a typical mechanism. Companies, from the same group and seated in a tax haven, are sold at dummy prices, to be sold again at full price in the international market. Thus, mispricing, along with the tax haven and fake enterprise system, costs the continent $60 billion a year, according to statements by Kofi

[25] *The Guardian*, June 10, 2015: http://dowbor.org/2015/06/claire-provost-e-matt-kennard-the-obscure-legal-system-that-lets-corporations-sue-countries-the-guardian-june-2015-5p.html/

[26] The Missing $20 trillion: special report on offshore finance - *The Economist,* February 16, 2013, Editorial, p. 13.

Annan, which is more than the sum of foreign aid and investment. The undeclared funds in Panama alone involve more than 250,000 companies around the world.

The system is planetary and the fact that it is solidly embedded in the international financial system shows to what extent it is not a parallel activity or an exception to the rules of financial behavior but is, instead, a fundamental structuring element of the whole modern productive process. One of the largest tax havens is a state in the United States (Delaware), the British Virgin Islands are indeed British territory, Luxembourg is at the heart of the European Union, and Switzerland continues to exercise a global impact: the islands we imagine as tax havens are in fact support points that hold the global corporate network together as a whole.

A study by Mark Peith and Joseph Stiglitz perfectly sums up what we face: "There is a growing consensus that tax havens—jurisdictions that undermine the global rules of corporate and financial transparency—represent a global problem of facilitating money laundering as well as fiscal tax evasion and avoidance, thereby contributing to crime and unacceptable levels of global wealth inequality." This study is particularly interesting as it presents the initiatives that have been taken, the type of impact, and the set of international agreements that have tried, since the 2008 crisis, to provide an institutional basis for recovering transparency of financial flows. There is not much mystery here: "In a globalized world, if there is any pocket of secrecy, resources will flow through that pocket" [27] (p. 1).

---

[27] Stiglitz, Joseph and Mark Pieth – *Superando a economia paralela* – Friedrich Ebert Stiftung – February 2017. http://dowbor.org/blog/wp-content/uploads/2017/04/17-Stiglitz-Pieth-Paraisos-fiscais-33p.pdf The very illicit dimensions of the international financial flow can be found in the World Bank study, *Illicit Financial Flows*, April 2016.
http://www.worldbank.org/en/topic/financialmarketintegrity/brief/illicit-financial-flows-iffs "In the vast majority of cases involving high-value financial crime, criminals or their accomplices will employ a legal entity (company or foundation) or arrangement (trust) to conceal their interest in the illegally acquired asset." The Institute on Taxation and Economic Policy informs us that the 9 largest US banks have paid only 18.6% of taxes between 2008 and 2015. The 6 largest banks administrate 2,342 branches in tax havens (Bank of America, Citigroup, JPMorgan Chase, Goldman Sachs, Morgan Stanley, and Wells Fargo):
http://inequality.org/wp-content/uploads/2017/04/Republican-Tax-Giveaways-to-Wall-Street-April-11.pdf

The logic of capital accumulation has changed. The resources, which ultimately come out of our pockets (financial costs are in the prices and interest we pay), are not only not productively reinvested in the economies, but they do not even pay taxes. It is not just the illegality of fiscal evasion and the injustice that generates inequality: in terms of simple economics—profit, reinvestment, job creation, consumption, more profits, and the cycle of reproduction of capital—this system blocks development. It is unproductive capitalism.

7- Financial control of commodities

The idea we have inherited is that profit is generated by the company, which pays workers less than the achieved value. This is undoubtedly true, whether we call this achieved value profit, surplus value, or, more neutrally, just surplus. There is not much to be added to this debate, what we want to show, instead, is how this surplus moves in the productive chain. Less and less it is the producer—and here we are referring to the worker as well as the productive entrepreneur—who appropriates the result of the added value of a particular production process. The surplus is increasingly going to unproductive intermediaries.

The graph below shows how the price chain of a product—in this case, coffee—is formed as we move along the production chain from the bean production by the farmer to when it becomes the coffee we drink. These figures are outdated—they are from 2003—but what is of interest here are the proportions of who appropriates the surplus.

If we look at the evolution of the price of coffee from the farm gate in Uganda to the bar in the UK, it increases from the 14 cents paid to the coffee grower to the equivalent of $42 paid at the bar. We have used the example of Ugandan coffee in order to illustrate the general trend. This information has been drawn from an excellent international study, *Agriculture at a Crossroad*, on the investment of science and technology in the agricultural economy.[28]

One should follow the evolution of the columns that represent the value reached at each step: farm gate, trader price, the port in Mombasa, Felixstowe in the United Kingdom, the cost of the product after processing in the factory, the price at the supermarket shelf, and finally the price when made into coffee. First and foremost, one notices the ridiculous participation of the coffee producer, who handles the bulk of the work. When we take the first five steps, we can see that the group of economic

---

[28] IAASTD – Agriculture at a Crossroad - International Assessment of Agricultural Science and Technology for Development – UNDP, UNEP, WHO, UNESCO, New York, 2009 – http://www.unep.org/dewa/agassessment/reports/IAASTD/EN/Agriculture%20at%20a%20Crossroads_Synthesis%20Report%20%28English%29.pdf

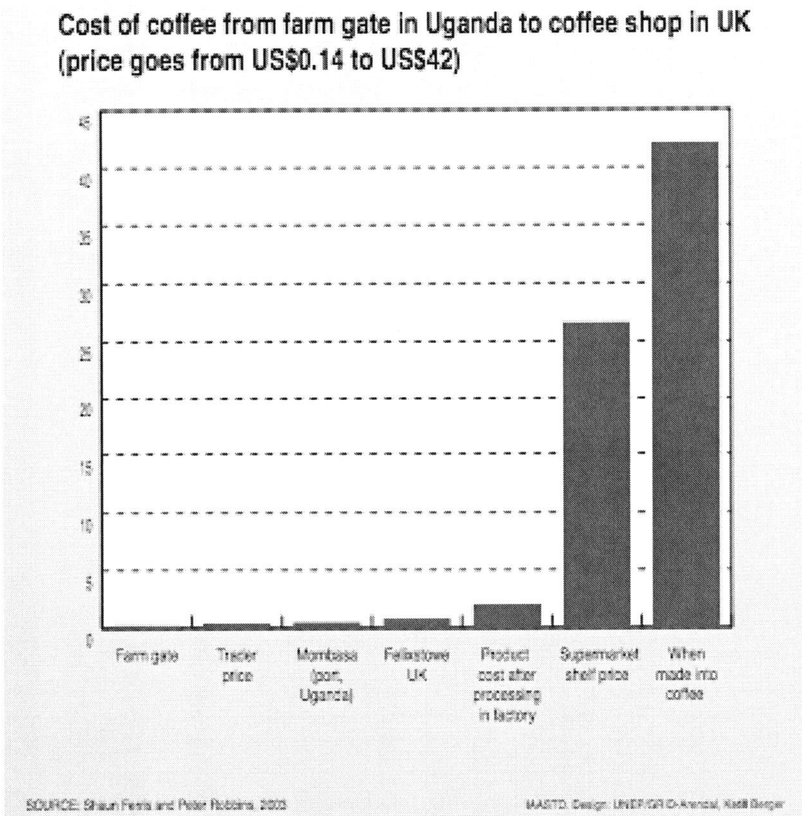

agents that can be considered productive (producer, primary commercial service, transportation, processing) still have a very small participation in the value payed by the final consumer. The boundless leap takes place in the price at the supermarket gondola such as Walmart or its equivalent. Another leap occurs when it is made into coffee, that is, when it is served as a beverage. The graph is self-explanatory. The values at each end, 14 cents and 42 dollars, give an indication of the deformation of the logic of remuneration factors and economic agents; this creates a difference of 1 to 300. Effective production only generates marginal yields. It is more profitable to mediate the production of others.

This is nothing new, as we are fully aware of the weight of a middleman: a concept invented precisely to reflect the negative dimension of the intermediaries in the productive processes, who earn not by helping, but by placing bottlenecks or tolls on the productive cycle. What stands out today is the existence of a very strong imbalance between efforts dedicated to the study and dissemination of price variations along time, essentially inflation, and about how little we study the variation of prices within the productive chains. This appears from time to time, such as in the "Globo Rural" TV program showing tomato producers in Paraná who refused to sell their product at the price of a few cents per kilo (four reais per 30 kilo case at that time) because they knew how much the consumer would pay at the supermarket (more than 40 reais).

The economic impact of this process is simple: on the producer side, profit is insufficient to develop, expand, or perfect production and, therefore, the supply does not expand. On the consumer side, the price is very high, which means that consumption is also limited. It is the intermediary who benefits, due to the very high margins on the relatively small flow of product. In addition, these intermediaries, increasingly, are huge marketing networks that decide the prices which generate oligopoly profits and create a toll-booth economy.

The logic of disintermediation, of course, is to reduce the profits extracted by the toll-booth and to redistribute this added value between the producer, who will be able to produce more and better, and the consumer, in the form of a lower price, which will expand consumption thereby absorbing a greater flow of products. This middleman could earn less per unit but on an increased volume of product, and would receive his share of the pie again, without jeopardizing the supply chain.

Where does this intermediary power to maximize profit come from? Another graph from the same study illustrates the situation of the small producer at the start of the process and the consumer at the end when facing a "bottleneck" created by the big intermediaries. It is essentially a matter of understanding the difficulty of small-scale agriculture; however, the argument suits a very wide range of productive activities.

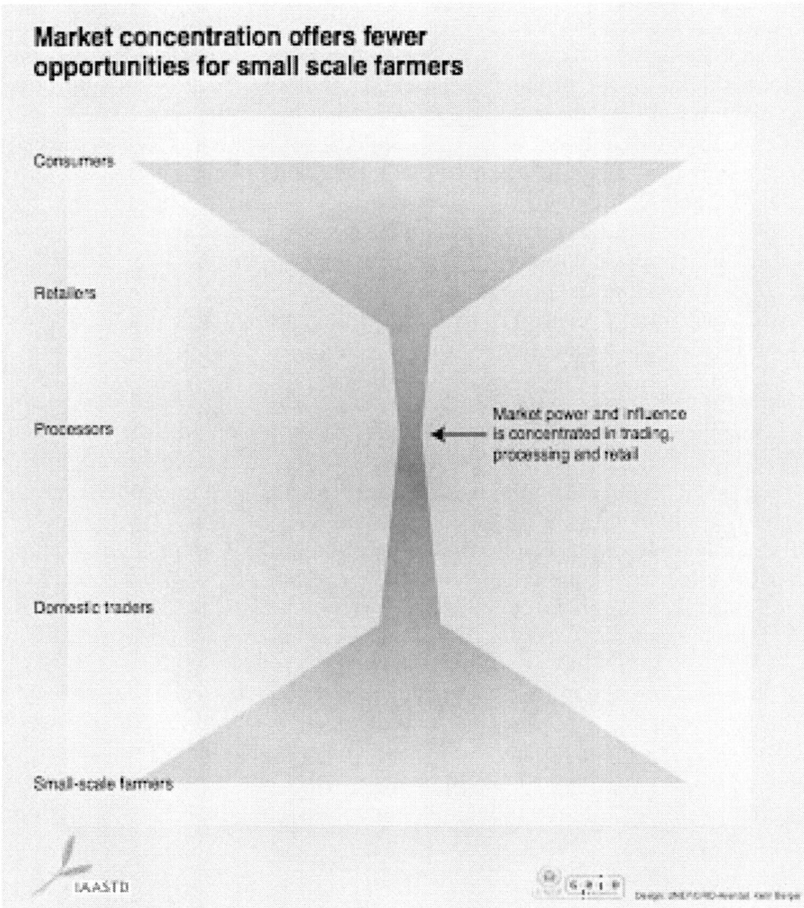

Source: IAASTD – Agriculture at a crossroads -UN 2009

The broad base at the bottom of the chart, representing small-scale farmers, is made up of many producers (more than four million in Brazil), who are scattered and with little force. A bottleneck is then formed at trader lever (bulk marketing) and becomes even narrower at product processor level, which remains concentrated at retailer level. At consumer level, the hourglass opens again in a radical way, due to the fact that millions are consumers, with no individual strength to influence prices. When we, consumers of the final product, ask why the price went up, we are told that the product "is becoming more expensive". At what point is it becoming more expensive?

This type of study, which appears only occasionally in some extreme cases, shows where inflation actually rises (the moment of the radical price “leap”) and, therefore, where the development of the productive processes is also blocked. Today, we have a number of institutions that keep a very detailed follow-up of inflation because it is important for the readjustment of rents, salaries, and so on. However, the analysis of where change happens in the general price level is limited to the sectors that stand out, for example food, and not to price changes within each production chain.

Virtually nobody studies which link of the productive chain creates increased prices. The two graphs we have presented above are seldom found and, in any case, not in a systematic nor regular way particularly with regard to shaping an image of evolution in time. However, all of the cost composition data exists because companies need this in order to set the final sales price. What we have to do is reverse engineering by taking an end product, for example a drug, and check the evolution of costs at each level of transformation and intermediation. This would also clarify the cost of financial intermediation in the production processes, which greatly increases the prices for the final product while reducing the productivity of the chain. Furthermore, it would stimulate additional investments in bottleneck areas in order to diversify supply and reduce cartelization. It would be a powerful tool for CADE (Administrative Body for Economic Defense) to identify incidence points of antitrust and create a defense of the market mechanisms to improve the power balance between producers and intermediaries, which is becoming increasingly unbalanced.

This hindrance, which is represented by different types of intermediaries for the dynamization of production and consumption, can no longer be sustained. Yet, no one produces adequate information on how to construct the final price of each product. To measure inflation does not suffice, we have to see how it is generated and who generates it. It is not particularly complex to compare the value of ascorbic acid, the very popular vitamin C, in the wholesale market with what is paid at the pharmacy.

In terms of the general dynamization of the productive process, the bottlenecks that generate extraordinary profits without aggregating a corresponding value must be identified. These are the links of the productive chain that inflate prices and block the expansion of the productive cycle. With large intermediaries in ever smaller numbers intersecting the main production chains, it would seem critical to shed a little light on how the price chain is formed.

Today the various institutions that follow inflation in such detail could easily start an array of promising activity and provide a good service for the rationalization of productive processes. In addition, the process of incorporating financial costs (high interest paid by producers) into price increases must become transparent. Looking at the price chain leads us to identify the bottleneck, where money is effectively earned and profits accumulate, without any equivalent productive effort or economic contribution. In particular, the value appropriated by financial and commercial intermediaries, with no proportional productive contribution, will then become clearer. This is the universe of commodity traders.

A dossier organized by Joshua Schneyer—who is not suspected of any dislike towards speculative systems—which was disclosed by Reuters, helps us to understand the process. "For the small club of companies who trade the food, fuels and metals that keep the world running, the last decade has been sensational. Driven by the rise of Brazil, China, India and other fast-growing economies, the global commodities boom has turbocharged profits at the world's biggest trading houses. They form an exclusive group, whose loosely regulated members are often based in such tax havens as Switzerland. Together, they are worth over a trillion dollars in annual revenue and control more than half the world's freely traded commodities. The top five piled up $629 billion in revenues last year, just below the global top five financial companies and more than the combined sales of leading players in tech or telecoms. Many amass speculative positions worth billions in raw materials, or hoard commodities in warehouses and super-tankers during periods of tight supply."[29]

As they work with physical assets, efforts to regulate financial speculation (such as the Dodd-Frank proposals in the USA and similar in the EU) do not affect them, which means that no one regulates them. "Outside the commodities business, many of these quiet giants who deal with the world's basic goods are little known. Their reach is expanding. Big trading firms now own a growing number of the mines that produce many of our commodities, the ships and pipelines that carry them, and the warehouses,

---

[29] Joshua Schneyer - *Commodity Traders: the Trillion Dollars Club* – http://dowbor.org/2013/09/joshua-schneyer-corrected-commodity-traders-the-trillion-dollar-club-setembro-201319p.html/ or www.reuters.com/assets/print?aid=USTRE79R4S320111028

silos and ports where they are stored. With their connections and inside knowledge— commodities markets are mostly free of insider-trading restrictions—trading houses have become power brokers, especially in fast-developing Asia, Latin America and Africa."

The way the process is presented, largely due to the uninformed or interested comments of the economic press, is that commodity price fluctuations result from variations in supply and demand: that is, market mechanisms. In fact, it is unthinkable that a commodity like oil, with such broad and balanced levels of production and consumption, will fluctuate between $17 and $148 a barrel in a few years, when production and consumption have been basically stable at around 95–100 million barrels a day, with minimum variations. It is a trade that deals with goods that are vital to the world economy, but whose prices and flows are essentially the result of mechanisms of economic speculation and political power.

Schneyer's study quotes a comment by Chris Hinde, editor of London's *Mining Journal*: "Most commodity buyers in the world are price takers. The top trading firms are price makers. It puts them in a tremendous position [of power]." The fact is that the set of products that constitute the "blood" of the economy, such as food, minerals. and energy, are not regulated by rules or market mechanisms, let alone by any planning system that would consider the depletion of resources or environmental impact. Formal regulation, by laws, agreements, and the like, does not take place, essentially, because it is a world market and there is no world government. Individual countries cannot cope with the process. When Argentina wanted to restrict grain exports to prioritize the food for its own population, the world came down hard on it, as if food production should not primarily satisfy the food requirements of the population.

The chaos created may be seen in simple numbers: the planet produces 2 billion tons of grain per year, equivalent to about two pounds per day per inhabitant, and we still have 800 million people starving. Here we have a regulatory void, where the large intermediary corporations navigate freely. The critical impact is the deformation of access to essential goods such as food, energy, and raw materials.

This chaos results directly from the oligopolization of the system. In practice, besides the five main operators, few have systemic importance. This means that these corporations can set prices and manipulate supply in an organized way. They call this the "market" in the press, but it is not a market in the economic sense: a free game of supply and demand. In the absence of effective competition, manipulation mechanisms become common practice. An example: in 2010, Glencore controlled 55% of world zinc trade and 36% of the copper trade. That year, Vitol and Trafigura sold 8.1 million barrels of oil per day, equivalent to oil exports from Saudi Arabia and Venezuela together (Schneyer, p. 2). For the general population, including the well-informed, the impression is that the price changes that reach our pocket are the outcome of unpredictable mechanisms, and not of a group of corporations that simply pick money out of our pocket. Who will blame an impersonal and anonymous mechanism?

Another vector of deformation is secrecy. Companies have little global visibility, only experts follow what happens in this small club. Additionally, no one has the formal authority to request the data in this global space. These practices would be illegal in any country that has regulations against market manipulation; this includes Brazil. The result is the accumulation of immense fortunes in the hands of those who do not produce any wealth but who still charge tolls on all significant transactions. This study details the major world groups, often unfamiliar names, even though they are key players in the global economy. This process is obviously part of the fantastic fortunes, concentration of wealth, and inequality that we looked at in the beginning of this book.

Here is some basic data about the main groups, alongside the names of the respective researchers, which can be found in the Schneyer report, as well as some complementary data from other sources:

Vitol: founded in 1996, based in Rotterdam and Geneva, and traded $195 billion in 2010. It mediates oil, gas, coal, metals, and sugar. "They sail as close to the wind as they possibly can legally," comments one analyst who asks for anonymity. They smuggled fuel for the rebels in Libya, which today gives them a position of strength (Richard Mably). More recent information indicates a revenue of $313 billion in 2012 and control of the American financial giant Blackrock, New York.

Glencore: founded in 1974 by Marc Rich, who was one of the founders of the global commodity toll system. Their headquarters are in Switzerland and they deal with metals, minerals, energy, and agricultural products. They traded $145 billion in 2010. Rich was sued in the USA but was later pardoned by President Clinton. South African Ivan Glasenberg is the largest shareholder, (Clara Ferreira Marques). In 2012 their revenue was $150 billion.

Cargill: founded in 1865, a family business, sales of $108 billion in 2010, and trades in grain, seeds, salt, fertilizer, metals, and energy. This company has a culture of confidentiality and aggressive behavior and attitudes, but uses advertising campaigns that create a friendly image. It seeks to dominate new markets for recyclable plastic and low-calorie products for Kraft, Nestlé, and Coca-Cola. When the Ukraine's government sought to encourage the population to favor internal grain consumption, Cargill, together with Bunge and ADM (also American corporations), "agreed to undertake a public relations effort with the goal of creating a political problem for the Government of Ukraine" which would "recruit the (Ukrainian) farmers to take an active role". It only became known when the instructions to the American ambassador were leaked by Wikileaks (Christine Stebbins).

ADM: former Archer Daniels Midland, founded in 1902, trades grains, seeds, and cocoa, and was worth $81 billion in 2010. "Corn goes in one end and profit comes out at the other." As a USA-based company, it has had numerous price manipulation and environmental crime suits against it, which have been regularly transformed into settlements. The company's criminal file can be seen when searching "ADM settlements" on Google. (Karl Plume)

Gunvor: founded in 1997 by a Swede, Tornqvist, and Russian-based Timchenko. This company trades in oil, coal, and gas. They are heavily leveraged by Russian political power. This company gives an idea of how quickly money is made in this area: it reached a high of US$80 billion in 2011 in comparison with US$5 billion in 2004. Political relations are essential in this area.

Trafigura: another Geneva-based company where bank secrecy allows for both tax evasion and undeclared sources of funds. Its trades in oil was worth $79 billion in 2010. Numerous illegalities did not prevent the expansion of the company, which went on to become the third largest independent oil intermediation company, and second largest in the metals area. It works a lot with storage because it has a huge infrastructure that can stock commodities and leverage prices (Dmitry Zhdannikov and Ikuko Kurahone). In 2012 its revenue stood at $124 billion. In 2013, Trafigura bought the Southeast port of Itaguaí (RJ, Brazil), in partnership with the Mubadala Development investment fund.[30]

[30] Carta Capital, October 9, 2013, p. 33

Mercuria: this is a very new company as it was founded in 2004 but it is already one of the five largest energy traders and earned US$75 billion in 2011. Its headquarters are, of course, in Geneva. The company owns mines and oil fields in numerous countries. They raised their capital from Jankielewicz and Smolokowski (J+S Group) who owe their fortune to Russian oil intermediation with Poland. (Christopher Johnson)

Noble Group: works with sugar, coal, oil, and grains. It grossed $57 billion in 2010. It was founded in 1986 by Richard Elman, who is British but based in Singapore, which is another tax haven with a strong commodity intermediation role with China and Hong Kong. (Luke Pachymuthu)

Louis Dreyfus: an old family-owned company (1851) today in the hands of Margarita Louis-Dreyfus, covers everything from wheat to orange juice and is worth $46 billion (2010). The owner says the family-name and that of Olympique de Marseille must be preserved. Everything in the company is a secret. (Gus Trompiz, Jean-François Rosnoblet)

Bunge: founded by the Dutchman, Johann Bunge, in 1818. It trades US$46 billion (2010) in grains, oilseed, and sugar and is a large intermediary of agribusiness in Brazil and Argentina for pig feed and other animals in China. The CEO is the Brazilian, Alberto Weisser, who was prosecuted for tax evasion worth $300 million in Argentina. This is the world's largest oilseed processor. In 2012, its revenue was US$50 billion and it has a very strong presence in Brazil.

Wilmar International: founded in 1991, led by Kuok Khoon Hong, and based in Singapore (another tax haven). It negotiated a wealth of $30 billion in 2010 and has 20% of the soybean market in China, due to its vertical integration of the entire production chain from planting to final marketing: including refining, bottling, transportation, etc. Heavily involved in palm oil. It is strengthening its position in the Brazilian sugar market (Harry Suhartono and Naveen Thakral).

Arcadia, founded in 1988 by Japanese Mitsui and owned by John Fredriksen. Reuters estimates its oil trades are worth $29 billion (2010). It was sued for oil price manipulation in 2008 and accused of storing gigantic quantities of product to create the appearance of a supply crisis and to profit in the derivatives market. Fredriksen changed his Norwegian nationality in 2006 to Cypriot where he pays less taxes. Wikileaks and Reuters disclosed their political manipulations in Yemen and Nigeria.

The giant **Blackrock**, as we saw above, is a case by itself. According to *The Economist*, the financial platform manages almost 7% of the $225 trillion of financial assets in the world.[31] It manages numerous other shadow banking groups, which are not subject to control that, theoretically at least, banks should respect.

What do we see in this small survey of a dozen groups? First, of course, the immense power that such a small number of groups have because they control the blood of the world's economy, in the form of grain, oil, minerals, energy, transportation systems, with corresponding financial infrastructure, and the gigantic supplementary speculative system of derivatives. It is not the "market" in the sense of the free market, where each competes to serve others better but, instead, it reflects systems where commodity end users have little to say and the countries of origin of these commodities have even less. To overthrow a minister or even a government is nothing new here.

Noteworthy, however, is the preference of these groups for venues in tax havens. They make money by mediating what they do not usually produce and by manipulating prices to make us pay more. The price to consumers at the end of the chain is included in the shelf products. In addition, they are all international enough to benefit from tax havens, where they do not pay taxes. In a way, this creates net profit. They also do not invest, in the sense of investing in production, but essentially make and manage financial and commercial transactions.

Likewise, one observes how most of these groups are recent. There are some very old ones like Cargill or Bunge, but even these have been converted to speculative processes on a gigantic scale. In general, good relations, and strong political and military support when necessary, allow leaps such as Guvnor which, in seven years, increased its revenue from $5 billion to $80 billion. This is a very present and evident process of the oligopolization of the system that has access to the essential raw materials of the planet.

There has been a significant geopolitical shift with a strong Russian expansion and an increased presence by China and Asia. As such, new actors enter into the traditional logic of speculative behavior, market manipulation, and political truculence, leading to an entrenched capacity of limiting access to raw materials that feed the productive chains of

[31] *The Economist* – Briefing BlackRock – the monolith and the markets – December 7, 2013, pp. 24–26

virtually all economic domains. As we have seen previously, these large global groups are simply above any legal system. Their transnational dimensions allow them to shift their legal headquarters according to the current pressures.

Large intermediary systems generally have little interest in the products themselves. They are essentially interested in market fluctuations in time and space, including the generation and exploitation of these fluctuations. This means the financial dimension of their activities is essential.

Their support mechanisms consist essentially of tax havens, derivatives and, in particular, future markets but also, of course, the political support of countries most interested, such as the United States and the UK. In a way, the giants of financial intermediation and those of commercial brokerage are the hand and glove of the process, although each naturally tries to maximize its piece of the pie.

Based on the tax havens, which we saw earlier, the derivatives system crowns the process. It is important to note that the volume of speculative transactions is incomparably higher than the volume of real transactions. The oil on a ship will typically change hands dozens of times during a day as it is traded by groups that have no interest in oil but who are focused, instead, on the game of price variations.

Outstanding derivatives in the second half of 2012 were in the order of \$633 trillion: nine times the total world GDP.[32] In 2017, they had reached 544 trillion. To illustrate this point, the graph below shows the impressive dance of commodity prices, while their production and consumption are essentially stable.

[32] "The over-the-counter (OTC) derivatives market shrank slightly in the second half of 2012. The notional principal of outstanding contracts fell by 1% to \$633 trillion" *BIS Quarterly Review*, June 2013, International banking and financial market developments – p. 19 http://www.bis.org/publ/qtrpdf/r_qt1306.pdf

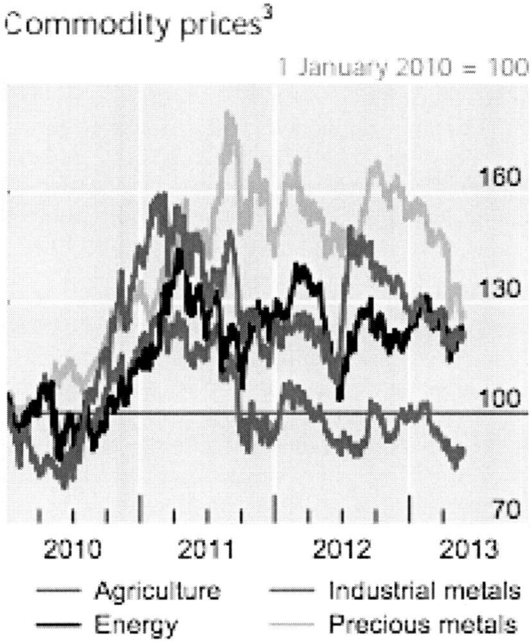

This directly affects both producers and consumers of commodities by generating a huge instability in prices at both ends. Speculation profits precisely from this instability. A country that relies on exporting grain to import the oil it needs must have certain guarantees that it can supply its domestic market. The futures market, as a derivative segment, guarantees a fixed sales price for grains, as well as buying options on oil. Therefore, the country knows at what price it will sell its commodities (for example grain) and how much it will pay for the oil that it will have to import. The risk of variations is taken by the trader, who guarantees a sale or purchase on a given date while demanding overly high prices. This system is often justified as having a stabilizing impact but, in fact, traders are quite keen to provoke the price dance, as it allows them to raise risk premiums. The huge storage capacity they have also enables them to manipulate prices. For intermediaries, fluctuations are a profit factor, as they allow them to charge increasingly higher tolls for production and consumption, without having to produce anything.[33]

[33] *BIS Quarterly Review*, June 2013, p.3 –

It must be mentioned that Wall Street and other centers of speculation have always sought academic justifications for these outrages. Much of Milton Friedman's renown is due to the aura of scientific respectability that his opinions have given to speculative activities. This bridge between the large scientific institutions and the world of speculation is described, for example, by the *New York Times* which cites several university professors, with work that is widely disseminated in the media but who are supported by financial groups (including the Trafigura group as discussed above), going so far as to state that speculative activities help to stabilize prices.[34]

The pricing system relies on induced speculative manipulations in a set of strategic areas, which is to the detriment of traditional supply and demand mechanisms and so it becomes mandatory to adopt a statistical analysis of the price chains. This data reflects where the changes actually take place, both in terms of excessive profits for intermediaries, and in the generation of inflation and pro-cyclical movements that destabilize the world's economy and reduce the ability to organize national economies.

***

The mainstay of change is the shifting of profit and economic and financial power from the producers—i.e., last century's manufacturing—to toll collectors of various kinds: such as financial intermediaries, commodity traders, and communication monopolies. The real profit, the big profit, is generated in the immaterial economy.

Returning to the analysis by ETH's Vitali, this shows the mechanism by which financial groups dominate by 75% the 147 groups that control 40% of the corporate world. This point of view naturally shifts the reasoning about corporate power structures. One thing is the revenue of each group. Another is each group's authority over a set of other activities through financial and stock control, as we saw previously. By including the term "control"—the indirect forms that a given group has to influence the use of resources of other groups—the research found that the concentration of

---

http://www.bis.org/publ/qtrpdf/r_qt1306.pdf
A 7-minute didactic YouTube video helps us to understand the mechanism: http://www.youtube.com/watch?v=rpM9XxJ-vo4&feature=youtube_gdata_player

[34] David Kocieniewski, *New York Times*, December 27, 2013
http://www.nytimes.com/2013/12/28/business/academics-who-defend-wall-st-reap-reward.html?pagewanted=1&_r=0&adxnnlx=1388405488-1DXVPx3vNxfy%20VclhdNkrg

power is ten times higher than would be supposed by the simple revenue of each group.[35]

The power of intermediaries has become planetary. There are few systemically significant groups, so price manipulation becomes perfectly feasible.[36] On the whole, it is no longer a matter of just evaluating from an ethical dimension the impact of the concentration of wealth among only a few but also of understanding the degree of the erosion of market mechanisms that were previously believed to generate balance by competition. Here, we are clearly evolving towards what in other studies we have termed a "toll-booth economy", where the losers are the producers and the consumers. It is really a new architecture of power.[37]

The extreme concentration of financial power in a few hands takes place in a very capillary way. From a dense, articulated, and online network, millions of fundraising points are covered in all parts of the world through simple things: such as the interest rate charged at a bank branch in a city in the interior of Brazil or India; the rates we pay for each use of our credit cards; the overpriced products that involve commodities; the absence of control over social and environmental impact, which extends to human rights. This all generates costs taken on by society (the so-called "externalities", see the Mariana example in Minas Gerais). The "big economy" has, with modern technologies and electronic immaterial money, managed to wire-tap us all, for example through the magnetic tape on the credit cards in our pockets. It has become a systemic mechanism for extracting a social surplus from every one of us, with very few productive counterparts.

The fact that oligopolies may refer to themselves as "the markets" while, at the same time, not having to submit to any market, creates this semblance of absence of power, or of an abstract power: i.e., "the

---

[35] Vitali (*et al.*): “This means that network control is much more unequally distributed than wealth. In particular, the top ranked actors hold a control ten times bigger than what could be expected based on their wealth” (p. 6) – http://arxiv.org/pdf/1107.5728.pdf

[36] “What are the implications for market competition? Since many TNCs in the core have overlapping domains of activity, the fact that they are connected by ownership relations could facilitate the formation of blocks, which would hamper market competition” (Vitali, ETH, p. 7)

[37] On the toll-booth economy (economia de pedágio), see Dowbor, *A Reprodução Social,* Ed. Vozes, Petrópolis 2003, http://dowbor.org

markets". However, when one says that the "markets are nervous" it usually means that half a dozen speculators are not content.

This power's freedom of action avoids any attempt to regulate the system which, in the "thirty golden years" (between 1945 and 1975), ensured a reasonable balance between the business world, the State, and civil society. In recent decades, we have seen an attack that has captured the political systems that could have provided a counterweight: governments, the judiciary, the media, international organizations, civil society organizations, and public opinion.

Manipulating the ground rules was the first step. The second step is the appropriation of the very institutions that define the ground rules. Changing the law can be much more efficient than bypassing it and when those who are already strong become those who hold the pen, anything is possible.

DEFINIÇÃO DE CAPITALISMO EXTREMO
ECONOMIA GLOBAL nas mãos de poucos grupos econômicos
fora do controle do governo
AO EXTREMO
Desigualdade
Concentração de riquezas
cada vez MENOS empresas
e
MAIORES
737 grupos
80% do mundo corporativo é controlado por apenas 737 grupos
147 grupos
e 147 grupos controlam 40% deste núcleo
no Brasil
em 2015
62 indivíduos detinham a mesma riqueza
que
3,6 BILHÕES de pessoas
riqueza
87%
13%
8% mais ricos
82% da população brasileira
CONGLOMERADOS EMPRESARIAIS E CONCENTRAÇAO DA RIQUEZA
empresas com propriedade cruzada
SOBRE A CAPTURA 12 / 13

8 - THE CAPTURE OF POLITICAL POWER

Looking at the 21st century through last century's lens does not help. When we think about the world of economics, we still think about economic interests and market mechanisms. Politics, formal power, taxes, and the public sector in general would normally be in another dimension. The rupture of these frontiers is not new, since we have a long tradition of the penetration of private economic interest groups in the public sphere. What is new is the scale, depth, and level of organization of the process. Belluzzo and Galipoli summarize the transformation thus: "Today, it is the logic of globalized finance that delimits the territory occupied by the options of democratic politics".[38]

What used to be fragmented deformations, punctual penetrations by lobbies, corruption and revolving doors between the private and the public sectors have expanded and, by osmosis, are turning into articulated political power. The public interest seldom emerges but when it does it is only after prodigious efforts by popular movements, fragile protests in the alternative media, rare independent politicians, and civil society organizations.

Corporate power has become systemic, capturing one by one the various dimensions of expression and power thereby generating a new dynamic, or a new architecture of power.

Expansion of traditional lobbies

One way of capturing power is the expansion of traditional lobbies. Google, for example, now has eight lobby companies in Europe alone, in addition to direct funding of parliamentarians and EU Commission members. It will probably have to pay EUR 6 billion for illegalities perpetrated in Europe. Google's expenditure in this area is already close to that of Microsoft. Google has mobilized USA congressmen to lobby the Commission as reported in *The Guardian*: "The coordinated effort by senators and members of the House of Representatives, as well as by a congressional committee, formed part of a sophisticated, multimillion-

[38] Luiz Gonzaga Belluzzo and Gabriel Galípoli – *Manda quem pode, obedece quem tem prejuízo* – FACAMP, Contracorrrente, São Paulo 2017, p. 183

pound lobbying drive in Brussels, which Google has significantly ramped up as it fends off challenges to its dominance in Europe".[39] Today, the money and pressure from corporations permeate the decision-making process everywhere.

Direct financing of political campaigns

While lobbies can still be presented as external forms of pressure, much more important is the direct funding of political campaigns, through political parties or by "investing" in candidates. In Brazil, the law enacted in 1997 authorized corporations to directly finance candidates, which had a disastrous impact on the behavior of parliamentarians, who formed internal pressure groups linked to major corporate interests.[40] In 2010, the United States followed the same path, leading Americans today to comment that "we have the best Congress money can buy."

Finally, in Brazil, the STF (Supreme Court) decreed the practice illegal from the elections of 2016. However, we still have an agribusiness group in Congress, besides the mainstream media interests, major construction corporations, banks, and the automotive industry. Congressmen that actually represent citizens can be counted on only a few fingers. The loss of representativeness by Congress tends to be viewed with some resignation, or even cynicism, but if we think a little then it becomes apparent that it is a dramatic deformation of the whole political system. The 1988 Constitution, in a pendular movement after decades of dictatorship, reaffirmed political rights and democratic principles, but not even the Constitution survived the attacks of corporate groups in Congress, which approved the self-serving access to corporate money. In the image below, some congressmen are for sale, others are for rent.

---

[39] The Guardian, *Revealed: How Google enlisted members of the US Congress* - http://www.theguardian.com/world/2015/dec/17/google-lobbyists-congress-antitrust-brussels-eu

[40] The funding is based on Law 9504 of 1997: "The donations may come from their own resources (of the candidate), from individuals, with a limit of 10% of the amount declared in assets during the previous year in the Income Tax; and of legal persons up to a limit of 2%, corresponding [to the statement] of the previous year" said Judge Marco Antonio Martin Vargas, advisor to the Presidency of the Regional Electoral Court (TRE) of Sao Paulo." - *Exame Magazine*, June 8, 2010, Elaine Patricia da Cruz, *Entenda o financiamento de campanha no Brasil.* The Congress that decreed the presidential impeachment in 2016 was elected on the basis of a system which was finally declared unconstitutional at the end of 2015.

These successive constitutional amendments have created the current deformed monster, which has frozen public investment into infrastructure and social policies while, at the same time, deregulating the financial system. The alterations to the Forest Code and the consequent destruction of the Amazon, as well as blocking taxation on financial transactions and so many other measures, such as the tax on fortunes or unproductive capital, result from these new power relations created by a literally bought out Congress. The widespread attack on social policies, among others, has, in a short time, brought about a generalized setback in the country.

The capture of the judiciary and the creation of a parallel legal system

We have already mentioned the capture of the legal area, which has acquired immense importance and takes place in various forms. The attempt by large Brazilian banks, through different types of financing, was noteworthy with regard to placing financial activities out of the reach of PROCON and other consumer protection bodies. In the United States, a judge from an American district decided to outlaw Argentina on behalf of the so-called "vulture funds"; thereby, clearly serving the legalization of international financial speculation, and ignoring the legal system of another country.[41]

---

[41]A synthetic explanation of this operation, allowing judge Thomas Griesa in the USA to treat the chaos in the Argentina debt negotiation, can be found in Michael Hudson, *Killing the Host* (p. 347). Additionally, debt renegotiation is not a default; it is part of the write-down that is a legal practice of reviewing an unpayable debt.

As we have seen, a particularly pernicious form of capture of the judiciary is through settlements, which are agreements where corporations pay a fine but do not need to avow guilt, thereby exempting managers from being held criminally accountable. As such, corporate managers and financiers are safe in terms of possible convictions. Joseph Stiglitz comments: "It has been repeatedly noted how none of those in charge of the big banks that brought the world's economy to the brink of ruin have been held accountable for their misdeeds. How can it be that no one is responsible? Especially when there have been misdeeds of the magnitude of those that have occurred in recent years?"[42]

Elizabeth Warren, an American senator, presents in *Rigged Justice* an excellent description of these mechanisms alongside company names and examples of financial crimes in student loans, car insurance, work safety, environment, trade, the manufacture of medical drugs, and others.[43]

This lack of accountability is now widespread and settlements even open a back door for government funding. George Monbiot calls this "a privatized system of justice for global corporations" and considers that "democracy is impossible under these circumstances" (p. 252)[44].

Control of information

Another powerful mainstay of the capture of the political space occurs through the organized control of information, which builds a consensus of the manufacturing system through which Noam Chomsky brought us precious analyses.[45] The planetary reach of the mass media and the

Moreover, the write-down should be legalized for a set of private debts in Brazil, which have been burdened with usury interest rates.

[42] Joseph Stiglitz – *On Defending Human Rights* – Geneva, December 3, 2013 http://www.ohchr.org/Documents/Issues/Business/ForumSession2/Statements/JosephStiglitz.doc

[43] Warren, Elizabeth – *Rigged Justice* – Jan. 2016 http://www.warren.senate.gov/files/documents/Rigged_Justice_2016.pdf and *New York Times* January 29, 2016 http://www.nytimes.com/2016/01/29/opinion/elizabeth-warren-one-way-to-rebuild-our-institutions.html?_r=0

[44] Monbiot, George – *A global ban on leftwing politics",* in *How Did we Get into this Mess,* Verso, London, New York, 2016 – http://www.monbiot.com/2013/11/04/a-global-ban-on-left-wing-politics/

[45] See the documentary *Chomsky & Cia*, subtitles in Portuguese, https://www.youtube.com/watch?v=IHSe9FRGpJU

expansion of corporate consensus-building giants have allowed, for example, to delay by decades the people's knowledge of the link between smoking and cancer, to block the expansion of the public health system in the USA, to sell the war over oil control to the world as a struggle to free the Iraqi people from dictatorship and as protection from weapons of mass destruction, and so on. The scale of these mystifications is impressive.

A similar attack on a global scale, in particular in the USA, has been organized to sell to the world not the absence of climate change—the data is too strong for that—but the assumption that "there are controversies", which postpone or halt the inevitable change in the energy matrix.

James Hoggan has completed interesting research on how this industry works. The articulation is strong and involves think tanks. It also includes conservative institutions such as the George C. Marshall Institute, American Enterprise Institute (AEI), Information Council for Environment (ICE), Fraser Institute, Competitive Enterprise Institute (CEI), The Heartland Institute and, of course, the American Petroleum Institute (API) and the American Coalition for Clean Coal Electricity (ACCCE), as well as the Hawthorne Group and many others. Exxon Mobil and Koch Industries are powerful funders: the latter being the great advocate of the Tea Party and Trump candidacy. It also always involves oil, coal, producers of vehicles and guns, much finance, many republicans, and the religious right.[46]

Campaigns of this genre are conveyed by media giants. Globally, Rupert Murdoch easily admitted that he was responsible for the rise of and the support for Margaret Thatcher in the 1980s. He financed a large-scale wiretapping system in Britain and still supports a climate of right-wing hatred through Fox, without getting more than a pat on the hands when they reveal the illegalities practiced. Cambridge Analytica is not an exception, we now face a global manipulation industry.[47]

---

[46] James Hoggan – *The Climate Cover-up: the crusade to deny global warming* – see http://dowbor.org/2009/12/climate-cover-up-the-cruzade-to-deny-global-warming-2.html/; about financiers see http://dowbor.org/2010/04/petroleira-dos-eua-deu-us-50-mi-a-ceticos-do-clima-6.html/; see also the article by Jane Mayer *The dark money of the Koch Brothers,* 2016, http://www.truth-out.org/news/item/35450-the-dark-money-of-the-koch-brothers-is-the-tip-of-a-fully-integrated-network.

[47] On what is aptly called "influence industry", see an excellent overview in Samantha Bradshaw and Philip N. Howard, *A Global Inventory of Organized Social Media Manipulation,* University of Oxford, 2018 http://comprop.oii.ox.ac.uk/wp-content/uploads/sites/93/2018/07/ct2018.pdf

In Brazil 97% of the households have televisions, which take up to 3–4 hours of a person's day and are also present in waiting rooms and transport; we are constantly being bombarded by messages coming from a few groups. With our world view being essentially controlled by four families—the Marinhos, Civita, Frias, and Mesquita—the very concept of free press becomes surreal. The impact in Argentina, Chile, Venezuela and other countries has been impressive in terms of promoting more retrograde standpoints and generating a climate of social hatred. The Brazilian 2018 presidential election used the media and the fakenews industry on a gigantic scale, with tragical results.

The links between media power and the global corporate system is largely indirect, but are still very important. Advertising campaigns have deeply influenced values and behavior, thereby generating obsessive consumerism. This binds the media in two ways: first, because negative news can be presented about the government but never about companies, even when they clog food with pesticides, misrepresent the function of medicines, or sell us products associated with the destruction of forests in the Amazon.

Second, since advertising is remunerated by audience points, it is essential to broadcast a rose-tinted world on the one hand, with crime and police persecution on the other. This is all done in order to attract punctual and fragmented attention, which creates a misinformed or frightened population that is, above all, obsessed with consumerism. Advertising is, of course, paid for in the price of the products we buy. The circle is complete. The outcome is an uninformed and consumerist society. Advertising, the kind of programs and information presented, consumerism, and corporative interests all shape an articulate and coherent universe, albeit ruinous in terms of the democratic functioning of society (p. 217).[48]

Control of schooling and academic publications

In addition to having the command of think tanks and media, the control of academic opinion has advanced radically in recent decades through direct corporate funding, with direct control, in particular, over scientific publications. In many countries, and especially in Brazil, universities have been bought by transnational groups that favor a corporate outlook. This trend is particularly open in economics studies. Helena Ribeiro gives an

---

[48] See the short but excellent commentary by George Monbiot, *How did we get into this mess,* with the same name - Verso, London/New York, http://www.monbiot.com/2007/08/28/how-did-we-get-into-this-mess/

example of this profound corruption of teaching at Notre Dame University in Indiana. Given that it was 2009 and that, according to all, the financial world was collapsing, students thought this would be a great topic for discussion in their macroeconomics class. The teacher's response was as follows: "The students were curtly informed that the issue was not in the discipline's planned curriculum, nor was it mentioned in the references attached and, therefore, the teacher did not intend to deviate from the lesson that was planned. And that is what he did" (*Jornal dos Negócios*, 2013). The Ribeiro paper shows the extent of this corruption, and describes the protests by students and the multiplication of alternative centers of economic research, such as the New Economics Foundation, the Young Economists Network, the Institute of New Economic Thinking and many other institutions.[49]

Less perceived but equally important, is the oligopolization of the control of scientific publications in the world. According to a Canadian study, the oligopoly of academic publishing houses in the digital age, "in social sciences, which includes specialties such as sociology, economics, anthropology, political sciences and urban studies, is quite striking: while the top five publishers accounted for 15% of papers in 1995, this value reached 66% in 2013." Here we have the impressive hold of world groups like Reed-Elsevier, Springer, Wiley-Blackwell, and others (Larivière, 2015).[50]

The conflict here is evident: numerous researchers are quitting the cartel of disseminating scientific papers for profit and, instead, publishing for free online using arXiv, PlosOne, and others. MIT, today one of the leading research centers in the world, makes its publications and research available with the use of OCW (Open Course Ware). Open educational resources systems and others are multiplying, including in China (CORE: China Open Resources for Education). In the USA there are already more than 15,000 scientists who refuse to publish with Elsevier and other oligopoly groups. However, in Brazil, the very system of classification and ranking

---

[49] Helena Ribeiro – *Os protestos nas universidades por um novo ensino da economia – Jornal dos Negócios*, Lisbon December 2013 – http://dowbor.org/2013/12/helena-oliveira-o-protesto-nas-universidades-por-um-no-ensino-da-economia-dezembro-2013-3p.html/

[50] V. Larivière, S. Haustein and P. Mongeon – *The Oligopoly of Academic Publishers in the Digital Era* – PlosOne, 2015, http://dowbor.org/2016/02/the-oligopoly-of-academic-publishers-in-the-digital-era-vincent-lariviere-stefanie-haustein-philippe-mongeon-published-june-10-2015-15p.html/

of teachers and academic institutions privileges those who publish in the oligopoly.

The Economist, with its solid tradition of advocating for private interests, also rebels: "In 2011 Elsevier, the biggest academic-journal publisher, made a profit of £768m ($1.2 billion) on revenues of £2.1 billion. Such margins (37%, up from 36% in 2010) are possible because the content is largely provided for free by researchers, and the academics who peer-review their papers are usually unpaid volunteers [...] The aim of academic journals is to make the best research widely available. Many have ended up doing the opposite. It is time that changed."[51]

In this case, the essential aspect for us is that the corporate control of academic publications favors the mass of pseudo-surveys that are of interest to the corporations themselves, as has been seen in the many publications that minimize the impact of smoking and cancer, neonicotinoids, climate change, the causes of obesity, and the like. David Miller's studies show how scientific research itself is largely funded and appropriated: "In the corporate world, managing science is simply a part of broader strategies for influencing government policies in ways that protect profits. Building up scientific controversy, in other words, is part of lobbying."[52]

Erosion of privacy: direct control of people

In addition to these power-capture mechanisms we have to add the radical erosion of privacy in the last decades. Today, the blood of our lives runs in magnetic media, leaving traces of everything we buy or read, our friends' networks, the medicines we take, and our level of indebtedness. Companies have access to an employee's pregnancy by purchasing information from laboratories. The Identification Number that the pharmacies ask for when purchasing medicine is part of this universe. Our life leaves traces that are visible, identifiable, and individualized.

The argument by large groups for holding all this information about people is that they use "anonymized" information, but the truth is that

---

[51] About this war of control of scientific publications, see Dowbor, 2011 - http://dowbor.org/2011/08/o-professor-frente-a-propriedade-intelectual-7.html/; *The Economist,* in an impressive turnaround, has come to attack the system that holds back the expansion of science in the name of protecting its quality see http://dowbor.org/2012/04/o-questionavel-mercado-das-revistas-academicas.html/

[52] David Miller – *Sweet'n'sour*, *New Scientist*, November 12, 2016, p. 20

cross-analyzing electronic traces allow persons to be perfectly individualized and this then influences potential political persecution, difficulties in employment, or higher financial costs from insurers or banks. Access to confidential business information also radically weakens smaller economic groups vis-a-vis giants who may have access to internal communications. It is not just a high level of espionage, as seen in the conversations recorded between Dilma and Merkel. This affects all of us and it has the support of global systems that can capture and process information the size of the NSA. *Big Brother is Watching You* is no longer just literature.[53] In fact, this happens with our generous contributions through social media in which we write permanent descriptions of our activities, which are then analyzed by powerful algorithms.

The general public tends to feel that no one will be interested in personal information about them, until they see that information come up when they are looking for a job, applying for a visa, or in need of a loan. With modern technology, which can amass detailed and individualized information about billions of people, privacy invasion is a reality and represents a potent instrument of power.[54]

Control of governments through public debt

Political power, which results from public debt mechanism, plays an important part in this game. Large financial groups have enough power to impose the appointment of officials at key posts such as central banks or treasury ministries, or even in parliamentary committees, with people from their own sphere, transforming external pressure into internalized structural power. The policy suggested to governments is that it is more popular to expand public debt than to levy taxes.

"These financial institutions are major owners of government debt, which gives them even greater leverage over the policies and priorities of governments. Exercising this power, they typically demand the same thing: austerity measures and 'structural reforms' designed to advance a

[53] Lane, S. Frederick – *The Naked Employee*- AMACOM, New York, 2003 http://dowbor.org/2005/06/the-naked-employee-o-empregado-nu-privacidade-no-emprego.html/

[54] An excellent presentation of how the system operates on the planet can be found in Glenn Greenwald, *No place to hide,* Picador, 2015

neoliberal market economy that ultimately benefits those same banks and corporations. It is the debt trap" (Marshall).[55]

We will return to this subject in detail when analyzing the impact of public debt in Brazil. In the world, in general, we can see the result from the obvious examples of Greece, Portugal, Spain, and others, but also the United States and other developed countries. The common denominator is the use of debt as a power lever and as a factor of appropriation of the surplus produced by society.[56]

The political dimension of tax havens

We have already seen the absolutely overwhelming dimension that tax havens have assumed, as they manage a stock that is equivalent to about a quarter to a third of the world's GDP. A similar proportion of GDP, about $520 billion, is the estimated share of Brazilian capital. We are concerned here with the political dimension of this process. We saw that in 2016 the government begged large groups to repatriate their resources and then gave them advantages to encourage this. These actions were then praised in the media because 46 billion reais was returned to the country, out of a total of R$1,700 billion . A trifle.

Indeed, the existence of tax havens means that any fiscal and monetary policy decision has to face the reality that if large fortunes are threatened, they have the option of simply disappearing from the map of the Treasury ministry by placing themselves under the shelter of offshore secrecy. Even more important is that any control of tax evasion, fraud in the invoices, mechanisms such as transfer pricing, and even the control of who owns what in the complex systems of cross-ownership with segments closeted, becomes precarious.

Nor is it secondary that in this era of largely white-collar organized crime repression becomes inefficient, while financial crime begins to penetrate the political machine and the judiciary. In times of piracy, there were islands in the Caribbean where pirates were considered untouchable and,

---

[55] Andrew C. Marshall – *Bank crimes pay under the thumb of the global financial mafiocracy* – Truthout, December 8, 2015 – http://www.truth-out.org/news/item/33942-bank-crimes-pay-under-the-thumb-of-the-global-financial-mafiocracy

[56] A particulalry well documented analysis can be found in Eric Toussaint, *Bankocracy,* Resistance Books, UK, 2015

therefore, they always had guaranteed refuge and could even trade and negotiate the proceeds of robberies. Frankly, today's tax havens are quite similar.[57]

More serious still is the fact that financial giants such as HSBC and others play a crucial role in managing criminal resources by making not only their cover up expertise but also their powerful legal advisories available. The fluidity of immaterial money, now a mere digital representation on computers that can be transferred and redirected in seconds, makes repression increasingly precarious. Additionally, the fact that crime navigates the planetary space, while control is limited to national spaces, makes the process even more difficult. Interpol is impressive. Unfortunately, just impressive.

Reducing the government's capacity to promote adequate monetary and financial policies to foster development affects all nations. This leads to the erosion of governance and the demoralization of politics and democracy. These resources are desperately needed today to finance a technological reconversion that will enable us to stop destroying the planet and ensure the productive inclusion of billions of excluded people; thereby reducing the inequality that has reached explosive levels.[58]

Financial profitability requirements and the corporate power pyramid

Today, with much more power in the hands of the financial giants in control of the real economic world of companies that produce goods and services, financial returns tend to become the central objective. This, in

[57] A French judge (*juge d'instruction*), Jean de Maillard, has organized the *Atlas mondial de la Finance Illégale,* which shows the main procedures. More recent studies on the world drug mafia show how global logistics, money laundering, international cocaine quotas, legal counseling and similar networks are organized. A country like Mexico has now become largely ungovernable. In the absence of power to confront organized crime, the United States focuses on mass incarceration. With 4% of the world population and 25% of the incarcerated population, they let organized crime loose. See Elizabeth Hinton, *From the war on poverty to the war on crime: mass incarceration in America* - Harvard, 2016

[58] We have seen in chapter 6 the research by Shaxson, Nicholas – *Treasure Islands: uncovering the damage of offshore banking and tax havens* - St. Martin's Press, New York, 2011 - http://dowbor.org/2015/10/nicholas-shaxson-treasure-islands-uncovering-the-damage-of-offshore-banking-and-tax-havens-st-martins-press-new-york-2011.html/

turn, precludes initiatives, at the level of the engineers and technicians who know the productive processes of the real economy, in order to preserve a minimum of professional decency and corporate ethics. We will then have chaos in terms of the discrepancy between financial profitability and economic and social development goals. There are undoubtedly tensions and wars among the financial giants; however, this is a directed and logical chaos when it comes to warranting a large flow of financial resources towards the top of the hierarchy. Their chaotic competition can lead to systemic crises, but when it comes to curbing control or regulatory initiatives, these corporations react in a united and organized way.

Money rules money and it is the big financial groups who control it. In Brazil, where the financial system sterilizes resources through exorbitant interest rates, it is impressive that an industrial pressure group such as the FIESP (Industrial Federation of the State of São Paulo), which should represent industries, joined the 2016 coup while entrepreneurs, who produce goods and services, are actually interested in reorganizing the financial system and ensuring access to cheap credit.[59]

The truth is that the decision-making control of the real economy companies by the financial system has become general. The resilience of traditional productive entrepreneurs is not only scarce but might disappear when greater profitability does not come from the assembly line but results, instead, from financial investments. Governments have had to face powerful and articulate resistance as they try to boost the economy. Recovering the “confidence” of the “market” does not mean generating better production conditions, but better conditions for the profitability of financial papers. Production, employment, sustainable development, and the welfare of families are not on the horizon of the present decision-making processes.

The basic reference point for capitalism from another era, in which the pursuit of business profit generated products, employment, and income, fell apart. The financial drain blocks the whole system. We face this paradox of fantastic technological advances that would allow so many economic, social, and environmental advances, but that generate the marasmus which was so well illustrated by the image of “general jelly” used in Brazil.

---

[59] This rare manifestation of common sense by Benjamin Steinbruch, Vice-president of FIESP and president of CSN is impressive: "In addition to trust, the consumer needs credit, but with a civilized interest, and not with the absurd current cost, which surpasses 300% per year." - Valor, Aug 25, 2015.

Capture of the UN decision-making process

Faced with the global power of corporations, which operate in all spaces of the planet, we do not have corresponding multilateral public instruments. In fact, on the contrary, we can see a documented capture of the UN's decision-making process by the same corporate groups.

The Global Policy Forum study directly focuses on the fact that corporate interests have had a disproportionate influence on the institutions that define the global ground rules. This document presents the "growing influence of the business sector in the political discourse and agenda-setting [of international organizations]", questioning whether "partnership initiatives allow the corporate sector and their interest groups growing influence over agenda setting and political decision-making by governments". In the timid and prudent way that characterizes so many international texts, the essential information is stated here. According to Leonardo Bissio, "this book shows how Big Tobacco, Big Soda, Big Pharma and Big Alcohol end up prevailing and how corporate philanthropy and private-public-partnerships twist the international agenda without government oversight, but it also clearly spells out some practical ways to prevent it and rescue a citizens-based multilateralism" (GFI, p. 1 and p. 9).

Do we need to remember that the UN has $40 billion for all its activities, while each of the SIFI financial giants we have seen above handles an average of $1.8 trillion? The BIS, the IMF, and the WB today, frankly, only follow what is going on. They publish interesting and sometimes surprisingly explicit reports.

The so-called risk assessment agencies Standard & Poor's, Moody's and Fitch, which attribute reliability ratings to countries and corporations, sell higher ratings for cash. Moody's, when convicted, agreed to pay $864 million. Standard & Poor has already paid over 1 billion. No one is arrested and so no one needs to acknowledge guilt. The money comes from contributing companies and it is in the prices we pay. This is systemic corruption and co-opted justice (money paid absolves the guilt). The irony is that they give us lessons about fiscal and financial responsibility.

Martin Wolf is the chief economist for the *Financial Times*. He is well-placed to provide the reality shock that we all need: "Widely shared increases in real incomes played a vital part in legitimizing capitalism and stabilizing democracy. Today, however, capitalism is finding it far more difficult to generate such improvements in prosperity. On the contrary, the evidence is of growing inequality and slowing productivity growth. This poisonous brew makes democracy intolerant and capitalism illegitimate."[60]

The dilemma of governments: who to serve?

In terms of economic mechanisms, at the current stage, the appropriation of social surplus is central not only through low salaries but increasingly through financial systems that appropriate the right over the social product through public and private debt. This form of wealth appropriation has become extremely powerful. Faced with the new global mechanisms of exploitation, which operates on a planetary scale, and even resorts to shelter in tax havens, national governments have become largely powerless.

We have structured global finance against a political power that is fragmented in 200 nations. This power in its various dimensions, within the nations themselves is being largely fractured by dissension and it is, therefore, easily captured. In this way, we have become systemically dysfunctional.

Wolfgang Streeck shows an interesting system for this capture of public power at government level. Through the indebtedness of the State and other mechanisms, as seen above, a process is generated in which the government has increasingly been accountable to the "market", forsaking citizenry. This way, for the survival of a government, the most important aspect is not to how it is meeting the interests of the population that elected it, but whether the market—that is, the financial interests—feel satisfied enough to declare it "trustworthy". As such, instead of a republic, or a *res publica*, we have a *res mercatori*: a thing of the market. An abridged chart helps us to understand the radical shift of these politics (p. 81).[61]

Citizen State	**Market State**
national	international
citizens	investors
civil rights	contractual rights

[60] Martin Wolf - Real World Economics Review - Sept. 8, 2016 https://rwer.wordpress.com/2016/09/08/capitalism-vs-democracy/

[61] Wolfgang Streeck, *Buying time* – Verso, London 2014 – http://dowbor.org/category/dicas-de-leitura/

voters	creditors
elections (periodic)	auctions (continuous)
public opinion	interest rates
loyalty	"trust"
public service	debt service

Of course, one is financed by taxes, the other by credit. A government thus depends on "two environments that set contradictory demands on their behavior" (p. 80). Between public opinion on the quality of government and the "risk assessment" of the same government to pay high interest on their debt, for example, the option of political survival tends more and more towards what we mysteriously call "the markets". Where there was welfare and social policies, we will now have austerity and financial profits.

This corporate power manages to generate tax systems that proportionally burden those who earn less. Financial power begets legal power, and the State has become an instrument of the privatization of its own taxes. A very significant and comprehensive standpoint, according to Streeck, is that we are not facing the end of capitalism but, instead, the end of democratic capitalism. When millions of diversified companies compete with each other in a loose and dispersed mass, the State could play an important stabilizing role and guarantee the larger interests of society. When facing today's articulated giants, the system dismisses democracy that so many market ideologies are believed to defend.

Also significant is the analysis by Saskia Sassen, the author of landmark research into governance and globalization, in her 2006 book *Territory, Authority, Rights*: "I assert that the specific institutional components of the national state begin to function as the space for the operation of powerful constituent dynamics of what we could describe as 'global capital' and 'global capital markets'. By doing so, these state institutions redirect their specific political activity, or more broadly, the state's agendas in the sense of the demands of global economy" (p. 412). Analyzing what she calls the State's denationalized agendas, the author writes that "central banks and governments seem to be increasingly concentrated on pleasing financial markets, rather than pursuing economic and social welfare goals. We recall here the governments of Argentina and Brazil after the Mexican crisis, in 1994, which promised not to devalue their currencies and do everything necessary to avoid it, even leading the middle-low classes into poverty [...] One critical issue is whether the citizens of their respective countries want the global capital market to exercise this discipline over their governments and impose such criteria on national economic policy, doing so at all costs—jobs, wages, security, health—and with no public debate" (p. 263).

The financial groups are absolutely not concerned if the economy breaks down or not: "The speculative character of many markets means that they will stretch profit-making opportunities to the best of their ability, whatever the implicit damage to the national economy" (p. 263). From Sassen's standpoint there is no longer the "national" versus the "global" because the global, particularly due to these financial mechanisms, has been included in the national.[62]

Research and understanding of the new power articulations are mandatory in order to understand the radically new mechanisms and scale of wealth accumulation in the hands of 0.01% of the world's population and the staggering figure of 8 billionaires who own more wealth than the poorer half of the world population. Equally significant is that the Brazilian economy is in recession when banks, such as Bradesco and Itaú, have declared profit increases between 25% and 30% in 12 months. Brazil is not an island.[63]

To a certain extent, when analyzing the mechanisms of the capture of power, we are unraveling the channels that allow the dramatic strengthening of inequality between and within nations, in addition to blocking economic growth by diverting resources from investment to financial allocations. Re-establishing regulation and control over these financial giants, who have come to rule the world's economy and the internal decisions of nations, seems to be unrealistic, due to the size and sophisticated organizational structure they have today and, of course, their degree of control over politics, the legal system, productive corporations, the media, and academia—and, therefore, public opinion—as we have seen above.

Here, the international dimension is crucial. Almost all of these groups are USA-based or European Union corporations. It is the dominant embodiment of a power that is global but which, in essence, pertains to what we have become accustomed to call the "West". Attempts to build a counterbalance through the articulation of the BRICs demonstrates both the importance of

---

[62] Sassen, Saskia - *Territory, Authority, Rights: from medieval to global assemblies* – Princeton University Press, 2006

[63] In relation to 2013, the Itaú and Bradesco banks have an increase in declared profits of 30.2% and 25.9%, respectively. See the Dieese report: http://www.dieese.org.br/desempenhodosbancos/2015/desempenhoBancos2014.pdf

the initiative and its fragility. Global financial power belongs to nations, but with governments duly appropriated by the same groups. The 2016 election in the United States and the appointment of the Exxon executive to be Secretary of State for the international politics of the most powerful country, as well as the choice of Gary Cohn from Goldman Sachs to head the president's economic council–already resigned, we are in Trump times–are significant signs of what we have qualified as a new architecture of power. In Brazil, we have a banker at the head of the Central Bank, and another banker at the head of the Ministry of Finance. A fulltime speculator is expected to take over in 2019. Processes are becoming openly cynical, and people are increasingly skeptical about the importance of voting.

***

The world certainly is not undergoing a shortage of resources. The immense progress of planetary productivity was essentially brought about by the technological revolution we are experiencing. However, the producers of these transformations—from fundamental research in public universities and public policies on health, education, and infrastructure, to technical advances in companies effectively producing goods and services—are not the ones who benefit. On the contrary, both the public and the corporate spheres are indebted to the giants of the financial system, which bestow fortunes on those who have never produced anything but who manage, by maneuvering the lines that control both the public sector and the private productive sector, to radically take us away from the sustainable development that is now vital to the world.

As for the population of a country like Brazil, which seeks to rescue some sovereignty in its peripheral position, what seems to remain is a feeling of powerlessness. Perplexed and in debt, families see their "stained name" pop up on Serasa-Experian—a multinational—if they do not bow to usury. In the chaos of financial rules, they contribute to the concentration of wealth and power through the high interest they pay in installment plans and banks, through surreal interest rates on public debt, and by the so-called "austerity" policies that deprive them of their rights.

These profoundly deformed ground rules will be seriously presented as the natural outcome of a democratic and legitimate process, for it is written in the Constitution that all power stems from the people. In practice, we can have democracy as long as we use it to favor the elites. The construction of democratic control processes and the productive allocation of resources is now a central challenge. Boaventura de Souza Santos rightly states the need to strengthen democracy. However, what we really must do is to retrieve it from the caricature it has now become.

9 - THOMAS PIKETTY: PRODUCTION AND APPROPRIATION

Considering the quality of his reasoning and the worldwide impact of his work, it is worthwhile to introduce the overview that Thomas Piketty has drawn in his *Capital in the 21st Century*. Many arguments help to clarify the analysis we have presented here of the new architecture of power and new forms of exploitation. Instead of dispersing quotes from Piketty in various parts of the present study, I have chosen to present his central ideas in this chapter, because they come together and form a particularly solid and cohesive analysis system. The pages we refer to here are from the original French edition, unless otherwise noted.

The appropriation of public resources

The world of economy is advancing at an approximate rate of 2% or 2.5% a year, which is perfectly respectable but could be higher due to technological advances, as well as the population growth. The remuneration of labor, however, has not accompanied productivity growth with robotization and other technologies. Almost all of the increase in the additional wealth produced goes to the richest 10% and mainly to the top 1%. This income in the hands of the richest, from a certain level of income, can no longer be transformed into consumption, and is invested in different financial products, whose profitability is in the order of 7% for average investments, which rises to 10% for large investments with professional financial managers.

With revenue on capital far surpassing the progress of the economy itself, a cumulative process of proportionally greater enrichment is generated by those who are already richer. The resulting imbalance cannot be reversed by simple market mechanisms. Indeed, we have already returned to the same level of imbalance of a century ago, when the more fortunate used to "live upon their revenues". This is the general dynamic, in which the advances generated by producers are appropriated by rentiers. It is "rentier capitalism" that is right at the center of the rationale.

The particular dynamic we see now, and which appears in the final part of Piketty's study, is that in addition to relatively low wages and household and business debt, financial management systems that manage large fortunes have developed a mechanism for appropriating our taxes through public debt. The pressures of the right to expand public indebtedness are explained thus: "Instead of paying taxes to balance public budgets, Italians—or at least those with the means—lent money to the government by buying Treasury securities or public assets, which allowed them to increase their private assets without thereby increasing national assets" (p. 291).

The Italian case here is just one example, the expansion of the public debt was generalized throughout the planet, while reducing taxes on fortunes and financial operations. Today the United States has a debt of the order of over $16 trillion. As we have seen, public debt in the world stands at more than $55 trillion. The world GDP is about $80 trillion, which represents an annual flow, but the figure helps us to have an order of magnitude: a reference point. Let us also remember that Brazil's GDP, the seventh world economic power, is of the order of $1.7 trillion. Financial transactions, interest on debts, and the like represent only transfers: a zero-sum process with regard to who is entitled to goods and services. "The level of national capital at first glance has not changed. Just its distribution between public and private capital has totally reversed itself" (p. 294). As a matter of fact, "public debt is no more than a right of one part of the country (those receiving interest) on the other party (those who pay taxes): therefore, it must be excluded from the national assets and included only in private assets" (p. 185). This is public rent (*rentes publiques*), which has a particularly disastrous impact when a country faces difficulties, because the investors in public debt bonds tend to force the interest upwards, generating self-reinforcing movement, as has been seen in Brazil, Italy, Greece, Spain, and so many other countries. The State, in this sense, has been transformed into one more vector of the transfer of wealth to the privileged. "There are two main forms for the State to cover its expenditures: through taxes, or through debt. In general, taxation is an infinitely preferable solution, both in terms of justice and effectiveness" (p. 883).

This option for the tax solution is explicit: "The tax on capital puts the burden on those who hold larger assets, while austerity policies generally seek to spare them" (p. 894). Given the international power balance, the common option seen in Europe was the policy of austerity, with restrictions on pensions and social policies, which affects the weakest link in both economic and political terms. Trump's administration attempts to exclude millions of poor Americans from access to health services by liquidating "Obamacare" is very significative.

The Brazilian case is emblematic and, in this sense, could very well illustrate the analysis made by the French researcher. The largest private appropriation of public resources in Brazil, in addition to being legal, uses as its ethical justification "the fight against inflation": this is the Selic rate. As many people know—but most, significantly, do not know—the Selic is the interest rate that the government pays to those who put money into government bonds, thereby generating public debt. The invention of the high Selic rate was a government initiative in the 1990s. From 1996 on, interest paid on government bonds was 25–30%, a fantastic level considering the inflation was around 10%. Thus, with government support, financial intermediaries created a formal and official system of access to our taxes. This allowed the government to buy, with our taxes, the support of the powerful class of rentiers and of the large banks, including transnational financial groups. Thus, the Brazilian rulers organized the mass transfer of public resources to private financial groups. Brazil received the coveted "investment grade" for being exceedingly finance-friendly.

We will see this mechanism in detail later, when analyzing the specific dynamics that this process took in Brazil. To understand the mechanism, see the explanation by Amir Khair, one of the best financial experts in the country, on what he calls "the poison of the economy": "The Copom (Brazilian monetary authority) establishes the Selic. It was set for the first time on July 1, 1996 at 25.3% per annum and remained at a high level, rising to a maximum of 45% in March 1999, justified by the inflation targeting system. It was only lower than 15% after July 2006, but remained in two digits until June 2009, when due to the crisis it was maintained between 8.75% and 10.0% for a year."[64]

By 2015, about 500 billion reais (9% of GDP) was taken from our taxes and transferred essentially to banks and other "investors". This was a cumulative process, as seen in Greece in a more scandalous way, since much of the interest that the State cannot pay is transformed into an increase in the debt stock. There is a monumental transfer of public

[64] Amir Khair, O Estado de São Paulo, September 9, 2012; see also, *A taxa Selic é o veneno da economia,* http://criseoportunidade.wordpress.com/2014/04/09/a-taxa-selic-e-o-veneno-da-economia-entrevista-especial-com-amir-khair-abril-2014-2p/

resources to rentiers who, in addition to costing us a lot of money, stop banks from making productive investments that would generate output and employment. This is because it is much simpler to invest in public debt: total liquidity, zero risk. Making productive investments, such as financing a shoe factory, involves project analysis and a follow-up, in short, activities that go beyond financial papers. That is what the intermediaries should do, at the very least, in order to foster and to irrigate economic activities, mainly because they are working with the money of others. But technically, what they achieve is the sterilization of savings as they take the money out of the economic circuit and transfer it to the financial area.

In our case, the political justification is that keeping interest rates high protects people from inflation. On this point, Piketty agrees with what Amir Khair and others have stated: "Inflation depends on multiple other forces, and in particular international competition on prices and wages" (p. 905). However, for a population who have suffered from past inflations, the argument is powerful, albeit false. With an impressive media campaign, high interest rates appear as positive (protect us from inflation), while taxes appear as negative (bloating the public machine and the like). In practice, the most fortunate people who should be paying their taxes instead invest in public debt and earn money which should have instead been paid back to society through public services.

The absurdity of using the pretext of inflation to raise interest rates only makes sense when we have a demand inflation: that is, when there is high consumer pressure, while producers are unable to increase production at a corresponding pace thereby generating the so-called overheated economy. By raising interest rates, which attract resources for financial allocations rather than consumption, the economy “cools”. Of course, in the case of Brazil, where productive entrepreneurs do not know what to do with their idle stocks and are working at 67% of capacity, this argument makes no sense. It is not an argument; it is an excuse. The fact that the mass media and even economists support this reasoning is simply shameful.

The analysis that Piketty's book presents about the public debt issue point to yet another problem: the financial chaos that has been generated. Cyprus is part of the European Union, however, no one had accurate information about the origin or interests of the holders of their public debt. In a way, these groups own parcels of the public system. It was diagnosed that, in Cyprus, they are predominantly Russian oligarchs and they have completely dismantled the country's attempts to balance its accounts. Moreover, throughout his book, Piketty gives us examples of the overall lack of transparency about stocks and financial flows: "Countries do not have automatic transmissions of international bank information or financial records to enable them to share transparently and effectively the gains or the efforts" (p. 908).

The financial system operates on a planetary scale and governments act in spaces delimited by national borders. The public finances themselves, as a result, are thrown onto this merry-go-round. The main idea that stands out is that the financial allocations and the movement of financial papers, yields more than production. The obvious result is that money will go where it pays more, thereby fattening financial fortunes and halting initiatives that boost the economy: such as household consumption, business investments, and public investment in social and infrastructure areas. The imbalance between those who produce and those who profit makes the system inoperative, or at the very least truncated, and throws away the immense potential for advancement that modern technologies could provide. To confront unproductive finance is the main vector for the recovery of systemic productivity.

The progressive tax on capital

How should we face the globalized patrimonial capitalism of the 21st century? This is the central issue that is addressed in the study by Piketty. The challenge tends to be discouraging. The author refers courageously to the "useful utopia" that he suggests. Even more so because he is a realist and fully aware "of the degree of foul play achieved by the economic and financial elites in defending their interests, as well as sometimes by economists, who now occupy an enviable position in the American revenue hierarchy, and who often have an unfortunate tendency to defend their private interests, which are always concealed behind a doubtful defense of the general interest" (p. 834).

What Piketty proposes will not be easy. The average congressman in the United States has personal assets of about $15 million, compared to the average American adult's assets of $200,000. We are reminded of Lincoln's dilemmas when trying to make a congress of slaveholders to vote for the end of slavery. Biographers comment on how a righteous man resorted to the most crooked methods in order to achieve the greatest civilizing advance in American history.

The broader propositive standpoint is along the lines of a progressive tax on accumulated financial capital. Since market mechanisms, instead of generating a balanced economy, create a cumulative process of inequality with an uncontrolled spiral of reduced enrichment linked to the lack of productive contribution, an institutional intervention to organize redistribution is mandatory. "The ideal tool", writes the author, "would be a worldwide and progressive tax on capital, accompanied by a very extensive international financial transparency. Such an undertaking would avoid a spiral of unending inequality and effectively regulate the disturbing dynamics of global concentration of wealth" (p. 835).

It is not only a matter of stopping uncontrolled dynamics, but of resetting and broadening social policies, for which public action is essential. Piketty is absolutely clear on the essential weight of social policies in the balanced post-war development phase. The State is not "a cost" or a financial burden, when it provides free universal public services that benefit families, in particular education and health services financed directly by the government. These "*in natura* transfers" have as much value as monetary transfers accounted for in available income as they exempt families from disbursing comparable sums—sometimes markedly higher––to private producers of education and health services.

Here Piketty converges with the contributions of Amartya Sen in his agreement that social policies, even if presented as expenditure, are in fact an investment in people, with generalized productive impacts.[65] Piketty is first and foremost a historian of economics. His long-term analysis allows—and this is felt throughout the book—a very broad view which reduces simplifications and ideological flag-waving. To see the indignant declarations of the rich a century ago when the collection of income tax was instituted with only a few percentage points from people of high income, give us the perspective that certain things that seemed absolutely impossible can become part of everyday life. In fact, it was the expansion of the tax burden in Europe and the United States that allowed civilized advances: "The development of the Fiscal State during the last century corresponds essentially to the constitution of a social state" (p. 765).

Piketty's study also shows that the various forms of basic income, with great social impact, represent very limited costs. The "social minima", as he calls them, "correspond to less than 1% of national income, almost

---

[65] A particularly well-presented systematization of these new trends can be found in document ECLAC, of the UN, *La Hora de la Igualdad*, with a short version in Portuguese.
http://dowbor.org/2010/11/cepal-la-hora-de-la-igualdad-brechas-por-cerrar-caminos-por-abrir.html

insignificant in the scale of total public expenditure." Here we can see the humanist, conscious of the ideological war: "These are, however, expenditures frequently facing the greatest violence: the beneficiaries are suspected of choosing to settle permanently in the aid, although the number of requests for these 'minimums' is generally much smaller than that for other benefits, which reflects that the effects of stigma (and often the complexity of provisions) often tend to dissuade those who would be entitled to them."

In the United States, the stigma against the poor pairs with thinly veiled racism: "One notices that this type of questioning of social minimums in both the United States (where the image of the single, black and idle mother plays the role of absolute rejection for those who despise the meager American Welfare State) and also in Europe." The author reports the "prison state" that sometimes replaces the provider state: 5% of black men in the United States are in prisons (p. 765). Incidentally, the catastrophic prison situation in Brazil cannot be forgotten. Where there are more than 600,000 imprisoned men, 40% are under provisional arrest. Roughly 63 thousand persons were assassinated in 2017 who, in the great part, were young, black, and poor men.

There are, therefore, immense gains to be found in social productivity through the redirection of resources and the taxation of their speculative and unproductive use. Another important vector of the wealth tax is the transparency that will be created. We saw above that something equivalent to about a quarter to a third of the world's GDP is hidden in tax havens, creating a vast disorganization of financial information, as well as tax evasion and opening doors to arms and drug trafficking. Tax evasion concerns is mostly done by those who should pay the most.[66]

Piketty's proposals are aimed at creating a progressive, yet limited, amount of tax on accumulated assets to begin reducing the planetary chaos. In fact, this proposal is close to the Tobin Tax (a proposal for taxation of international financial transactions) generating resources and, above all, allowing the recording of flows. An example of a possible tax would be exemption or 0.1% for those who have no wealth at all or below EUR 1 million, of 1% between EUR 1 million and EUR 5 million and so on (p. 943).

---

[66] On this subject see http://dowbor.org/2012/11/os-descaminhos-do-dinheiro-os-paraisos-fiscais-parte-v-novembro-2012-7p.html/; see also Kofi Annan, *How global tax could transform Africa's fortunes, http://dowbor.org/2013/09/kofi-annan-g20-how-global-tax-reform-could-transform-africas-fortunes.html/*

The strongest argument is that we need to commit this unproductive capital, which yields rents without productive contribution, often by the simple transfer of our taxes (as our Selic rate), the reduction of public debt, and funding more social policies in addition to financing technological and productive investments in general. The tax on capital already exists in an incipient form in several countries. It is just a matter of fostering a policy that has now become vital at a planetary level.

Utopian? No doubt. However, income tax ("the rich would never accept"), basic incomes, the right to strike, and so many other impossibilities used to be considered utopian until they became lodged in people's minds. A strong argument is that those unproductive fortune holders, faced by taxes on idle capital, would consider doing something useful with their money. Upon finding out that the tax on unproductive capital reduces their stock, they could remember their capitalist past, open a business, hire people, and generate the goods and services needed by society.

A useful utopia?

Piketty has a clear position against the excesses of inequality. Without giving way to hatred or prejudice, he offers extremely solid empirical grounds for understanding how detrimental the rentiers' reign has become to economics and politics. In my opinion, it is the most useful tool in the last decades, helping us to understand the current economic, social, and political dynamics. Faced with the unbridled and cumulative concentration of wealth in a few hands and the chaos that is progressively settling in, he considers that inequality has become the main challenge and the progressive tax on accumulated capital, the main tool:

> The world tax on capital is the ideal instrument for regulation, it has the merit of preserving economic openness and globalization, while at the same time regulating it effectively and fairly sharing benefits within and between countries. Many will reject the capital tax as a dangerous illusion, just as the income tax was rejected a little over a century ago. However, with a close look, this solution is far less dangerous than the alternative options (p. 837).

Ignacy Sachs declares himself adept at understanding the mixed economy. I tend to follow this line, as can be seen in my former publications. A curious example is China who, with 20% of the world's population, is responsible for the 70% decrease in the world's poor population: "China's economic system relies on public property to serve as its main structure but allowing the development of all types of property. Both public and non-public ownership are key components of the socialist market economy. This is a diversified ownership economy".[67] We will return to the Chinese example, but here it is noteworthy that more importantly than faithfully adhering to a certain "ism", we can study the various experiences that yield positive results.

After overcoming the major ideological simplifications of the last century, today we seek innovative governance. At the end of his book, Piketty stresses that "the nation-state remains a relevant level for the profound modernization of numerous social and fiscal policies, and also, to a certain extent, to develop new forms of governance and shared as well as private ownership, as one of the great challenges of the future. But only regional political integration allows us to consider an effective regulation of the globalized equity capitalism of this beginning century" (p. 945).

In this passage, he characterizes a phase of capitalism (globalized and patrimonial), the expression of different territorial scales (the nation-state and regional policy), and the articulation of diverse forms of property, in particular, "shared ownership". What he seeks is, like Stiglitz, a civilized capitalism. It may not be ideal, but in face of the catastrophes that are growing, it would be considered to be reasonable progress.

This is more than an ideological positioning as when characterizing the challenges, Piketty expresses the complexity of the current transition and argues that national politics does not regulate an economy that has become globalized. Financial power has come to dominate not only the productive economy but also democratic mechanisms. We have diverse forms of ownership (public, private, associative), of management (concessions, sharing, co-management), control (local, national, regional jurisdiction) and legal frameworks (from local to global). This is the challenge of governance in a much more complex and diversified economy.[68]

Property is no longer sufficient to define the type of economic animal that lies ahead. We may have a publicly-owned hospital, managed under concession by a medical cooperative, under the control of a municipal

---

[67] China Daily, 2014, *The Decision on Major Issues,* http://dowbor.org/2014/04/the-decision-on-major-issues-concerning-comprehensively-deepening-reforms-in-briefchina-daily-november-2013-12p.html/ About recent transformations in China, see the excellent *China's Economy* de Arthur Kroeber, Oxford, 2016

[68] For an overview of property alternatives, see Marjorie Kelly, *Owning our Future: the emerging ownership revolution,* BK Publishers, Oakland, 2012

health council, and within a state or federal regulatory framework. It is the age of complex society. However, our guiding line remains the same: we cannot continue to destroy the planet for the benefit of a minority that disrupts even the productive processes and we must prioritize what effectively works. By this we mean democratic access, rather than functionality for minorities. Managing for the privileged is easier, but inevitably leads to deadlocks.

The work of Piketty and his team is not a revolutionary proposition, but it has helped to clear the midfield by providing instruments for thinking about tools and alternatives. In theoretical terms, it approaches the line of institutional economics; it does not seek to overthrow capitalism, but to rescue the capacity of the political level—where we can have some democracy—to exert its regulatory role over the whole process. I have been working along the lines of "Economic Democracy", that is, the concept that the economy itself has to be democratized, with new mechanisms of regulation, transparency, participation, and democratic control. Together with Ignacy Sachs and Carlos Lopes, in *Crises and Opportunities in Times of Change*, we tried to outline propositive mainstays along this line.[69]

The creation of a progressive global tax on capital, as proposed by Piketty, is a necessary point of reference. Coupled with this proposal—and as explained throughout the book—is the need to create informative systems and to be able to enlighten the black box that has today become the financial flow. This can be initiated at a national level, but it requires a worldwide system of information and control.

There remains, of course, the big question: is the present political-institutional framework conducive to such modest advances?

---

[69] See here in the Attachment, the 13 propositive lines, which form part of the 2013 study, *Crises e Oportunidades em tempos de mudança* http://dowbor.org/2013/05/crises-e-oportunidades-em-tempos-de-mudanca-jan-2.html/; *Economic Democracy*, Lambert Academic Publishing, Saarbrucken, 2014 - http://dowbor.org/blog/wp-content/uploads/2012/06/12-DemoEco1.doc

10 - APPROPRIATION OF SOCIAL SURPLUS BY FINANCIAL CAPITAL

Sometimes we need a mirror. When it comes to the Brazilian reality, with the degree of ideological deformation of arguments, it is fundamental to follow the international debate on the rescue of the financial system. We are not an island and the deformations of our financial system are basically the same but magnified. A solid collection of research, launched after the 2008 crisis, shows how far the financial system has strayed from its initial goals which were to finance investment and economic growth. As the United States plays a structuring role in financial dynamics, a study of their mechanisms helps us to understand our own deformation.

One of such studies is that by Epstein and Montecino from the Roosevelt Institute. The title speaks for itself: *Overcharged: the high cost of high finance*. This provides an overview of the economic impact of financial intermediation, as it works in the USA, showing that this system not only does not foment the economy, but drains it. It inhibits activities, thereby generating more costs than productive stimuli. We have here a systemic and integrated overview of how this financial machine has grown and been radically distorted. This study also helps us to understand the Brazilian system, insofar as the deformations presented are the same; however, they do present as more radical in Brazil as they instituted a national system of legalized loan-sharking.

The international financial system works at full throttle. The culture of financial intermediation does not vary much between the City in London, Wall Street, or the system of usury that was established in Brazil. There is a global financial culture. In the Brazilian case, the mismatch is evident when we find that after 2014 the GDP dropped sharply while interest and profits of financial intermediaries increased between 20% and 30% a year. The Brazilian financial intermediation system does not serve the economy but is, instead, served by it. This is negative net productivity. The financial machine is living at the expense of the real economy. It helps and provides confidence to the ongoing research in Brazil when reading this simple remark by Stiglitz: "While finance used to be a mechanism for putting money into companies, it now draws money out of them".[70]

There are people who find it difficult to imagine a large international bank extorting money from their clients. They believe that in the USA these things would be serious, let alone in Europe. Curiously, many people think that even in Brazil banks are serious. One must remember some obvious things. Despite its millions of customers, in September 2016 Deutsche Bank was convicted of fraud by the USA courts and fined $14 billion; to put this in context, this is one and a half times the amount that the "Bolsa Família" which took 50 million people out of misery. This is not an isolated case: a bank as serious as Citigroup has been ordered to pay $12 billion (although this was settled for $7 billion), Goldman Sachs paid $5.06 billion, JPMorgan Chase & Co paid $3 billion, and the Bank of America $16.7 billion. We are talking about large banks, who are permanently audited, who have committed crimes that include giving fraudulent information to customers, the most diverse forgeries, plundering clients, cheating the tax office, laundering dirty money, and forging information on interest rates, amongst others.[71]

Everybody has heard of financialization, but few realize the depth of the overall distortion of the economic, social, and environmental processes which has been caused by the migration of our resources from economic development (through investments) to unproductive gains (through financial allocations) via banks. The media refers to "investment", which sounds more noble than financial/asset allocations or speculation. *The Economist* even invented the term "speculative investors", and Stiglitz refers to "productive investments" to differentiate, since in English the

---

[70] Epstein, Gerald and Juan Antonio Montecino – *Overcharged: the high cost of high finance* – The Roosevelt Institute, July 2016 – http://rooseveltinstitute.org/overcharged-high-cost-of-high-finance/; the book by Stiglitz, *Rewriting the Rules of the American Economy,* may be found in full at: http://dowbor.org/blog/wp-content/uploads/2015/06/report-stiglitz.pdf

[71] *The Guardian* of September 16, 2016 provides a short summary, see: https://www.theguardian.com/business/2016/sep/16/deutsche-bank-must-pay-14bn-fine-to-settle-us-mortgage-case?CMP=share_btn_fb. In the *Financial Times* this is a daily affair; one example is the case of the manipulation of 2 million customers by Wells Fargo, as reported on Sept 20, 2016 and reproduced in *The Guardian* on the same date. *The Economist* of August 30, 2014 argues that "Corporate America is finding it harder and harder to stay on the right side of the law" (p. 21). The traditional "too big to fail" has now become "too big to jail" (idem p. 24).

term “financial allocation” or “asset allocation” is seldom used and, instead, everything is called an “investment”. This financial casino is referred to as financial industry, which sounds very productive.

There is no escaping the simple reality that starting a business, hiring workers, producing and paying taxes is much more difficult than investing in public debt bonds, but still this is what drives the economy. When you buy securities, it might be profitable, but you have not produced anything, you have only generated earnings with no counterpart and, from a certain level, it becomes a dead weight on economic activities in general. In terms of economic functionality, Epstein and Montecino refer to a spectacular failure: "A healthy financial system is one that channels finance to productive investment, helps families save for and finance big expenses such as higher education and retirement, provides products such as insurance to help reduce risk, creates sufficient amounts of useful liquidity, runs an efficient payment mechanism, and generates financial innovations to do all these useful things more cheaply and effectively. All of these functions are crucial to a stable and productive market economy. But after decades of deregulation, the current U.S. financial system has evolved into a highly speculative system that has failed rather spectacularly at performing these critical tasks" (p. 1).

With regard to positive measures, the issue is to retrieve and restructure the system of regulation so that the financial system serves the economy and is not merely served by it. We have to generate alternative systems of financial intermediation, allowing people to regain their capacity of choice: "These excessive costs of finance can be reduced and the financial sector can once again play a more productive role in society. To accomplish this, we need three complementary approaches: improved financial regulation, building on what Dodd-Frank has already accomplished; restructuring the financial system to better serve the needs of our communities, small businesses, households, and public entities; and public financial alternatives, such as cooperative banks and specialized banks, to level the playing field" (p. 3).

How has the financial system gradually been deformed so that it currently imposes enormous costs on the real economy, forcing it to sustain an immense speculative superstructure? “We show how the asset management industry charges excessive fees and delivers mediocre returns for households trying to save for retirement; how private equity firms grab excessive levels of payments from pension funds and other investors while often worsening wages and employment opportunities for workers in the companies they buy; how hedge funds underperform; and how predatory lenders exploit some of the most vulnerable people in our society. From this bottom-up perspective, we can see more clearly how the levels of overcharging we identified at the macro level actually come about in practice" (p. 3).

The practical result is that the trillions of dollars raised by the financial intermediation system and that various funds, in net terms, represent a drain on the American economy. This system, as in Brazil, presents a negative productivity, generating gains without a corresponding productive counterpart: "That is, finance has operated in recent years as a negative sum game. This means that it costs us more than a dollar to transfer a dollar of wealth to financiers—significantly more. So even if you think our financiers deserve every penny they get, it would be a lot cheaper simply to write them a check every year than to let them continue business as usual" (p. 4).

Small and medium banks in the USA continued to perform their commercial banking activities, but 10 giants came to dominate the financial system, concentrating on other products, which were essentially speculative. This dominant group, according to the survey, focused on "the new financial products and practices associated with the financial crisis—including securitization, derivatives trading, and proprietary trading, all financed by very short-term borrowing" (p. 10). Oligopolization is central here, supported not only by the non-transparency of products, but also by its political power to obtain subsidies (which is, in fact, the high Selic rate in Brazil). It is the "monopoly or oligopolistic power that financial institutions could exercise because of non-transparent financial products, and easy access to massive amounts of capital because of their too-big-to-fail subsidy" (p. 19).

According to the authors, many smaller banks in the USA end up being tributaries of these giants: "The large Wall Street banks sit at the epicenter of the financial system. As a result, virtually all of the major aspects of finance that we have discussed so far—hedge funds, private equity, predatory lending, the mortgage market, and the so-called shadow banking system—are all tied to some extent to the core banks". These large banks, in turn, now exercise a political power that makes any reform non-viable: "In the case of financial reform, the power of the financial sector in the political process has been a difficult force to reckon with" (p. 41).

This pyramid of power in the financial system involves even small local or regional commercial banks. It also has control over the political decision-making process that should allow regulation, which has led to the development of a machine that draws resources from the economy in a way that is disproportional to their productive contributions. "We should emphasize that in our analysis, we are estimating the NET costs of our financial system: the costs over and above what an efficient financial system would cost society. Financial rents measure how much more customers and tax payers have to pay bankers to get the level of services (benefits) they are receiving" (p. 14).[72]

The concept of the net cost of the financial system is very useful, as it directly involves the question of systemic productivity of a country's finances. For Brazil, considering the costs of the crisis that began in 2013, of which the financial system was the main cause, we could also calculate the systemic cost. In the case of America, the authors consider that "we must incorporate the costs of financial crises associated with excessive speculation and destructive economic activities that are now well understood, to have been a key to the recent economic crisis" (p. 16). The difference is that the USA recognizes the roots of the 2008 financial crisis, while here the crisis is attributed to the ridiculous fiscal deficit of less than 2% of the GDP. Blaming government has proved very effective. The gap in the public accounts, in our case, was actually created by the surreal level of interest put on the public debt—the Selic rate—which in 2015 alone meant a transfer of 501 billion reais (9% of GDP) from our taxes for financial groups.[73] The parallels between Brazil and the United States is very interesting here.

Also important is the concept of financial rent. Indeed, this concept of "rent" (which is different from income) has to be introduced in our analysis of Brazil. The conceptualization of "rent" as resources obtained without the corresponding productive contribution helps us to understand the process. In Brazil, curiously, we use the term "rentierism", but the concept of "rent" (*renta*) does not exist yet. In English, the productive

---

72 "Renta" here corresponds to income without a productive counterpart: It is "*unearned income*" in the words of Joseph Stiglitz. See the explanation below and the glossary at the end of this volume.

73 Data researched by António Correia de Lacerda.We will go into the details of these figures later, when analyzing Brazil. See also the corresponding study of the financial system in Brazil, in *Resgatando o potencial financeiro do país:* http://dowbor.org/2016/08/ladislau-dowbor-resgatando-o-potencial-financeiro-do-pais-versao-atualizada-em-04082016-agosto-2016-47p.html/.

mechanism that generates income and the unproductive financial allocation that generates "rent" are clearly distinguished. In French the difference between "revenu" and "rente" is also clear. There is no way to understand, for example, Piketty's works without this distinction and this concept is, of course, quite present in the classics of political economy. We will address this issue in the glossary.

According to the authors, "In the case of modern finance, rents come in two basic forms: One form is the excess payments made to bankers—top traders, CEOs, financial engineers, and other highly paid employees of banks and other financial institutions; the other form is excess profits, or returns over and above the long-run sustainable returns that accrue to shareholders as a result of the financial services provided by a firm" (p. 19). Since the 1990s, financial gains of this kind have hugely increased. The costs of rentiers' activities that hinder economic activities, rather than promoting them, have to be borne by society. "The cost of finance to society is not only a result of transfers of income and wealth from society as a whole to finance; there are additional costs if finance itself undermines the health of the economy for households and workers" (p. 22). Here the parallel is equally interesting: the Brazilian Constitution has been amended to block government investments in social policies, while releasing them for interest payments on public debt.

An interesting quote from the authors is that of James Tobin, who in 1984 warned: "We are throwing more and more of our resources, including the cream of our youth, into financial activities remote from the production of goods and services, into activities that generate high private rewards disproportionate to their social productivity." Tobin was one of the first to note this systemic distortion of financial intermediation (p. 23). I have seen this quote in various authors, as it is very relevant, particularly since it uses the concept of "social productivity": that is, usefulness for the economy and society in general, not only for the bank or other group that performs an intermediation activity.

The concept of SROI (Social Return on Investment) is also beginning to be used more widely.[74] At a personal level, many financial operators are starting to wonder whether, regardless of how much they earn, the activity they perform is socially useful. When it is clearly harmful, contradictions

---

[74] On the subject read my technical note *Produtividade sistêmica do Território,* 2009, p. 4.
http://dowbor.org/2009/11/produtividade-sistemica-do-territorio-nov.html/

and existential crises arise, as studied, for example, in Luyendijk's excellent *Swimming with Sharks*, which focuses on the high officials of the City.[75] These are not philosophical ramblings: more and more people want their efforts to make sense and have come to realize that they are working against their clients who, in turn, can hardly escape the banking system.

The diversion of resources from productive activities to speculative gains hinders the economy as a whole, but indignation is restricted, simply because the system is extremely opaque. This opacity helps to expand the main trend: "Larger private financial systems might be associated with more 'speculative finance', greater trading, and a sector less associated with providing credit to the 'real economy' [...] This orientation is also likely to lower productivity growth and investment and therefore economic growth" (p. 23).

Epstein and Montecino cite the work of J. W. Mason who notes that between the 1960s and 1970s, every dollar of additional gains and credit led to an increase of investments of about 40 cents. Since the 1980s, it led to an increase of only 10 cents. This is a radical change in terms of the productivity of financial allocations. According to Mason, "This is the result of legal, managerial, and structural changes that resulted from the shareholder revolution of the 1980s. Under the older, managerial, model, more money coming into a firm—from sales or from borrowing—typically meant more money spent on fixed investment. In the new rentier-dominated model, more money coming in means more money flowing out to shareholders in the form of dividends and stock buybacks" (Mason, p.1)[76]

We do not have comparative data for Brazil, but if we have the same proportion of only 10% of the interest obtained becoming an investment, while the other 90% enters the financial merry-go-round, we cannot recover and create dynamic economic growth, even if the earnings for financial investors rise sharply. These unproductive assets increase and sterilize resources. It is also interesting to draw a parallel here with the United States, where with the crisis of 2008 the mass of public resources that the government handed over to the banks, instead of turning into productive investment that would renew the economy, was directed

[75] Joris Luyendijk – *Swimming with sharks* – Guardian Books, London, 2015 http://www.theguardian.com/business/2015/sep/30/how-the-banks-ignored-lessons-of-crash

[76] J.W. Mason –*Disgorge the Cash* – Roosevelt Institute, 2015 – http://rooseveltinstitute.org/wp-content/uploads/2015/09/Disgorge-the-Cash.pdf

towards purchase of more stock, bonuses, and the like. In the case of Brazil, the various subsidies and incentives did not boost the economy either, since those favored only bought more financial papers, especially public debt bonds. Here the mechanism of so-called gross fixed capital formation broke down.

As the dividends are sparingly burdened by the tax system—which has been achieved through political pressure—the circle of financialization and unproductive wealth closes. Joseph Stiglitz proposes the following definition of rent-seeking: "The practice of attaining wealth, not by means of economically profitable activity but by extracting it from others, often by exploitation." It is part of what he calls unearned income, earning with no productive counterpart. The new system of financial intermediation also generated a mass of lawyers, counselors, accountants, fund managers and the like, all eager to maximize returns and to receive the corresponding bonuses. "Asset management services have grown from $4 billion in assets managed by 51 firms in 1940 to more than $63 trillion in assets with more than 11,000 advisors and almost 10,000 mutual funds registered with the SEC in 2014" (Epstein, p. 41). It is the defense battalion of the system.

For comparison, let us remember that the world's GDP is in the order of $80 trillion, while the fortunes being managed are in the order of hundreds of trillions. A mass of professionals generated a significant cluster of power, with a strong influence, in particular, on the whole of the financial communication in the mainstream media, which almost exclusively presents the standpoints of the large financial groups. We rarely see an economist that is not part of the so-called "market" and what we are presented, instead, are opinions of professionals interested in maximizing the system's earnings. The task of the government is basically to regain their confidence, the so-called "market confidence", so that the economy can thrive. However, in fact, it will only work for them.

In the Brazilian case, the political power that these interests generate trampled any attempt to control, regulate, or render the level of their profits reasonable. It became clear when the Dilma government attempted to reduce the absurd interest rates (on both public and private debt) by 2013: we ntered a full-scale war. The financial world and the rentiers reacted *en bloc*, and this movement was taken advantage of by several spheres of political and legal opportunism, leading to impeachment.

This parallel with the United States is interesting. Huge public resources (trillions of dollars) were transferred by the American government to the big American banks as from 2008. The difference is that the protests there were not against the attempts to regulate the system (Dodd-Frank Law), but against the speculators themselves. The large manifestations of the Occupy Wall Street movement, which were strongly suppressed, were not against the government, but against who had taken over it: the big banks. Despite these manifestations and the latent anger in the USA against the banks, the dominant role of the financial system has not been touched. Donald Trump has already begun to dismantle the little that was achieved with the Dodd-Frank Act. In Brazil, banks remain in the shadows, solidly protected by the media, the legal system, the ministries, and the Central Bank that they control. Anger was directed against the government.

How did we get to this level of damage to the financial system, which was once so essential to productive processes but now blocks them? The authors of *Overcharged* identify five mechanisms: "As with much of finance, the keys to excessive rents obtained by financial firms and traders are: (1) opaqueness, often deliberately created, by excess complexity, lack of disclosure, and outright misleading information facilitated by light regulation; (2) high market concentration within specific lines of business leading to low competition; (3) government subsidies of various types, including bailouts, tax subsidies, accounting rule enabling, and legal advantages created by legislative, administrative, or legal engineering; (4) withdrawal of public provision that makes a ready market for finance and makes people vulnerable to all of these channels for excess income and returns and (5) weak fiduciary rules that allow conflicts of interest to flourish" (p. 35).

The bulk of society bears the biggest shock of this reorganization: "Households receive false and costly information from advisors who have an incentive to mislead and are able to do so because of a relatively lax legal and regulatory environment" (p. 36). This in turn generates deeper inequality: "Financial practices and incomes have contributed greatly to income and wealth inequality in the U.S. in recent decades. In addition, some financial practices contribute to the creation and maintenance of poverty. Nowhere are these connections between finance, inequality, and poverty more apparent than in the provision of banking services for poor and financially stretched households" (p. 40).

The parallels with the exorbitant interest rates in Brazilian installment plans and banks is evident. Actually, in Brazil, which has three-digit interest rates, the distortions are simply much more scandalous. For the authors, the profound reorganization of the financial system becomes an obvious necessity: "Broadly speaking, to address the issues we raise here concerning the enormous costs of our current financial system, we need three broad, complementary approaches: financial regulation, financial reconstruction, and financial alternatives. To achieve these goals, we will likely need a new Glass-Steagall law to eliminate the social safety net for highly speculative financial activity, stricter limits on leverage and bank size to break up the largest and most dangerous financial institutions, and stricter regulation to limit financial pay for highly risky activities" (p. 43).

The authors of the research also highlight the subsequent reformulation of the financial system's objectives, to render it useful (and less harmful) to the economy and society. "Our financial system needs to be restructured so that it better serves the needs of our communities, small business, households, and public entities, such as municipalities and states. Eliminating subsidies for the too-big-to-fail banks will help level the playing field for smaller and more community-oriented financial institutions; however, this is unlikely to populate the financial system with enough institutions to support the needs of our communities. As a result, we are likely to need many more financial alternatives: public banks, cooperative banks, and specialized banks such as green banks and infrastructure banks" (p. 43).

This type of survey in the United States stresses the need for us to study the integrated financial flow in Brazil and seek to rescue the economic productivity of financial intermediation in its various dimensions. Basically, we have found that the profound deformation of the Brazilian financial system is not only present here and that the methodology used to analyze the integrated financial process in other countries helps us to see more realistically what is going on in Brazil. We are all on a quest to find new routes.

11 – THE QUEST OF NEW COURSES: ROUTES AND DETOURS

As we have seen above, understanding the shortcomings of America allows us to gauge the challenges for Brazil. Two more recent studies contribute in this sense. One is by Joseph Stiglitz, *Rewriting the Rules: an agenda for shared prosperity*. The other is by Michael Hudson, *Killing the Host: how financial parasites and debt destroy the global economy*. Both are powerful works that enable us to structurally rethink the system.

Joseph Stiglitz has organized a document that is an agenda for the United States, which is today trapped by elites who insist on fighting social policies—thereby promoting greater inequality—and attacking environmental policies. Radically reversing mainstream standpoints, the large group of economists in this report rejects "the old economic models." The text states: "New research and thinking that has emerged as a result suggests that equality and economic performance are in fact complementary rather than opposing forces." In other words, the idea that concentrating income to place more money in the hands of capitalists who will invest more and develop the economy, and that trickling down will, in the long run, benefit the population, is simply wrong. The direct investment in reducing inequality is what reinforces economic performance.[77]

As obvious as it may be, this theoretical turnaround in the United States is important. It discards the standpoint that austerity, by forcing the population to save money, is a condition for the rich to invest and thus generate growth. The reduction of inequalities is now seen as the main drive. Although the outlook that the concentration of income and wealth stimulates investments continues to be mainstream in economic theory,

---

[77] Nick Hanauer, an American billionaire, in his short video on income provides an impressive testimony about what he calls the transformation of productive capitalism into the neo-feudal society of unproductive rentiers. The main argument is that downward-directed money invigorates the economy by creating stronger demand, while the money that goes to the 1% feeds financial fortunes and unproductive rent, thereby deepening inequality. Nothing like a billionaire to explain this to us mortals. https://youtu.be/q2gO4DKVpa8 (TED Talks, 20 min., 2014)

and unfortunately in Brazil, the trend presented in the Roosevelt Institute research can be also found in *Real World Economics*, *New Economics Foundation*, *Alternatives Economiques* and many others institutions worldwide, which focus on finding solutions to reduce inequalities, increase mass consumption, expand social and environmental policies, and reduce interest rates. The *Next System* movement, launched in March 2015 by Gar Alperovitz, Gus Speth, Jeffrey Sachs, and others is part of this reconstruction.

American economists are waking up and building new routes, not only in the academia, but in many local governments. One paragraph sums up well the displacement of standpoints and gives us the "temperature" of the report: "This is not about the politics of envy. The evidence of the last 35 years and the lessons of stagnation and low-wage recovery since the 2008 financial crisis show that we cannot prosper if our economic system does not create shared prosperity. This report is about how we can make our economy, our democracy, and our society work better for all Americans" (Stiglitz, p. 15).

Stiglitz is an international reference point today. A Nobel laureate, he was chief economist for the Clinton administration and the World Bank and has been a beacon in the chaos that is modern economic science, combining theoretical solidity and excellent insight over what is required in practical terms. Politically, he is not a revolutionary, but he does seek the retrieval of a civilized capitalism: one that is less unequal and more open to generate opportunities than fortune owners' clubs, which less destructive in environmental terms and more democratic in decision-making processes. The Roosevelt Institute is a progressive think tank that greatly helps to rethink the course and spread progressive ideas in the United States. These ideas may have a significant impact, for the US still has strong influence on the dissemination of scientific ideas throughout the world.

Basic finding: "The American economy no longer works for the majority of the population in the United States" (p. 169). In 40 years, between 1973 and 2013, the productivity of the economy increased by 161%, but the wage base by only 19%. Between 2000 and 2013 the average family income actually declined by 7%. It is a system that only works for a restricted group at the top, thereby generating a new era of inequality.

Second basic finding: capitalism, particularly in its financial form, does not regulate itself, and the rush to raise and capture more resources seems uncontrolled, generating "fraud, incompetence, and negligence beyond the imagination of even the sector's critics" (p. 162).

These two dynamics are obviously interconnected, which becomes evident both in the indebtedness of the public sector and in the indebtedness of productive enterprises, households, senior citizens, and more recently the financial plight of students, who enter professional life to pay banks. Credit cards alone, even without reaching the absurdities of Brazil, form a toll collection on all commercial transactions of daily American life (p. 116).

The financial system generates the appropriation of resources, not by those who produce them, but by those who handle stock, which in turn deepens inequality because financial investors are in the upper part of wealth. The worker merely tries to meet his bills. Rentierism, mentioned all through the study, does not only happen in Brazil. Stiglitz calls the USA credit system predatory lending (p. 107). In a long interview in Brazil with Paulo Moreira at EBC in 2016, he was appalled by Brazilian interest rates. Here we strangled the economy with a relatively moderate volume of debt, but on which we pay usurious interest rates.

A third dynamic worsens the process: concentrated wealth allows appropriation of politics and decision-making about how the economy is regulated. It is as if one of the teams had the right to rewrite the ground rules according to its own interests. "Enacting the bold reforms we outline in this report, as well as other measures to address wealth and income inequality, is as much about political will as it is about economics. The concentration of wealth in our economy has created a concentration of power in our democracy" (p. 166).

As such, inequality of wealth generates political inequality. Stiglitz considers that "it is critical that we create a campaign finance system less dominated by large contributions" (p. 167). Any similarity to Brazilian problems is, of course, no coincidence. A vicious circle is created, because as more political power is appropriated by the oligarchies, reversing the trend becomes more difficult. "As inequality rises, the political system becomes increasingly over-run by corporate interests, and the public policies required to provide real equality of opportunity become harder and harder to enact" (p. 178). The reduction of taxes on corporations by the Trump administration is a show case.

The trap closes. This is what we call "capture of power" that encompasses economics, politics, the legal system, and the mass media. The system has not only ceased to function for the general population, but also as a system because financial interests have no limits: while they spread their dominance, they merely reinforce the unproductive dimension of wealth.

The distinction by Stiglitz between capital and wealth is helpful. "In this analysis, we make a distinction between capital and wealth. Only an increase in the former necessarily encourages growth; therefore, the productive capacity of the economy may not be increasing in tandem with measured wealth. In fact, productive capacity may be falling even as wealth is increasing" (p. 14). Buying financial papers which feed rentiers and investing in producing shoes (or giving lessons) belong to different economic dynamics. Being an administrator and intermediary of other people's assets, earning bonuses, and posing as a generator of wealth, is the utmost glory. We have entered the era of unproductive wealth: that is, sterile capital.

This report also proposes a set of alternatives aimed at redirecting the American economy; it mainly focuses on "shared prosperity": ideas that can help us to define our own course. This is not as a model to copy, but as a mirror with which we can rethink our reality. Measures such as taxing unproductive capital (wealth), reducing political capture by corporations, strengthening the bargaining power of the working classes, reducing inequalities, and other proposals show a country that has, on another scale and with variations, very close challenges to those of Brazil. This report thus enables us to better understand our own dynamics. Financial capitalism, in essence, is the same animal everywhere, even if with different colors. Our solutions, whether we like it or not, will not be just national.

A second essential survey is that of Michael Hudson, *Killing the Host*, which is less condensed than Stiglitz's, but certainly with more bite as the work's own subtitle points out: “How financial parasites and the debt destroy the global economy”. As in the studies by Epstein and Montecino, as well as Stiglitz, Hudson's research reveals the significant similarity of the financial model imposed on American society with our Brazilian dramas.

"What critics of government expenditures really want to oppose is public funding from the general budget, including progressive taxes paid by the wealthier classes for Social Security, Medicare, and other social programs.

Hypocrisy becomes apparent when Wall Street lays claim to debt generation, when governments create currency to save banks" (p. 187). Here in Brazil, of course, it is not to save banks, but to sustain them, nevertheless the process is the same. In Brazil, the absurd interest rates on the public debt and in America, Quantitative Easing (QE), thereby attack welfare and dismantle Obamacare, respectively.

The impact on both societies are also quite similar: "The middle class is being crushed while markets are shrinking. The result is post-2008 austerity. Debt settlement is being squeezed out through real estate debts, student loans, and credit card debt. Real wages and 'markets' stagnate because consumers have little to spend after paying a larger proportion of their income in debt service" (p. 186). What are the volumes of resources? As an order of magnitude, although contributing less than 10% of the economic added value, "by mid-2013 the share of the banking system in corporate profits had reached 42%" (p. 194). Participating in more than 40% of the profits while contributing less than 10% of the value it extracts, gives an idea of the financial domination over all productive processes, but above all, lays open the fact that the financial system drains the economy, instead of financing it.

The series surveyed in the USA since 1947 shows that, in that year, the share of banks corporate profits was 11%.[78] The corresponding reduction of wages is part of this transfer, as well as the difficulties of productive companies which face reduced demand. The system has turned into a giant vacuum cleaner of resources for the top of the pyramid. What happens is not the proclaimed trickling down, but a mighty trickling up. Hudson clearly shows how the economy is stalled through various forms of indebtedness: "Paying real estate debts, student loans, credit card debt, business debt, state, local, and federal government debt all transfer income and more and more property to bankers and bond holders. This debt deflation hinders economic growth by shrinking spending on goods and services and, as a consequence, new investments in capital and employment" (p. 266). Indebtedness is strongly present as an essential mechanism of appropriating added value from producers. "Consumer demand deteriorates to the extent that income is diverted to debt service" (p. 266). The wage earner may even receive better pay, but if interest rates increase his actual purchasing power will decline.

---

[78] Hudson, p. 194. See also Richard Eskow, *The "Bankization" of America* – Common Dreams, August 16, 2013,
http://www.commondreams.org/views/2013/08/16/bankization-america

How was it possible to silently set up this gigantic system of exploitation? The following argument, in Hudson's direct style, attempts to answer this question: "We are brought back to the fact that in biological nature the parasites produce an enzyme that sedates the host's perception that it is being dominated by a free lunch. In today's financially savvy economies, the enzyme consists of junk economics." In terms of junk economics, Brazil has provided an interesting lesson, by justifying the ousting of President Dilma with the argument that a good housewife only spends what she has. This fantastic housewife's tale has been increasingly repeated on mass media thereby creating the conviction that our recession originated in irresponsible expenditures by the poor. Serious economists (in the sense of reputedly serious) thus justified the transfer of public money from social policies that would serve the population to the payment of the huge interest on the public debt, which serves the bankers and actually increases the deficit.[79] Let us leave aside the insult that this argument represents for housewives.

The overall mainstay of Hudson's study tends toward the retrieval of control over the financial system. In the case of the United States, "only a government strong enough to tax and regulate Wall Street can control the current capture of financial and rentier power" (p. 267). In 1999, in the United States, they revoked the Glass-Steagall Act that regulated the financial system. In Brazil, in the same year, Article 192 of the constitution that regulated the national financial system was revoked. As a result, the banks' freedom to charge what they want in Brazil means that the financial logic absorbs, in a deformed and speculative dynamic, any subsidy, exemption, transfer, or other privileges granted to productive enterprises.

The parallel between the attempts of the Brazilian government to try to subsidize productive sectors in trouble and similar initiatives in the United States is impressive: "The new easy money was not 'invested in the economy' by financing public services or investing in public infrastructures. It was not given to homeowners or used to relieve debt. Instead, the Federal Reserve provided credit to Wall Street banks at interest rates close to zero, under the Quantitative Easing (QE) framework. The excuse was that the banks would lend this money to reactivate the economy. Bank credit was presented as more efficient than the spending of government bureaucrats—as if all public expenditures were simply a loss. This misleading logic has

[79] An impressive synthesis of *junk economics* may be found on page 177 following "how junk economics paved the way for 2008." See also M. Hudson, *J is for Junk Economics,* Islet, 2017

proven to be completely false, and indeed, a deliberate reversal as to where bank credit actually goes and where it will be spent" (p. 263).

We are talking here of $4 trillion in the United States, and EUR 1 trillion in Europe, as subsidies, "to help the layer at the top of the economic pyramid, not to reduce or write down debts or reactivate the real economy through public expenditures. This huge act of money creation could have allowed debtors to free themselves from debt, so that they can resume spending to keep the circular flow of production and consumption moving. Instead, governments left the economy mired in debt, creating currency just to give it to financial institutions" (p. 178).

The enlightening impact of Hudson's book is largely tied to the fact that he has worked in the area—none of these mechanisms are taught in universities—and, in particular, because he has been examining a set of social surplus appropriation subsystems. Public debt securities, stocks, patents, insurance, real estate speculation, oligopolies, appropriation of natural resources, systems of commercial brokers, tax evasion, and the most diverse para-legal or illegal systems involving the real financial system, all lead to the formation of a rentier class whose interests are deeply divorced from real population progress and sustainability. Not even private health insurance escapes.

The United States is not an island in terms of financial mismanagement. I return to the argument that it is worthwhile to understand how the system works in a global way, in order to grasp the Brazilian case that, with less governance, is even more serious. We will now consider, for example, the City (London), the second world financial center after Wall Street, which is very close to the USA case.

Joris Luyendijk, a leading Dutch investigative journalist, was invited by *The Guardian* to make a book about how finance works in the City. The outcome is an extremely readable book. Luyendijk builds his understanding of the financial system along with the reader, disclosing to the non-specialist the cogwheels and, in particular, the interests and conflicts that arise. Since London is linked to the largest network of tax havens, frauds, and illegalities with third party resources, disclosing how things happen in practice is very interesting. Unfortunately, these are dynamics whose costs fall on all of us.

The first point: it is a general mess. Prosecuted for fraud are banks such as Deutsche Bank, HSBC, Barclays, and any of these giants you can imagine.

Additionally, 7 years after the bankruptcy of Lehman Brothers, we are still stuck, waiting for the next crisis. The logic is simple: "Megabanks and huge financial institutions operate globally, say the politicians of this school, while the policies and ground rules are organized at the national level or at best in continents or blocks. Financial institutions can throw countries or blocks of countries against each other, and do so shamelessly" (p. 258). In other words, there is a scattered and fragmented regulation in some 200 countries with their respective central banks, while financial giants navigate the globe, as we have already seen, without any regulation, other than some goodwill recommendations from the BIS (Basel Bank for International Settlements). It is the age of the financial free-for-all.

Second, this high finance is all about each one of us. Whether you like it or not you use a credit card, you may be paying a mortgage or for a commercial purchase, you may have money invested, or you simply do not understand how a bank can charge 633.21% on revolving credit card debt (as charged by Santander in Brazil). Consider that millions of Americans are outraged that they were taxed on a second account opened in their names, unknown to them, by Wells Fargo. "In the case of the Libor and FX scandals, traders in large banks and brokerage houses manipulated crucial rates of interest and exchange for personal gain over years and years" (p. 234). What is the importance of this? "The world of finance is not some distant land that can be safely ignored. If money is for society as blood is for the body, then the financial sector is the heart" (p. 261). Ethics in the process? "In the City, you do not ask if a proposal is morally right or wrong. You examine the degree of 'reputation risk'. Using loopholes in the tax code to help large corporations and rich families in tax evasion is 'tax optimization' through 'fiscally efficient structures'. Financial lawyers and regulators who accept anything you propose are 'business-friendly', cases of proven fraud or abuse are known as 'mis-selling', and exploiting inconsistencies between regulatory systems in two countries constitutes 'regulatory arbitrage'" (p. 106). In Luyendijk's successive interviews, financiers would rather say that they are not immoral, only amoral. “Welcome to the world of globalized finance”, writes the author (p. 109).

Should economists explain how this system works? "It took me months to realize the architecture and culture of investment banks, and what struck me was how little economists help—you would imagine that this very segment of experts could enlighten the world of high finance. However, economists do not do field work" (p. 45). This is the strength of Luyendijk's book. He visits institutions, talks, interviews, checks, and works himself into this world, listening to drunken complaints and moral indignation. It becomes clear, for example, why customers are internally called “muppets”.

An interesting standpoint addressed is that these institutions are "too big to know what is going on" (a problem we have seen in Lumsdaine's study above): "In many banks, the front, middle and rear-end offices follow different systems in different countries [...] readers would be shocked to know just how crappy are information technology systems in many banks, as well as corporations and government ministries” (p. 141). As a matter of fact, financial corporate giants do not leave the state bureaucracy far behind. Worse, not even the internal systems of control (i.e., the compliance departments), which by law must exist, understand what is going on (p. 132).

This closeness to the bureaucratic systems of the State is not just a similarity. The author also works on capture of power: "Over the past few decades, mainstream political parties, as well as regulators, have come to identify with the financial sector and its people. The term here is 'capture', a form of herd behavior in cognitive terms [...] The capture is more subtle and no longer requires the transfer of funds, as the politician, the academic or the regulator have begun to believe that the world works the way the bankers say it works" (p. 257). We are in a universe that we know well: "In America, France, and the United Kingdom, the law allows banks and bankers to buy political power—a process known in other examples of obscured language as 'campaign donations' rather than 'corruption'" (p. 256).

What are the necessary measures? "This requires better laws and it would not be difficult to see which four changes these laws should set forth. First of all, banks need to be divided into smaller units so that they are no longer too large or too complex to break, and that means they could no longer blackmail us. Banks should not have under one roof activities that generate conflicts of interest, such as trading, equity management and negotiation, bank holder activities, and higher risk banking activities. Thirdly, banks should not be allowed to build, sell or own excessively complex financial products so that customers can understand what they are buying and investors can understand bank accounting. Finally, the bonuses but also the criticisms should fall on the same heads, meaning no one should have any better reason to stay up at night worrying about the risks to the bank's capital or its reputation than the bankers who take these risks" (p. 254).

Actually, whether it is in the USA, London, or Brazil, the only thing we see of the financial system, as mere customers, is advertising that clearly does not explain any "product" but aims, instead, to associate the bank's name with human values and friendliness through familiar images. The cashier or account manager at the end of the system is generally completely unaware of the system as a whole. It is up to them to push the products, even if they know they are damaging the customer, because they have to meet the goals, win points, and avoid jeopardizing their colleagues. For those who are more aware, the malaise is growing.

***

The principle of political equilibrium to which we are subjected is simple: we must keep "investor confidence" up (i.e., keep them fat and well fed) or they will revolt. Obviously, these are not investors, in the strict sense of productive investors, but rather financial investors, who make money based on what the stock yields and is, therefore, unrelated to what they contribute to the economy. On the contrary, by extracting more than they contribute, they generate a net negative impact on the whole economy. We saw the evaluation by Epstein and Montecino which revealed that out of every dollar that is acquired by financial intermediaries, only 10 cents return to productive investment. I do not know any data that will allow me to evaluate the corresponding proportion in Brazil because we do not have the elements to assess the productivity of the country's financial system. Nevertheless, we are always following the same logic: returns over financial investment are higher than returns on productive investment, and money flows to where it yields more. The productive economy is simply drained.

Generally, the population sees the results of their efforts literally sucked out of them through three converging mechanisms. The most traditional is brought about by the fact that worker productivity increases without a corresponding increase in wages. Here we have the traditional surplus value, extracted by lowering the workers' compensation. Along the same line is the reduction of, or no increase in, wages when they are consumed by inflation.

A second way of reducing workers' earnings has to do with indirect wages: access to public schools, health services, social security in general, and the various forms of access to the collective consumption of goods and services. When this other form of earnings is attacked, for example, by transforming taxes into payments on public debt, or by blocking the government's capability to expand social policies, the result is another way of reducing the majority's share of the social product.

A third way of reducing the population's right to access goods and services is to raise the interest rate for both private individuals and legal entities. When private individuals are obliged to pay more than 100% on a product sold in installments—a discomfort avoided by the rich people who can pay cash—their purchase capacity has been divided in two and they have become poorer. When a small business suffers extortion by the bank's interest rates—something a multinational in Brazil avoids when borrowing overseas or through the headquarters with incomparably lower interest rates—it is their capacity to invest and produce that is drastically reduced.

If we add the interest rates on the public debt that restrict the population's access to public goods, as well as the interest rates that reduce family consumption and thus reduce activity in the productive sector, we are looking at a process of widespread misappropriation: the withdrawal of a growing part of the socially produced surplus by those who have done nothing more than control and expand the yield of their financial investments.

This process has radically expanded since the time of Marx. However, one cannot lose one's good humor when reading this excerpt from the old bearded man: "Public debt becomes one of the most powerful levers of primitive accumulation. Like a wand, it endows money with creative capacity, thus transforming it into capital, without it being necessary for its owner to expose himself to the hassles and risks inseparable from industrial investments and even the usurer. State creditors really give nothing, since the sum becomes easily transferable public debt securities, which continue to function in their hands as if it were money. The public debt has created a class of idle capitalists and, suddenly enriched the financial agents who serve as intermediaries between the government and the nation. The parts of their issuance acquired by the tax collectors, merchants and private manufacturers provide them with the service of a capital fallen from the sky. But above all this, the public debt made corporations prosper, in short, the stock market and the modern bankocracy".[80]

---

[80] Karl Marx, *The Capital*: critique of political economy, Book I, Vols. I and II, p. 868 - Rio de Janeiro, - Civilização Brasileira, 2008. It is due to Marcos Henrique do Espírito Santo that I have located this pearl on today's reality. In the French edition, La Pléiade, Le Capital, Livre I. Chapitre, p. 1217

Marx points out in the same chapter of *The Capital* that the public debt system leads to an increase in taxes to cover their interest: "As public debt is based on public resources, which should finance its annual service, the modern tax system with the necessary outcome of the indebtedness of the nation" (La Pléiade, p. 1218). What we are facing today is basically the same process, only radically more expanded in sophistication and breadth.

What is new, therefore, is the expansion of the mechanism, which now extends to every small purchase we make in installments and to each time we insert the credit card in a shop. Financial costs that burden producers or commerce are added to the prices we pay to the cashier and all this financial surplus ends up draining our pockets. The system of financial intermediation has increased, collecting tolls on practically all our activities, with a huge difference compared to the effective investor in productive activities. It is unproductive capital because only a small part returns to the real economy. Indeed, it is wealth, or equity, that ceases to be capital. The financial system becoming a vector of decapitalization is really interesting. Rentiers should go back to work, to earn their bread honestly, like any other worker or entrepreneur. Many financial intermediaries are undoubtedly working themselves to death and they earn lots of money. However, this is not the point because the fact is that their work appropriates the benefit of the work of others, and reducing overall economic productivity.

New technologies, by allowing financial corporations to closely track our immaterial money, our account or our debt, through algorithms that facilitate mass treatment, generate a new national and global reality. Our right to the goods and services of society relies on the magnetic signs recorded in the computers of the banks and the card in our pocket. Like it or not, we are inside the system. In 1993, Joel Kurtzman, in *Death of Money*, was right to speculate over the change of economic power that money as a digital expression would allow.[81]

The fight for decent living conditions, in addition to battling for decent wages, today involves the struggle for indirect wages through public policies, and the fight against the extortionate interest that drains our purchasing power. The need to fight is not reduced, it expands. Therefore, the need for the general population to understand the new exploitation

---

[81] Joel Kurtzman – *The Death of Money: how the electronic economy has destabilized the world's markets and created a financial chaos* - Simon & Schuster, New York 1993 – Kurtzman's study is quite helpful for understanding the decoupling between the "money" economy and the "real" economy.

mechanisms becomes essential. We could make some sense of productive even if low-wage activities, they at least generate jobs, provide goods and services, and pay taxes. But this new system is absurd.

12 - THE BRAZILIAN DIMENSION: THE FOUR ENGINES OF THE ECONOMY

It is not by chance that advertising by financial agents is so full of images of tenderness and security: a smiling girl, old ladies who play with their cell phone, a mother with children or a baby. It is essential that they imply tranquility and security. However, few sectors of activity are as truculent in their impact as we can see as millions of Americans have lost their homes, Greeks have lost their savings, or the masses of lower-class Brazilians who are penniless without even understanding the mechanism that deprives them of their resources. The dominant information systems do not help, as Michael Hudson so well sums up when he states that "the implicit aim of the marketing departments of banks—and of lenders in general—is to tie the whole of the economic surplus to the payment of debt service" (p. 3).

Everywhere in Brazil we see sophisticated information systems qualified as "taxmeters" (impostómetro). This resonates strongly with the emotions of a population that feels overwhelmed by taxes and forgets about banks and interest rates. Additionally, the population does not even understand that taxes are so high because they are largely transferred to the banks: the leap in the tax burden in Brazil, from 27% to 34% of the GDP, took place in the 1990s in order to pay interest on the public debt. The final nail in the coffin is that the biggest receivers of the resources appropriated in this way are precisely the ones who pay fewer taxes.

But let us go step by step. What we have seen above, both in terms of the new architecture of power and the examples of mechanisms for extracting the surplus produced by society, provides important reference points. What we want to see now is how this system is organized in Brazil and how it has blocked the economy in general.

The economy is driven by four engines: exports, household demand, business initiatives, and public policies. In our case, beginning in 2014, these four engines were blocked and the financial system played a key role in this blocking. Understanding this process allows us to understand the main cogwheels that move the economy.

Foreign trade

In Brazil, exports are by no means the main engine. The $200 billion worth of exports, equivalent to about 700 billion reais, represents 10% of the GDP. This is particularly significant, because it allows the import of goods and services, which is important for the economy but it is still nothing crucial. We are by no means an economy like some Asian countries where the engine of foreign trade is essential. With a population of 208 million inhabitants and a GDP of $2 trillion , we are, above all, an economy linked to the domestic market. If the internal dynamics do not function, the foreign sector will hardly be a solution.

Nevertheless, it is sufficient to contribute to our present difficulties. The commodity Price Index, for example, fell 21.14% in the 12 months from April 2015 to April 2016, and our exports depend heavily on these products. It has recovered somewhat, but there is not much that we can do, because it relates to the evolution of the world market. In fact, export activities remain steady in terms of production and volume, but they yield much less today. Export monoculture and large-scale mining generate few jobs and, therefore, have a limited effect on boosting demand. That is not going to be our saving grace.

Although these are physical goods, such as iron ore or soybeans, the fact is that at an international level the variations are directly linked to modern financial activities, as we saw in the chapter on commodities. There are no significant reasons, in terms of world production and consumption volumes to justify the huge commodity price variations in the international market. Oil production and consumption volumes, for example, are around 95–100 million barrels per day, with very few changes. However, the daily moves of speculative exchanges on oil surpass 3 billion barrels, which is about 30 times greater. These are the speculative moves that allow us to understand why, with a steady flow of a real product that is oil, prices may fluctuate considerably in a few months.

What drives prices in this case is not the Chinese economy, or a Saudi decision, or Iran's entry back into the market, but rather the expectation of speculative gains from traders: nowadays 16 groups that control world commodity trade. These groups, concentrated in Geneva, feed the so-called derivatives market, which now is in the order of $500 trillion, for a world GDP of 80 trillion. Within this system are all the major financial groups in the world, creating immense instability for both producing and consuming countries, as seen in more detail in Chapter 7.

The key to our reasoning here is that the short and medium term solutions for the Brazilian economy mainly depend on the domestic market, household consumption, business activities, and public investments in infrastructure and social policies. With the international instability generated by the lack of regulatory instruments, solutions for Brazil appear mainly in its internal dynamics. In fact, we depend on the expansion of the internal market in order to compensate for the fragility of international perspectives. It is not a matter of underestimating the impact of our losses on exports as a factor of the economy's collapse, but rather of understanding that by far, the main dynamics are in activities that are directed toward domestic demand. An improvement in the prices of our exports helps, but it is just trimming: the central mainstay is here in the country.

Domestic demand

Family consumption, the main driver of the economy, is incomparably more important. It is also a dynamic that generates the products we need: the rice and beans on our table and the schools for our children. When domestic demand wanes, companies have no interest in producing, while when demand is strong, there will be people to invest and generate profit and taxes, thereby boosting the economy.

The two Lula governments and the first Dilma term strongly raised the popular consumption base through a set of income distribution programs, minimum wage increases, productive inclusion, and other measures that enabled tens of millions of people to be released from poverty. This served to create dynamics of strong growth, which in turn generated taxes, thus funding social policies. It is what has been called a virtuous circle, in which one progress fosters another. From 2013, however, the process was abruptly stalled. The truth is that banks and other financial intermediaries lost little time to learn how to drain the increased purchasing power of the lower class by largely sterilizing the redistributive process and growth dynamics.

What was presented to both the country and internationally is that excessive generosity aimed at economic and social inclusion generated a catastrophic deficit. Actually, the story has been told upside down. The culprit is essentially the sterilization of the country's resources through the system of financial intermediation which drains, in impressive volumes, the resources that should serve to foster productive and economic development. The figures are quite clear, and known, and all we need to do to understand the impact is to connect them.

Let us begin with the interest rates to the final borrower, private individual, practiced in commerce, the so-called installment plans. ANEFAC (National Association of Executives of Finance, Administration and Accounting) shows the data for February 2018:

Interest rates of Installment Plans by Sector (2018)

SETORES	jan/18		fev/18		Variação %	Var.pontos percentuais ao mês
	Taxa Mês	Taxa Ano	Taxa Mês	Taxa Ano		
Gdes.Redes	2,76%	38,16%	2,79%	39,13%	1,09%	0,03
Med.Redes	5,68%	94,05%	5,73%	95,15%	0,88%	0,05
Peq.Redes	6,61%	115,56%	6,67%	117,02%	0,91%	0,06
Emp.Turismo	4,60%	71,55%	4,64%	72,33%	0,87%	0,04
Art.do Lar	7,10%	127,76%	7,16%	129,29%	0,85%	0,06
Ele.Eletron.	5,30%	85,84%	5,35%	86,90%	0,94%	0,05
Importados	5,98%	100,76%	6,01%	101,45%	0,50%	0,03
Veiculos	1,99%	26,68%	1,97%	26,38%	-1,01%	-0,02
Art.Ginástica	7,62%	141,39%	7,67%	142,74%	0,66%	0,05
Informática	5,11%	81,86%	5,15%	82,69%	0,78%	0,04
Celulares	4,78%	75,12%	4,82%	75,93%	0,84%	0,04
Decoração	7,30%	132,91%	7,36%	134,48%	0,82%	0,06
Média Geral	5,40%	87,97%	5,44%	88,83%	0,74%	0,04

Source: ANEFAC, https://www.anefac.com.br/uploads/arquivos/2018315161835543.pdf, 2018

First of all, a methodological note: interest rates are almost always presented in Brazil as "monthly rates", as in the first column above. It is technically right, but commercially and ethically wrong. It is a way of confusing credit takers, because no one can mentally compute compound interest. What is used worldwide is the resulting annual interest rate. Banco Itaú, for example, presents interest rates in its website only in the monthly format, because the yearly rate would appear, as it is, extortionate. The procedure is not simply shameful; it is an abuse of economic power and shows the absence of Central Bank regulation.

The average interest rate on installment plans—88.83% in the bottom line of the table above—simply means that this type of trade, instead of decently providing commercial services, has been essentially transformed into a shadow banking system. They take advantage of the fact that people do not understand financial calculations, and have little money in cash, to extort them. Here, the seller of "Household Appliances" (Art. do Lar in the table above) charges an interest rate of 129.29% on its products which affects demand because it will be impounded for 12 or 24 months, while the installments are paid, and it also means that families are then paying more than double. It also restricts the producer, who receives little for the product. This is what we have qualified as a "toll economy". So, in June 2014, with the bankers in power, the average interest rate for installment plans was 72.33%, and for "Household Appliances" it was 104.89%. It was extortion that has now become an assault.

Ironically, stores say this "makes it affordable" because the monthly payments "fits your pocket". In the process as a whole, half the consumer's purchasing power is left to the intermediary, who produces nothing. Additionally, because the producer receives little, his investment capacity is reduced. Since all big stores keep basically the same level of interest on installment plans, people come to think of that as "normal." They have no choice and the media fails to report on this scandal. This is partly due to the fact that for a poor family able to own a fridge for the first time, in a country like Brazil, any sacrifice is good. In comparison, a large comparable network of household appliances in Europe, Midia@markt, works with an interest rate of 13.3% (equivalent to 1.05 per month) and has handsome profits. It allows people to buy, but does not ruin the families.

Consumers end up buying on credit, paying an average rate of 88.83% as can be seen in the bottom line of the table above. However, they also use credit cards and other forms of financial instruments, which are little understood by the vast majority of consumers.

Interest rates for private individuals (Pessoa física) in 2018

LINHA DE CRÉDITO	JANEIRO/2018		FEVEREIRO/2018		VARIAÇÃO	VARIAÇÃO
	TAXA MÊS	TAXA ANO	TAXA MÊS	TAXA ANO	%	PONTOS PERCENTUAIS
Juros comércio	5,40%	87,97%	5,44%	88,83%	0,74%	0,04
Cartão de crédito	12,70%	319,84%	12,67%	318,50%	-0,24%	-0,03
Cheque especial	12,12%	294,64%	12,18%	297,18%	0,50%	0,06
CDC – bancos-financiamento de automóveis	1,99%	26,68%	1,97%	26,38%	-1,01%	-0,02
Empréstimo pessoal-bancos	4,10%	61,96%	4,22%	64,22%	2,93%	0,12
Empréstimo pessoal-financeiras	7,44%	136,59%	7,50%	138,18%	0,81%	0,06
TAXA MÉDIA	**7,29%**	**132,65%**	**7,33%**	**133,70%**	**0,55%**	**0,04**

Source: ANEFAC, https://www.anefac.com.br/uploads/arquivos/2018315161835543.pdf, 2018.

Looking at the data for February 2018, we find that financial intermediaries have charged 318.50% on credit cards, 297.18% on overdrafts, and 26.38% on car purchases. Personal loans cost on average 64.22% in banks and 138.18% in non-banking financial institutions. We have left out street loan-sharking, which in fact is not very different from the banks who simply practice legal loan-sharking. The argument becomes clear when comparing the interest rates above with the annual rates practiced in Europe using the data from the European Central Bank and different credit lines in several EU countries.

Bank interest rates—ECB Statistical Data Warehouse—2002/2016

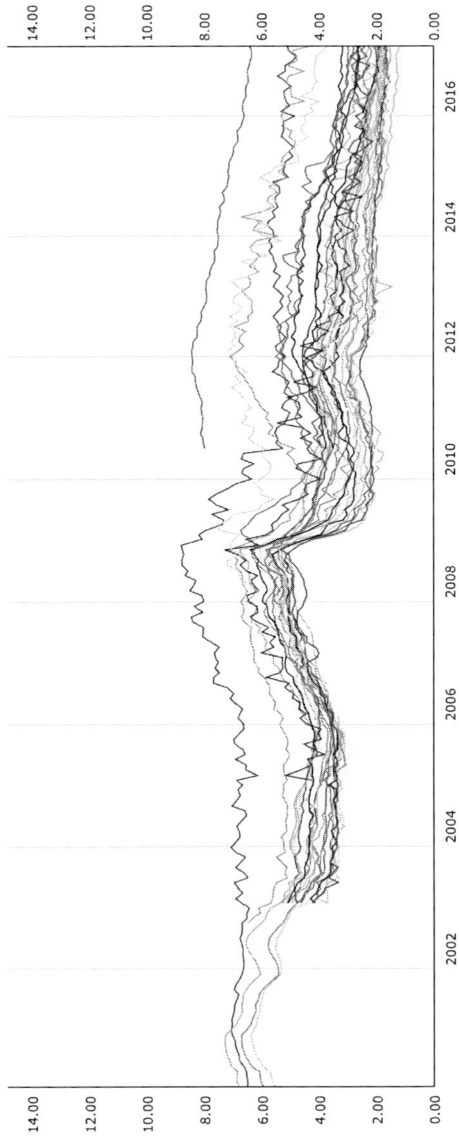

Euro area (changing composition), Loans for consumption excluding revolvi...->	5.05	Euro area (changing composition), Lending for house purchase excluding r...->	1.76
Euro area (changing composition), Lending for house purchase excluding r...->	1.87	Euro area (changing composition), Lending for house purchase excluding r...->	1.8
Greece (GR), Loans (defined for cost of borrowing purposes, sum of A2A a...->	4.91	Austria, Lending for house purchase excluding revolving loans and overdr...->	1.85
Austria, Loans (defined for cost of borrowing purposes, sum of A2A and A...->	1.62	Belgium, Lending for house purchase excluding revolving loans and overdr...->	2.02
Belgium, Loans (defined for cost of borrowing purposes, sum of A2A and A...->	1.75	Germany, Lending for house purchase excluding revolving loans and overdr...->	1.77
Germany, Loans (defined for cost of borrowing purposes, sum of A2A and A...->	1.7	Spain, Lending for house purchase excluding revolving loans and overdraf...->	1.91
Spain, Loans (defined for cost of borrowing purposes, sum of A2A and A2Z...->	1.96	Finland, Lending for house purchase excluding revolving loans and overdr...->	1.1
Finland, Loans (defined for cost of borrowing purposes, sum of A2A and A...->	1.82	France, Lending for house purchase excluding revolving loans and overdra...->	1.5
France, Loans (defined for cost of borrowing purposes, sum of A2A and A2...->	1.55	Greece (GR), Lending for house purchase excluding revolving loans and ov...->	2.62
Ireland, Lending for house purchase excluding revolving loans and overdr...->	3.17	Ireland, Loans (defined for cost of borrowing purposes, sum of A2A and A...->	2.5
Italy, Lending for house purchase excluding revolving loans and overdraf...->	2.03	Italy, Loans (defined for cost of borrowing purposes, sum of A2A and A2Z...->	1.95
Luxembourg, Lending for house purchase excluding revolving loans and ove...->	1.68	Euro area (changing composition), Loans other than revolving loans and o...->	1.22
Euro area (changing composition), Loans other than revolving loans and overd...->	2.68	Euro area (changing composition), Loans other than revolving loans and overd...->	1.39
Euro area (changing composition), Loans other than revolving loans and overd...->	2.8	Euro area (changing composition), Lending for house purchase excluding r...->	1.76
Euro area (changing composition), Revolving loans and overdrafts, Total,...->	2.64	Euro area (changing composition), Revolving loans and overdrafts, Total, Tot...->	6.35
Euro area (changing composition), Extended credit, Total, Total, Households ...->	16.62	Estonia, Lending for house purchase excluding revolving loans and overdr...->	2.17
Estonia, Loans (defined for cost of borrowing purposes, sum of A2A and A...->	2.53	Cyprus, Lending for house purchase excluding revolving loans and overdra...->	2.96
Cyprus, Loans (defined for cost of borrowing purposes, sum of A2A and A2...->	3.86	Lithuania, Lending for house purchase excluding revolving loans and over...->	1.95
Lithuania, Loans (defined for cost of borrowing purposes, sum of A2A and...->	2.29		

Source : [1]European Central Bank (ECB), [2]Oesterreichische Nationalbank (Austria), [3]Banque Nationale de Belgique (Belgium), [4]Central Bank of Cyprus, [5]Deutsche Bundesbank (Germany), [6]Bank of Est Finland (Finland), [9]Banque de France (France), [10]Bank of Greece (Greece) (GR2), [11]Central Bank of Ireland (Ireland), [12]Banca d` Italia (Italy), [13]Bank of Lithuania, [14]Banque centrale du Luxembourg

URL of the page: (copy the link, enlarge and open on internet)

https://sdw.ecb.europa.eu/browseChart.do?dc=&removeItem=&ec=&rc=
&legendPub=published&oc=&node=9691393&df=true&pb=&legendNor
=&activeTab=&legendRef=reference&DATASET=0&DATASET=2&SE
RIES_KEY=124.MIR.M.U2.B.A2A.D.R.1.2240.EUR.N&SERIES_KEY=
124.MIR.M.U2.B.A2A.D.R.2.2240.EUR.N&SERIES_KEY=124.MIR.M.
U2.B.A2A.Q.R.1.2240.EUR.N&SERIES_KEY=124.MIR.M.U2.B.A2A.Q
.R.2.2240.EUR.N&SERIES_KEY=124.MIR.M.U2.B.A2B.F.R.A.2250.E
UR.N&SERIES_KEY=124.MIR.M.U2.B.A2C.F.R.A.2250.EUR.N&SERI
ES_KEY=124.MIR.M.U2.B.A2C.I.R.A.2250.EUR.N&SERIES_KEY=12
4.MIR.M.U2.B.A2C.O.R.A.2250.EUR.N&SERIES_KEY=124.MIR.M.U
2.B.A2C.P.R.A.2250.EUR.N&SERIES_KEY=124.MIR.M.U2.B.A2Z1.A.
R.A.2240.EUR.N&SERIES_KEY=124.MIR.M.U2.B.A2Z1.A.R.A.2250.
EUR.N&SERIES_KEY=124.MIR.M.U2.B.A2Z3.A.R.A.2250.EUR.N&S
ERIES_KEY=124.MIR.M.AT.B.A2C.AM.R.A.2250.EUR.N&SERIES_K
EY=124.MIR.M.AT.B.A2I.AM.R.A.2240.EUR.N&SERIES_KEY=124.
MIR.M.BE.B.A2C.AM.R.A.2250.EUR.N&SERIES_KEY=124.MIR.M.B
E.B.A2I.AM.R.A.2240.EUR.N&SERIES_KEY=124.MIR.M.CY.B.A2C.
AM.R.A.2250.EUR.N&SERIES_KEY=124.MIR.M.CY.B.A2I.AM.R.A.2
240.EUR.N&SERIES_KEY=124.MIR.M.DE.B.A2C.AM.R.A.2250.EUR.
N&SERIES_KEY=124.MIR.M.DE.B.A2I.AM.R.A.2240.EUR.N&SERIE
S_KEY=124.MIR.M.EE.B.A2C.AM.R.A.2250.EUR.N&SERIES_KEY=1
24.MIR.M.EE.B.A2I.AM.R.A.2240.EUR.N&SERIES_KEY=124.MIR.M.
ES.B.A2C.AM.R.A.2250.EUR.N&SERIES_KEY=124.MIR.M.ES.B.A2I.
AM.R.A.2240.EUR.N&SERIES_KEY=124.MIR.M.FI.B.A2C.AM.R.A.2
250.EUR.N&SERIES_KEY=124.MIR.M.FI.B.A2I.AM.R.A.2240.EUR.N
&SERIES_KEY=124.MIR.M.FR.B.A2C.AM.R.A.2250.EUR.N&SERIES
_KEY=124.MIR.M.FR.B.A2I.AM.R.A.2240.EUR.N&SERIES_KEY=124
.MIR.M.GR.B.A2C.AM.R.A.2250.EUR.N&SERIES_KEY=124.MIR.M.
GR.B.A2I.AM.R.A.2240.EUR.N&SERIES_KEY=124.MIR.M.IE.B.A2C.
AM.R.A.2250.EUR.N&SERIES_KEY=124.MIR.M.IE.B.A2I.AM.R.A.22
40.EUR.N&SERIES_KEY=124.MIR.M.IT.B.A2C.AM.R.A.2250.EUR.N
&SERIES_KEY=124.MIR.M.IT.B.A2I.AM.R.A.2240.EUR.N&SERIES_
KEY=124.MIR.M.LT.B.A2C.AM.R.A.2250.EUR.N&SERIES_KEY=124
.MIR.M.LT.B.A2I.AM.R.A.2240.EUR.N&SERIES_KEY=124.MIR.M.L
U.B.A2C.AM.R.A.2250.EUR.N

The table above shows the different interest rates for various types of credit in Europe. Data may be analyzed based on the link on the European Central Bank's website, which provides the detail for each line. Here, in the static image on paper we see the overall trend: interest rates ranged between 1.5% and 3.5% per year and the only line slightly out of the curve is that of overdraft and revolving loans, which reach around 6.5% per annum. European banks are clearly profitable. Remember that in 2018 in Brazil the overdraft is in the range of 300% and revolving credit around 320%. It would not even be possible to represent Brazilian interest in this chart. This is legally organized loan-sharking which is simply scandalous, and confronting it is an absolute priority if we wish to rescue the Brazilian economy. Displaying interest rates by month is deliberately intended to confuse people, as it makes our interest appear similar to the international ones that are annual.

It is important to stress that even when paying cash with a credit card, the banks charge between 2.5% and 5% of the value paid. These 5% may be less for large stores with power to bargain with the financial system, but this is still a gigantic private excise tax that drastically reduces consumer purchasing power, because the store adds this cost to the price. We are speaking of an absurd overcharge on tens of millions of daily purchases.

Abecs, the national association of credit card services, believes that this system "is responsible for boosting consumer credit in the country." It is a positive way of presenting the issue but it is credit that is boosted, not consumption. In the case of frequent use of revolving credit, people will pay three or four times the value of the product. Miguel de Oliveira, director of Anefac, summarizes the situation well: "The person who cannot pay cash and needs to buy on credit, or to access revolving credit, is actually financing credit card debt with another type of credit. The problem is that this debt has no end. People do not realize the interest they will have to pay" (DCI, B1, 08/20/2014).

Since people have difficulty imagining that the system has been so grossly deformed, we have presented below the interest rate charged by Banco Santander. The "Total Effective Cost" of the revolving credit in Santander, for example, reported in a table sent to customers, is 633.21%. Inflation is under 5%.

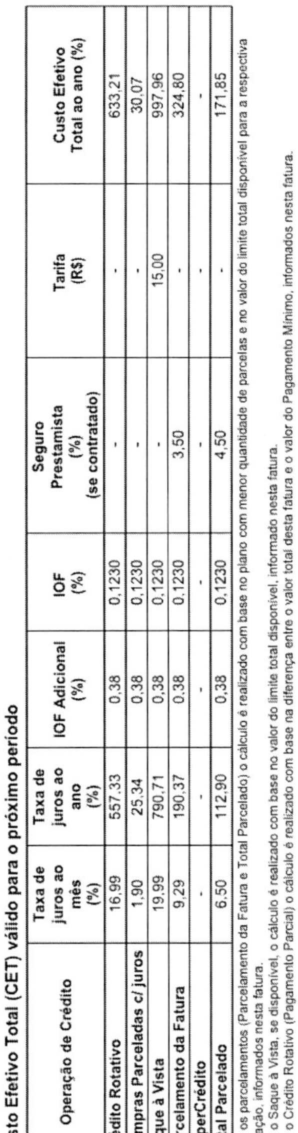

Custo Efetivo Total (CET) válido para o próximo período

Operação de Crédito	Taxa de juros ao mês (%)	Taxa de juros ao ano (%)	IOF Adicional (%)	IOF (%)	Seguro Prestamista (%) (se contratado)	Tarifa (R$)	Custo Efetivo Total ao ano (%)
Crédito Rotativo	16,99	557,33	0,38	0,1230	-	-	633,21
Compras Parceladas c/ juros	1,90	25,34	0,38	0,1230	-	-	30,07
Saque à Vista	19,99	790,71	0,38	0,1230	-	15,00	997,96
Parcelamento da Fatura	9,29	190,37	0,38	0,1230	3,50	-	324,80
SuperCrédito	-	-	-	-	-	-	-
Total Parcelado	6,50	112,90	0,38	0,1230	4,50	-	171,85

Para os parcelamentos (Parcelamento da Fatura e Total Parcelado) o cálculo é realizado com base no plano com menor quantidade de parcelas e no valor do limite total disponível para a respectiva operação, informados nesta fatura.
Para o Saque à Vista, se disponível, o cálculo é realizado com base no valor do limite total disponível, informado nesta fatura.
Para o Crédito Rotativo (Pagamento Parcial) o cálculo é realizado com base na diferença entre o valor total desta fatura e o valor do Pagamento Mínimo, informados nesta fatura.

Source: original image of the Santander Bank mailing to clients, Brazil, 2016

After 2014, with bankers already holding power in the economic area, the process worsened radically. For example, in the product "Santander Master" the credit would have cost the customer 481.96% in February 2016. In December 2014 this product was 372.62% (*Extrato Inteligente*, a Santander publication sent to clients). Of course, it is not surprising that a staggering 63.3 million adults in Brazil are excluded from the credit system because of the so-called “nome sujo” (dirty name) according to SPC (Credit Protection Service, June 6, 2018), which is 5 million more than in December 2016. If we consider that adult population in Brazil represents about 130 million persons, we are speaking of roughly half the Brazilian population.[82]

Additionally, with the total lack of regulation of credit, the system can charge anything. According to the Anefac report: "We emphasize that interest rates are free and are stipulated by the financial institution itself, as so there is no control of prices or ceilings for the amounts charged." Let us recall that Article 192 of the Constitution that regulated the national financial system was repealed in 1999, by a Congress elected with corporate money, and the system included in the Constitution in 2003 (Emenda Constitucional 40, 2003) represents a free-for-all system.

Obviously, with these interest rates, when making a purchase on credit, people spend more on interest than on the value of the product they purchased. Families not only become heavily indebted, but also end up buying very little. The calculation is clear: in practical terms, they pay almost double, sometimes more. In other words, they buy half of what their money could buy if it were in cash, and cash purchases obviously already include commercial intermediation profits.

According to data from the Central Bank, in March 2005 household debt amounted to 19.3% of a family’s income. In March 2015, the accumulated debt represented 46.5% of their income. This level of debt, in terms of debt stock, is lower than that of many developed economies. However, in these countries interest rates are in the order of 2% to 6% per year. With the interest paid in Brazil, families evidently are unable to expand their consumption and their purchasing power has been appropriated by financial intermediaries. Demand has been curbed by high interest rates

---

[82] SPC Serviço de Proteção ao Crédito, https://www.spcbrasil.org.br/imprensa/noticia/4768 June 6, 2018: “It is estimated that approximately 63.29 million Brazilians have their fiscal number restrained from installment purchases or credit concession.” In December 2016 this number stood at 58.3 million. https://www.spcbrasil.org.br/imprensa/noticia/2415

for private individuals, and this holds back the economy as a whole (BCB, DEPEC, 2015).

Taxes are not the villain, although the dominant weight of indirect taxes only worsens the situation: it is the stifling of demand for the benefit interest payments. Families were spending much more, as a result of the high level of employment and increase in the purchasing power in the general population; however, interest payments have gradually sterilized the stimulation impact of demand on the economy. One of the main drivers of the dynamization of the economy has been blocked, and the economy thrown into recession.

An economy essentially benefiting financial intermediaries was generated. The households that need the goods and services are hampered and also indirectly producers see their stocks pile up. Much of the impact of the economic dynamization of redistributive policies is lost. Payroll loans help but only account for 23.5% of credit for consumption (DCI, 2014), and they still charge 25–30% interest. It is certainly cheaper credit, but only by comparison with the exorbitant level reached by the other forms of credit.

Some examples help us to understand the dynamics. Installment plans charge, for example, 129.29% for "household appliances" purchased by installments (see table above). Those unable to keep paying frequently resort to using an overdraft—more than 300% in Brazil—only to sink further in the accumulated debt, and if they enter revolving credit—in the order of 320%—the noose gets even tighter. It should be noted that the interest on the overdraft and the revolving credit card does not exceed 20% per year in developed countries. In our case, a large part of the purchasing power of new consumers is drained to benefit financial intermediaries, thereby sterilizing the dynamization of the economy on the demand side.

Should a person seek credit in a bank, the interest for private individuals, notwithstanding the payroll deductible loan, which is the range of 25 to 30% (still scalping but used in less than a quarter of credit transactions), is in the order of 64.22% according to ANEFAC (National Association of Executives of Finance, Administration and Accounting). In France the corresponding costs are in the range of 3.5% per year.

People who are either more aware or have greater resources, pay cash using their credit card, generally ignore that in the "credit" modality of a purchase of 100 reais, 5% of what they pay goes to the banks, and in the "debit" mode this stands at about 2.5%. The already abolished CPMF tax on transactions was 0.38%—paid to government and used for investment in health—was widely criticized by the mainstream press. It was low, and useful, particularly since all financial transactions were registered, and helped to reduce illegal operations. Presently the bank discounts 5 reais on a purchase of 100 reais, for cash payment with a credit card—therefore, in the mode of "credit"—when the cost of the operation (card management) barely reaches 10 cents. This is a cost-benefit ratio of 50 to 1. With millions of credit card payment transactions carried out every day, all economic activities have become more expensive for the consumer, since the transaction costs are included in the price. It is a huge drain on the entire economy.

It should be added here that many of the new installment buyers have little credit experience. As seen, a particularly nefarious practice is that intermediaries, and today, also banks, present interest on a monthly rather than a yearly basis, which masks the compound interest mechanism. An untrained person in the area will think that 6% interest per month is three times higher than 2% per month. However, an interest of 6% per month represents about 100% per year, while an interest of 2% per month represents 26% per year. Three times 26 is 78%, not 100%. Will the buyer do these mental calculations?

Indeed, it is even stranger to note that no one has ever had a lesson on how money works. The main structuring mechanism of our society is simply absent from education throughout the entire school cycle, and even in universities, except in areas specializing in financial economics. No wonder Stiglitz won his "Nobel" prize for showing the importance of the asymmetry of information in the economic process.

The result is that the population gets highly in debt in order to purchase very little. The installment that "fits in the pocket", actually weighs down the pocket for a long time. The demand effect is blocked. When 63 million adults in Brazil have "stained names", as they are called in Brazil, and are unable to pay their debts, it is the system that is deformed. Brazilians work hard, but the results are diverted from productive activities to the so-called financial merry-go-round, which does not reinvest in the real economy. You cannot have your cake and eat it too. The main driver of the economy—household demand—is stalled.

The truth is that Brazil has in its vast domestic market a gigantic opportunity for expansion. The effectiveness of this process on the performance of the overall economy became evident during the phase of increased family income in the Lula administration, but it was also evident in the impressive advance of Europe in the post-war period, and today in China. In economic terms, that is what works. In addition, cheap credit must be made available for the dynamization of mass consumption, as well as for the productive sector.

At the initial stage of the crisis in Brazil, it became fashionable to repeat that this stimulus to the economy had been exhausted, as if the little progress achieved by the poor of the country was the limit. Nothing like taking a walk in a popular neighborhood, or checking statistics in the "Data Popular" publications which present studies on the level of consumption of the lower classes, to realize the idiocy of this argument. The mass of the population has a lot to improve both in quantitative and qualitative levels of consumption, not only in terms of the "out of pocket" consumption from available income, but also collective consumption with access to education, health, and other public goods of universal access.[83]

A specific example of personal indebtedness:

A freelance professional, without a formal contract, at the age of 40, Maria do Carmo spent two months without receiving a salary, which forced her to apply for a loan at Santander, the bank where she had had an account for more than twenty years. Very sympathetic, her credit manager offered her a loan of R$5,790.00, which was enough to carry her over this hard time. This amount would be paid in 25 installments of 497.45 reais. A pretty smooth deal for Santander, who would lend R$5,790.00 and then receive R$12,436.25.

The manager presented the interest rate that would be charged to Maria do Carmo: 6.89% per month. Interestingly, she did not mention the value of the rate per year: 125.02%. This is more than double the amount requested in the loan, yet it was not explained, only described in the contract. As Maria do Carmo does not know anything about the interest system, she did not question her manager about this and only acknowledged the 6.89% value that did not mean much to her. The manager also offered other

[83] João Sicsú sums up this evolution of consumption: "Brazil has progressed in terms of economic rights, that is, expansion of employment, distribution of income, real improvement of wages, reduction of extreme poverty and democratization of consumption. It is time to radicalize the development project by offering quality public services in the areas of health, education, transportation and social and life security." João Sicsú – *O que é e o que produz o ajuste fiscal* – May 19, 2015

products to Maria do Carmo, including the Van Gogh card, which is charged more than the card she used until then. Life insurance was also suggested.

In November 2016, Maria do Carmo was offered help to pay off her debt and called the bank's manager. At the beginning of November 2016, she had paid five installments of R$497.45, or R$2,487.25. If she did not pay off the debt, she still had 20 installments to pay, totaling R$9,949.00. When you repay a debt, the bank calculates the reduction in interest. The total that Maria do Carmo needed to repay her debt was R$5,672.61.

Note that between June 25 and November 16, in just five months, Santander earned R$2,369.86 on Maria do Carmo's loan: lending R$5,672.61 and receiving from her R$8,159.86 (R $ 2,487, 25 in five installments paid between June and October and R$5,672.61 paid in November to pay off the total debt). Obviously, for Santander it would have been preferable if Maria do Carmo had not paid off her debt. If she had not received help, in 25 months (two years) the bank would have snapped up R$6,646.25 from Maria do Carmo (R$ 12,436.25 total, minus the R$ 5,790 loaned).

Maria do Carmo is just one example. Imagine the number of people who are in her situation, generating this kind of profit to Santander, which in Spain would act in a completely different way. In Europe, typically this loan would have an interest of 3.5% per year, not 125.02% and we are not talking about overdrafts or revolving credit on credit cards where the latter is in the range of 633% at Santander.

When foreign economists visit me in Brazil, I have to show them the original banking instructions, they can hardly believe this can go on.

Producers

The collapse of household demand—the great mass of the people's consumption—has had an immediate effect in the initiatives of companies that see their inventories of unsold products accumulating. It is natural that they reduce the rate of production, which in turn affects employment. An even larger impact results from the reduction of company investments. If demand is reduced by 5%, for example, then it will create uncertainty about the production perspective, new investments will fall as companies go on hold, and any new initiative will be suspended.

Effectively productive entrepreneurs—unlike intermediaries—generally work with relatively small margins. A stove can be purchased in installments for 840 reais and in cash at 420 reais, which already includes the 40% tax and store profit, but it will have left the factory at just over 200 reais. The result is that those who do not have money to pay in cash will pay more than 800 reais for a 200-stove. The producer here receives little and will have difficulties when they expand activities, since the bulk of the profit goes to intermediaries who, instead of providers of good commercial services, have become financiers: i.e., credit sellers. These are banking activities although they are often not assumed as such. In practice, they are financial intermediaries.

Interest rates for legal entities are, proportionally, as scandalous as those for private individuals. The study by Anefac shows an average practiced rate of 63.08% per year, with 28.93% for working capital, 34.96% for discount of trade bills, and 146.83% for guaranteed accounts. No one in their right mind can develop productive activities, open a company, face the period of market entry, and balance accounts paying this type of interest. Here, private sector production and investment are directly affected. The inflation rate is around 3% and so we are speaking of huge real interest rates.

Interest rates for legal entities (2018)

LINHA DE CRÉDITO	JANEIRO/2018		FEVEREIRO/2018		VARIAÇÃO	VARIAÇÃO PONTOS
	TAXA MÊS	TAXA ANO	TAXA MÊS	TAXA ANO	%	PERCENTUAIS AO MÊS
Capital de Giro	2,12%	28,63%	2,14%	28,93%	0,94%	0,02
Desconto de Duplicatas	2,55%	35,28%	2,53%	34,96%	-0,78%	-0,02
Conta garantida	7,76%	145,18%	7,82%	146,83%	0,77%	0,06
Taxa Média	4,14%	62,71%	4,16%	63,08%	0,48%	0,02

Source: ANEFAC, https://www.anefac.com.br/uploads/arquivos/2018315161835543.pdf (2018).

There are official lines of credit that up to a certain point offset the appropriation of results by financial intermediaries, but these concern basically large loans for large corporations, through the official development bank, BNDES. The small and medium-sized entrepreneur will look for credit at the branch where he has his account, and the request for subsidized forms of official credit does not enter in his sphere of decision. In the euro zone, the average cost of credit for a legal entity is around 2 to 5% a year, which is directly available at any bank. Nobody can develop productive activities with interest rates like the ones we practice. Companies end up seeking self-financing, which means that the immense engine of a dynamic economy (i.e., cheap credit for the producer) is lost.

In addition to reduced household consumption and expensive credit, in the case of Brazil, a third factor discourages the producer: he has the alternative to invest in "Tesouro Direto", public debt bonds, which yield 7.5% for an inflation of 3.0% at the beginning of 2018, but had yielded over 10% net of inflation, with full liquidity and zero risk, during many years. This is an alternative that allows the entrepreneur to obtain monetary gains without having to face the efforts and risks of productive activities. Even when inflation is reduced, it is an excellent remuneration, which has influenced a large part of the business community and enlarged the class of rentiers: those who earn without having to produce, since they are paid by our taxes, as it is a service of the public debt. This last mechanism, because of the burden it represents for the budget, blocks the fourth engine of the economy: public investment in infrastructure and social policies.

Public investment and social policies

Let us look at the fourth item of the cogwheels: the Selic rate levied on the public debt. The mechanism is simple. In 1996, in order to compensate for the losses that the banks faced when hyperinflation was halted, the government created a mechanism of financing the public debt with high interest rates. My savings, for example, are in the bank, but yield very little. The bank, in turn, invests this money in public debt bonds that yielded, during the FHC government, on average 25% to 30%, reaching a maximum of 46%. The justification was to reassure "the markets", that is, the big financial intermediaries, national or international. To be "reliable" for international finance and risk rating agencies has become more important than to be trustworthy.

To pay these intermediaries, the government had to increase taxes, and the tax burden, as we have seen, rose by 5 percentage points in the 1990s. For example, in 2016, with a Selic interest rate of 14% and low inflation, government transfers a large part of our taxes to banks. This is at a lower rate than in the Fernando Henrique Cardoso phase, but it is levied on a larger stock of debt and lower inflation. The mechanism is simple. I am a saver and so I take my money from one pocket and put it as savings into the bank, which pays me a symbolic interest rate that barely protects me from inflation; now, from the other pocket, I take 14% to give to the government who also transfers it to the bank. In other words, I pay the bank, through my taxes, for it to have my money. It is important to remember that interest rates on public debt are in the range of 0.5% to 1% a year in most countries in the world.

Brazil has a GDP of about six trillion reais, which means that every time 60 billion is drained from productive activities for speculation, it is 1% of GDP that is lost to the real economy. If public debt expenditures reach 8.5% of the GDP, as in 2015, it is about 500 billion reais of our taxes that are essentially transferred to financial groups. This restricts a very significant part of the government's capacity to finance infrastructure and social policies. Furthermore, the high Selic rate discourages productive investment in companies because it is easier, as we have seen, to gain from public debt interest. Additionally, for banks and other intermediaries, it is easier to profit from public debt than to boost the economy by supporting good productive projects, which would require identifying clients and projects, as well as analyzing and following credit lines: i.e., doing their homework and using our savings to foster the economy. The major profits extracted from the real economy by financial intermediation end up contaminating all the economic agents. The following chart was sent to me by António Correia de Lacerda and clearly explains where the gap in the budget comes from (the higher 2015 figure includes 100 billion in exchange swaps).

The tale of the housewife sold to the population by huge propaganda efforts indicates that the government has to behave like a good housewife, who only spends what she has. However, the government has not spent more than it has on public policies but has instead spent this money on the debt service. The new government issued from the coup began to reduce public policies, such as investments and social policies, but not the transfer of money to the banks. The EC95 amendment to the Constitution, called "expenditure ceiling", makes it illegal for government to raise investment on infrastructure or social policies such as health and education, but not expenditures on debt servicing. The political coup basic aim was to keep and even increase the transfer of financial resources to financial intermediaries. Bleeding the state obviously does not help, and reducing investment in social policies in a country like Brazil is a drama.

In terms of economic impact, public investments are essential to energizing any modern economy. The two mainstays of dynamism in the public domain are investments in infrastructure such as transport, energy, telecommunications, water supply, and sanitation, as well as social policies

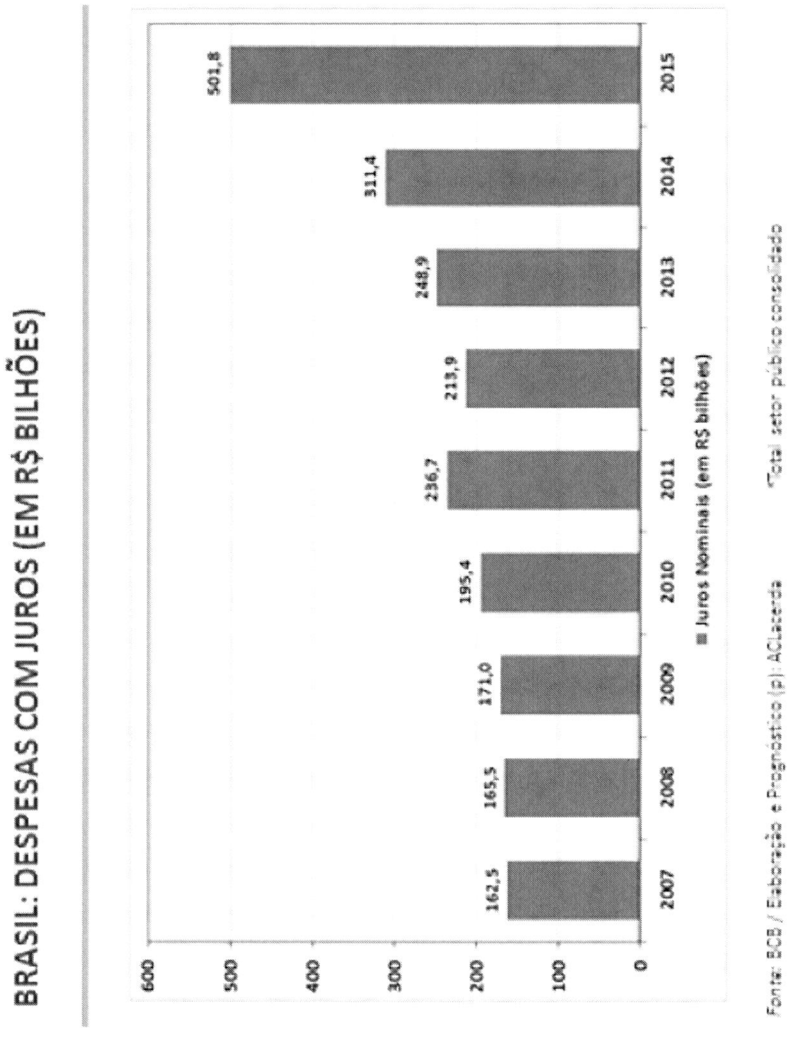

such as health, education, culture, leisure, sports, housing, security, and other activities that essentially are an investment in people and expand collective consumption. By diverting a large part of the public resources from investments to the remuneration of financial intermediaries and rentiers in general, the fourth engine of the economy was blocked.

In political terms, this perverse mechanism became explosive, because if the system initially favored the banks today, with the opening of asset allocations in the “Tesouro Direto” bonds to any saver, it is a mass of entrepreneurs and upper middle-class people that have become accustomed to see their money profit from the high Selic rate. When the Dilma government attempted reduce the bleeding of public money by lowering interest rates in 2013, from 14% to 7.5% (for 5% inflation), the rebellion was essentially among the rich. In addition, a perverse synergy was formed between financial interests in the banking sector benefitting the high-middle-class, who are accustomed to a large flow of rent on their financial investments, and right-wing political activists eager to come back to power. This is a financial and political crisis with one aggravating the other. We will see this in detail in the next chapter.

It is essential to understand that people with a lower income—3/4 of the country—invest very little in financial products and can hardly make ends meet, in particular because of the debt that chokes them. This population is also in dire need of public investments, such as health, education, basic sanitation, social housing, and other initiatives. When the resources that would serve to finance these sectors are diverted to those who have important financial investments, that is, to the richest segments of the country, a deepening of inequalities is generated. This then reverses all efforts from the past 12 years of expansion of social policies and of mass consumption during the Lula and Dilma governments. Brazil thus returns to a "narrow-based" economy, and the essential historical aim of bringing harmony through the social rising of the poorer population is blocked.

It is important to mention that the perverse mechanism created in the country is found in many countries, albeit in various forms. The common denominator is that large financial groups take over public policies through swelling public debt. Survival of the government will then depend less on its commitment to ensure policies that favor the population at large, and more on showing that it is "reliable" for the national and global system of financial speculation. There are countless countries that elected governments with progressive programs and which, in the end, implemented right-wing policies. Meanwhile they do manage to convince the population that it is the public deficit—the excessive dimension of government “expenditures”—that is responsible. Social policies are presented as populist irresponsibility, generating deficit and a stalled economy. When one compares the few tens of billions that the "Bolsa Família" (family support) costs (around 0.5% of the GDP) through its investment in people, with 500 billion (8,5% of GDP) transferred to rentiers, who earn without producing, the argument becomes ridiculous. In fact, Jorge Abrahão de Castro's work at IPEA shows that for every single real invested in the "Bolsa Familia", the multiplication effect leads to a GDP increase of 1.78 reais.[84]

A perverse mechanism

We are witnessing a paralysis of the country more in financial than economic terms—our productive capacity remains largely intact—which has been aggravated by a political stalemate, resulting in the impressive drop in GDP and surge in unemployment (4.3% to 13%) during the more than 3 years of the new administration.[85] The first economic engine, foreign trade, depends on the international dynamics over which we have little influence. However, for the other three engines of the economy we can risk very reliable orders of magnitude. Here is a preliminary assessment of the size of the gap generated by financial intermediaries and rentiers. When we try to reach gross figures, we must face the fact that the various statistical subsystems do not form a coherent universe that may simply be added up. Nevertheless, the orders of magnitude are evident.

According to the Central Bank report of February 2017, the balance of credit operations of the financial system, including free and targeted resources, reached 3,074 billion reais, 48.7% of the GDP. On this stock of debt interest is paid, with an average value in the same period of 32.8% per annum (the equivalent in Europe is in the order of 3 to 5%). This means that the interest burden paid by private individuals and legal entities

---

[84] The study shows the multiplication effect of redistribution programs: "The *Programa Bolsa Família* (PBF) becomes the most effective income transfer program: in the simulation, the GDP would increase by R$1.78 for a marginal investment of R$1.00 in the program. That is, if the supply is perfectly elastic and the other assumptions are respected, an additional 1% of the GDP in the program would translate into a 1.78% increase in economic activity. The *Benefício de Prestação Continuada* (a pension fund for the poorest or disabled) the unemployment insurance and the salary bonus come next, also with multipliers higher than one". Interest on public debt has an inverse effect and, therefore, reduces the GDP.

[85] Formally, the Temer administration from the coup has been in charge since May 2016, but actually the new policy directed by bankers started at the beginning of 2014. See the following chapter.

amounts to 999 billion, which is almost one trillion reais and about 16% of the GDP. This is the interest drawn, not the volume of loans. A mass of resources of this size transforms the economy. We will return to the details of these figures further on (BCB, ECOIMPOM 26/01/20177).[86]

O ESTADO DE S. PAULO

Crise de crédito tira R$ 1 tri da economia e piora recessão

Contra crise, Temer busca perfil técnico para Casa Civil

Complicações do aborto matam 4 mulheres por dia

"O Estado de Sao Paulo" Sunday headline, December 18, 2016: "Credit crisis takes 1 trillion reais out of the economy and deepens recession". The open mouth of the whale and the volume of money swallowed up by the banks are here just a coincidence or, maybe, a humorous touch by some journalist.

As we saw, this results in the collapse of the purchasing power of households, whose debt stock was equivalent to 46.5% of their income, in March 2015. When one pays 100% interest, it is the total stock of debt that drains the family's resources. We do not have the corresponding figures

[86] BCB – *Política monetária e operações de crédito do SFN*, February 27, 2017, http://www.bcb.gov.br/htms/notecon2-p.asp

for the business world. It would be important to be able to exhibit the degree of indebtedness, for example, of small and medium enterprises in various sectors. However, the bottleneck is certainly powerful; therefore, the second and third engines of the economy, the consumption of families and business activity are blocked here.

As for the fourth engine, public investment, about 500 billion diverted from our taxes represent 8% of the GDP. The system represents a scandalous appropriation of public resources. If the banks and others favored by the system invested these financial gains in productive activities of goods and services, we would certainly have a strong economic growth. However, these are resources that are dominated by financial rent, via public or private debt, and partly placed abroad in tax havens.

If we add up then it becomes apparent that around 15% of the GDP, which is practically one trillion reais, is diverted to the remuneration of financial intermediaries through the debt of private individuals and legal entities, while 8% is diverted through public debt. Several parts of this return to the productive circuit; this is significant, although minor, and it is no overstatement to estimate that we are restricting more than 15% of our resources by diverting them from economic activities to unproductive rentiers.[87]

In this context, it is understandable that the declared profits of financial intermediaries are soaring, while the economy is in recession: an impressive 3.8% fall in 2015 and 3.6% in 2016, and practically zero growth in 2017, possibly 1% in 2018. The graph below shows an "alligator's jaw" (*boca de jacaré* as we call it in Brazil) which is characteristic of these strongly diverging trends.

---

[87] It is striking to note that in the assessments of analysts that supported the figure of 1 trillion reais taken out of the real economy, as mentioned in the headline in *Estadão* above, the problem of the crisis which justified impeachment, after all, not be of fiscal adjustment (see section B in the same edition).

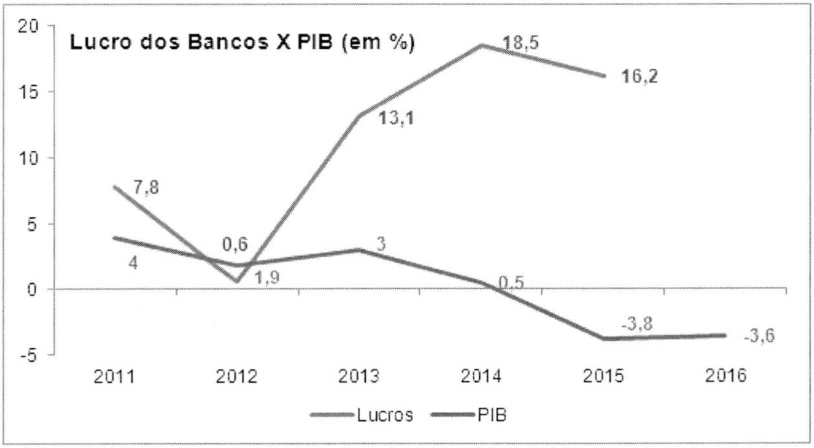

In red GDP and in blue profits of major banks. This is the sum of profits of the banks Itaú, Bradesco, CEF, Banco do Brasil, Santander, and HSBC. The years 2011, 2014, and 2015 do not include HSBC's profit. The bank's balance sheet in 2016 was not yet available in early 2017. Source: DIEESE based upon the balance sheets provided by financial institutions. Prepared by Marcos António do Espírito Santo.

No economy can work under such circumstances. Data simply does not allow access to how many of these resources return to the economy. As we saw in the Epstein and Montecino study, as well as Mason's, in the American economy, once appropriated by financial groups, little returns to the real economy: their estimate is 10%. Here, much of these benefits turn into more financial papers, particularly public debt bonds and, therefore, drain the real economy even more. Importantly, these financial resources are drained into tax havens or become new usurious loans for the population. I have conservatively estimated the net drain to be of more than 15% of the GDP and this is already large enough to stall the economy.

No member of the elite would be willing to let the financial mechanisms appropriate the surplus, which generates so much profit with so little effort, to be reduced to civilized levels. Dilma did try and was faced with a ferocious backlash. To say that the recession they generated is due to government expenditures on social programs is simply ridiculous. What we are facing is not a fiscal adjustment problem or some minor deficit problem but a deep deformation of the overall financial flow, which will then demand the restructuring of the financial system in general. In particular, banks need to go back to their traditional homework, which is to identify projects and productive investment opportunities and thereby boost the economy.

The key issue is that financial intermediaries do not finance production, but drain it. This logic allows us to understand how the economy entered a recession, while at the same time, in 2014, that the Bradesco bank increased its profits by 25.9% and Itaú by 30.2%; this is a dynamic where the more the banks profit, the more the economy is stalled. It is difficult not to see this connection. The fact that similar processes are taking place in other countries only strengthens the need to focus on this dynamic. The immense effort by economists from financial institutions and the media to attribute the recession to the excess of public expenditures represents a scandalous scam.

The fiscal dimension

We must now consider what happens to the many earnings that land in the hands of the financial agents. The Tax Justice Network (TJN) has produced the most reliable data on tax evasion through tax havens. Long before the Panama or the Paradise Papers, with the pressures of the G20 and the impact of the 2008 crisis, the figures were becoming evident. As an order of magnitude, resources invested in tax havens are equivalent to somewhere between 1/4 and 1/3 of the world's GDP (accumulated stock of resources, not annual flow).

As such, Brazil is not isolated in this planetary system, nor is it particularly corrupt. The data for Brazil, $519.5 billion in terms of offshore capital, is impressive in every sense: we are fourth in the world. These resources, which also represent something like 28% of the GDP in terms of accumulated capital, should not only pay taxes, which would allow public investments to be increased, but be invested to foster the economy where they were generated. This was envisaged by Article 192 of the Constitution, until the article was repealed, in full, in 1999. In 2016, with great fanfare, the government was able to repatriate the equivalent of 46 billion reais from stocks in tax havens amonting to around 1,700 billion reais, which stands at roughly 3%.

We have seen this data in Chapter 6 in our discussion on tax havens. Here, we see in more detail the accumulated capital in tax havens for specific countries. We only have the information for this up to 2010: see the figure referring to Brazil and the US $519.5 in flight stock. It is also important to note that Latin America is not the onlyculçprit.

UNRECORDED CAPITAL FLOWS, OFF SHORE ASSET, AND OFF SHORE EARNINGS, 1997-2010

Latin America and Caribbean Region
FOREIGN DEBT ADJUSTED FOR CURRENCY CHANGES, RESCHEDULINGS, AND ARREARS
(Nominal and Real $2000 Billions)
(40 countries in region—33 with data)

	Country	Original Outflows		Offshore Earnings ($B)	CF/GNI	CF/Sources	Flight Stock ($B 2010)	External Debt ($B 2010)	CF Stock Ext.Debt	Offshore Earing % Outflows
			Real #B		Period Merinas					
		Nom $	$2000)	($2000)	%	%	Nominal	Nominal	%	%
1970-2010	Brazil	$345.0	$362.6	$247.3	1.7%	43%	$519.5	$324.5	160%	68%
1970-2010	Argentina	$213.9	$259.3	272.8	3.4%	68%	$399.1	$129.6	308%	105%
1970-2010	México	$223.7	$263.5	$299.1	1.8%	36%	$417.4	$186.4	224	113%
1970-2010	Venezuela	$269.1	$278.2	$202.0	5.7%	82%	$405.8	$55.7	728%	73%
1970-2010	*All Others (29)*	$205.1	$211.9	$169.1	1.7%	41.5%	$316.	$317	100%	
	Lac Total	**$1,254.8**	**$1,375.5**	**$1,190.3**	**2.5%**	**51%**	**$2,058.3**	**$1,013.4**	**203%**	**87%**

Source: World Bank IMF/ UN /central bank/CIA (data); JSH analysis @JSH2012
Adjusted for Currency of Debt; 75% Reinvestment Rate; Ave Yielt: $US 6 mos CD rate

Source: http://www.taxjustice.net/cms/upload/pdf/Appendix%203%20-%202012%20Price%20of%20Offshore%20pt%201%20-%20pp%201-59.pdf

It is not illegal to open a tax haven account but it is obviously illegal to use it for tax evasion purposes. The "Sindicato Nacional de Procuradores da Fazenda Nacional (SINPROFAZ)" (National Union of Treasury Attorneys) estimates tax evasion in Brazil stands at 9.1% of the GDP in 2016, which is equivalent to about 570 billion reais: "Supposing, furthermore, we consider only the average indicators of misappropriation of the most relevant taxes (ICMS, Income Tax and Social Security Contributions), an indicator of evasion of 27.6% of the collection could be estimated (the same as the VAT misappropriation indicator in countries of Latin America, which was of 27.6%). Considering this last indicator for the misappropriation, it could be said that if there were no evasion, the weight of the tax burden could be reduced by almost 30% and still maintain the same level of collection. These estimated R$571.5 billions of tax evasion are practically equivalent to almost 90% of the total collected by the states and municipalities together, which is estimated at R$638.0 billions."[88]

One particularly interesting study is from the Global Financial Integrity (GFI), which was coordinated by Dev Kar, *Brazil: capital flight, illicit flows and macroeconomic crises, 1960–2012*. We are talking about a bleeding of resources by evasion, estimated at about US$35 billion per year between 2010 and 2012, equivalent to more than 115 billion reais a year. Thus 2% of our GDP evaporates annually through these operations alone. These are resources that in turn will supply a good part of the stock in the order of 1.7 trillion reais in tax havens, as seen above. According to the report, "the government must do much more to fight export under-invoicing and import over-invoicing, actively pursuing additional deterrent measures rather than retroactive penalties" (GFI, 2014).

In fact, profits made by the financial system are not only not invested in the economy, but are also largely not even taxed. An interesting poster was

---

85 Sindicato Nacional dos Procuradores da Fazenda Nacional - SINPROFAZ National Union of National Treasury Attorneys" *Sonegação no Brasil – Uma Estimativa do Desvio da Arrecadação do Exercício de 2016* - Brasília/DF, March 2017, p. 27 - http://www.quantocustaobrasil.com.br/artigos-pdf/sonegacao-no-brasil %E2%80%93uma-estimativa-do-desvio-da-arrecadacao-do-exercicio-de-2016.pdf. It should be noted that the TJN survey estimates Brazilian tax evasion at US$280 billion in 2010, which is a much higher level than the SINPROFAZ estimate. *The cost of Tax Abuse: The Cost of Tax Evasion Worldwide*, 2011, see table on p. 4: http://www.taxjustice.net/wp-content/uploads/2014/04/Cost-of-Tax-Abuse-TJN-2011.pdf

seen at the pro-coup demonstrations on Av. Paulista: "Tax evasion is not robbery." Of course, those who are fortunate and evade the treasury are also very happy to have their offspring enrolled at USP (University of SãoPaulo), studying free of charge on the back of others who pay their taxes. The ethics of the elites tend to be flexible.

In reference to the level of the flows abroad, the control of leaks could be improved, particularly with regard to under and over-invoicing: so-called transfer pricing. The GFI report points to these possibilities and acknowledges a strong advance in Brazil until 2012. At an international level, BEPS (Base Erosion and Profit Shifting) was finally approved in 2016, with an agreement endorsed by 40 countries that represent 90% of the world's GDP; this aimed to organize the control and gradual reduction of tax evasion by transnational corporations. The resistance of large international groups promises to be fierce. The election of Trump in the United States greatly reduced the scope of this agreement.[89]

At a domestic level, the very structure and incidence of taxation in Brazil is surreal. Inesc's research shows that "taxation on assets is almost irrelevant in Brazil, as it amounts to 1.31% of the GDP, accounting for only 3.7% of the 2011 tax revenue. In some countries of central capitalism, taxes on assets represent more than 10% of the tax collection: for example, Canada (10%), Japan (10.3%), Korea (11.8%), Great Britain (11.9%), and the United States (12.15%)" (Inesc, 2014, p. 21).

The top income tax rate (27.5%) is very low, and we must add the exemption from tax on distributed profits and dividends (since 1995, under the Cardoso administration), the absence of wealth tax, a ridiculous level of inheritance tax, and the fact that indirect taxes account for 56% of the collection. This is in addition to the fact that large debtors often resort to massive tax evasion. Therefore, we have, on the whole, a situation that is simply unsustainable. The critical economic situation in Brazil does not need arcane explanations. Just follow the money.

---

[89] On the structure of the BEPS agreement see OECD, 2014: http://publicintegrity.us4.list-

Incidence of taxes in Brazil (2011)		
	% of collection	% of GDP
Consumption	55.7%	19.7%
Income	30.5%	10.8%
Equity	3.7%	1.3%
Others	10,1%	3,6%
Total	100%	35.4%

Source: Inesc, Implications of the Brazilian tax system, September 2014, (part of table 1 p. 13)

"It should be highlighted that the tax burden is very regressive in Brazil, since it is concentrated on indirect and cumulative taxes that burden the workers and the poor, because more than half of the revenue comes from taxes levied on goods and services, with low taxation on income and assets. According to information from the 2008/2009 Household Budget Survey (POF) by Ipea, it is estimated that 10% of the poorest families in Brazil allocate 32% of the available income for the payment of taxes, while 10% of the richest families spend 21% of income on taxes" (Inesc, 2014, p. 6). It should also be remembered that wage earners have their income declared at the source, while the corporate world and large fortunes resort to the banking machine with specialists in tax evasion or tax avoidance, as seen in the HSBC data published in early 2015. Tax evasion in banking jargon is called tax optimization.

The lack of control is impressive. We, therefore, have the immense inventory of resources in tax havens, which is equivalent to 28% of the GDP (accumulated assets, not annual flow); a flow of evasion through fraud in invoices (transfer pricing) of around 2% of the GDP per year; and general tax avoidance, here estimated conservatively at 9.1% of the GDP. Add in the fact that the very incidence of taxation is greatly deformed because it is centered on indirect taxes on consumption alongside a very fragile taxation on profits and dividends. There is no tax on fortunes and taxation on inheritance is very limited, while wage earners have their taxes collected at source. The combination of these elements becomes disastrous for the functioning of the financial system in general, thereby radically affecting a key point of reference for any economic reasoning: the proportion of who becomes wealthier and by how much, and who effectively contributes to economic development. We are facing a deep divorce between the ends and the means.

The awareness that we are literally rewarding parasites is unavoidable. It is not about specific deformations. When we see how judges increase their already impressive salaries, we find that it is a culture of organizing niches of privilege that promotes solidarity between banks, representatives, judges, media giants, and many international groups. In the name, of course, of the welfare of the nation, whose very development they paralyze.

13 - Chronology of Disaster

The crisis that struck Brazil from 2013 onwards followed a series of advances that must be qualified here. A chronology of the transformations of the last three decades helps us to have an overview, which is necessary if we want to go beyond the search of who to blame.

The institutional framework

The starting point for the current process is the 1988 Constitution. Article 192, in particular, defined the economic and social usefulness of the national financial system as the guiding mainstay, and recommended a maximum annual interest rate of 12% above inflation. With a set of more balanced norms after years of arbitrariness and violence during the military dictatorship, the country had ground rules again and returned to the universe of democracies.

Between 1993 and 1994, hyperinflation was defeated; this was a key element to ensure the economic management of both governments and companies, by finally recovering the currency as a stable benchmark for value measurement. Let us recall that at the time, according to *The Economist*, there were 44 countries with hyperinflation, such as Argentina, Mexico, Israel, and many others. Hyperinflation was eliminated in all of them between 1993 and 1995.

On the 26th of December 1995, as a generous gift, a new law (Lei nº 9.249) exempted the rich from paying taxes on distributed profits and dividends; this was a monumental deformation which would directly favor all the financial intermediaries. The owners of large fortunes are the ones who invest in financial papers and are exempt from paying taxes on this source of revenue. The corporation pays 15% on profit, and once transferred to personal fortunes they are exempt from this under the justification that double taxing should be avoided.

In July 1996 the government established a system of high interest rates on public debt, thereby allowing banks to finance themselves by investing in bonds rather than seeking to boost the economy. The remuneration of securities was, from the beginning, at levels above 20% and reached 46%

at its peak. What the banks lost with the breakdown of hyperinflation, they would recover with the new Selic rate. Since then, for financial investors, it has become more profitable to invest in government bonds, paid for with our taxes, than to pursue projects, invest, and foster the economy. Economist Luiz Gonzaga Belluzzo estimates that the real average (deducting inflation) the banks were paid in the Cardoso presidency period was in the order of 20%; this is public money that has been transferred to the banks.

Since, as we saw, profits and dividends for legal persons are taxed 15%, but once they become private money in stake-holders hands, they are free from taxation, which means that the billions earned by the wealthiest families pay zero taxes on these gains, Brazil became a paradise for financial corporations. I, as a professor, am charged 27.5% on my salary, deducted at source. This impressive gift to the top of the pyramid was quietly approved, while the population was benefiting from the elimination of hyperinflation.[90] The two gifts to the financial system and rentiers in general, which allowed them to gain huge rewards from the public debt and to be exempt from paying the corresponding taxes, are clearly an economic monstrosity. In this way, by 1996, financialization had achieved an impressive foothold in the productive economy.

In 1997 Congress approved a law that authorized corporations to finance election campaigns. This, of course, meant congressmen as well. With the power of their money, economic groups could now elect their representatives, turning the basic clause of the Constitution, that all power stems from the people, into fiction. This capture of power would, evidently, have a dramatic impact on Brazilian politics, meaning that those elected no longer represented the population. Therefore, the deformation of the financial system now gained corresponding political teeth. It would take 18 years (at the end of 2015) for the supreme court to decide that corporations purchasing political representatives was unconstitutional. The Congress that ousted President Dilma and supported the political coup and approved austerity measures for the population, was elected by corporate money (Cruz, 2010).

---

[90] http://www.planalto.gov.br/ccivil_03/leis/L9249.htm: "Lei nº 9.249, de 26 de dezembro de 1995 que altera a legislação do imposto de renda das pessoas jurídicas, bem como da contribuição social sobre o lucro líquido, e dá outras providências". See Senator Lindbergh Farias at
https://www12.senado.leg.br/noticias/materias/2015/09/14/imposto-sobre-lucros-e-dividendos-geraria-r-43-bi-ao-ano-diz-estudo

In 1999, with PEC 53/1999, later turned into constitutional amendment EC 40/2003, all the paragraphs of Article 192 of the Constitution, which regulated the national financial system, were repealed. The date coincides with the repeal by president Clinton of the Glass-Steagall Act which had ensured a minimum of regulation and discipline in the American financial system and the rest of the world. Granted full power and free of regulation, the financial globalization exploded without barriers. Finances no longer foster the economy, either here or in other countries. It is worth remembering that the repealed Article 192 of the Constitution stated that "interest rates above this limit [12% per annum plus inflation] will be considered a usury crime, punished in all its modalities, under the terms set by law." The law, by the Congress elected via corporation money, did not set anything but simply revoked the article and then the pathway was opened.

In June 2002, at an event at the Anhembi Park in São Paulo, the then presidential candidate Lula read the "Letter to the Brazilians", in which he committed himself to respect the financial system as it had been established. In his words, he read this letter because he wanted to be elected. Once elected, President Lula maintained the high Selic rate, appointed a banker to manage public finances, and banks entered a spiral that increased private interest rates for both private individuals and legal entities thereby deepening financialization. This commitment was clearly a condition for his eligibility, not in legal terms, but in terms of actual power relations: the so-called political clout.

Notwithstanding the tricky situation in which the presidency was placed in 2003, with relatively limited resources and with the financial sector bleeding the economy, it was possible to implement a policy of inclusion on a previously unknown scale. A policy of the general reduction of inequalities began, one that today inspires countless political and economic actors in the world. We will not go into the detail of the immense success that these ten years, between 2003 and 2013, represented for Brazil. The eventual skeptics are essentially uninformed, and misinformation is understandable if we consider the role of the media oligopoly. The World Bank called this period “the golden decade of Brazil” for solid reasons. (World Bank, 2016).

In the two Lula governments and in the first Dilma government, there was clearly a State policy of social inclusion and modernization of the economy. However, the structural framework was not affected and the endlessly deferred basic reforms, such as tax reform, agrarian reform, and other structural modernization initiatives, were simply not scheduled. In

Brazilian history, their mere appearance on the political horizon has generated successive coups, beginning with the dismissal and suicide of Vargas in 1954, as well as the 1964 military coup.

What is important for us to understand here is that the immense effort to promote inclusion in the country was undertaken within a very restricted institutional framework, which was closely watched by broader political, financial, and media interests; this also includes international pressures. The most that could be done within the existing institutional framework was indeed successfully achieved. Although, clearly, there was not enough strength to transform the framework itself. With hindsight, many question why Lula did not use his 80% population approval to make these basic reforms. He clearly considered that power at the top is different, and that he did not have the political strength to promote them. He would make the most within the given straightjacket.

The logic of achievements

It helps us to perceive the breadth of what has been achieved. The Atlas of Human Development in Brazil 2013 shows the evolution of indicators in the 5,570 municipalities of the country. Reliability is very important here. In this case, it is the joint work of UNDP—which has years of international and national experience with human development indicators––IPEA, and the João Pinheiro Foundation from Minas Gerais, as well as many foreign consultants. The data is from IBGE: the official statistical institution. There is no way to manipulate figures, or to create an unbalanced interpretation, with this range of research institutions.

Another important factor is that the study covers the years 1991 to 2010, encompassing a long enough period to provide an overall picture, rather than to dramatize each oscillation according to media interests. Evaluating two decades also favors a more exempt political interpretation, since these are different administrations. Basically, the two fundamental factors, the 1988 Constitution and the overcoming of hyperinflation, led to the beginning of a process that was strengthened in the Lula government and continued with that of Dilma; this process essentially lasted until 2013.

For the layperson, let us remember that the HDI shows the combined evolution of per capita income, education, and health. This allows us to overcome, in part, the deformation linked to statistics that only center on the GDP, which measures the intensity of resource use, not the results. To give an example, an environmental disaster like the oil spill in the Gulf of

Mexico raised the US GDP by generating additional decontamination costs, thereby "heating up" the economy. The fact that it damages the environment and the population does not count. Crime also increases the GDP. In 2013, Britain and other countries have included prostitution and drug trafficking as a contribution to the GDP, which explicates to what extent it is an indicator with little scientific basis, but of great value in ideological and political manipulations.[91]

The global data shows that in these two decades the Municipal HDI went from 0.493, ("Very Low") to 0.727 ("High"). This represents a leap of 48% in the period. In 1991, Brazil had 85.8% of Brazilian municipalities in the Very Low group (below 0.50) and in 2010 there were only 231 municipalities which is equal to 4%. This was an absolutely amazing result, because a HDI below 0.50 is a black hole particularly in areas as essential as income, education, and health. The advances are impressive, but we still had a long way to go. The Northeast region still had 1,099 municipalities (61.3% of the total) with a Low index, which is in the range of 0.50 to 0.59 in the HDI. Overall, with the wide internalization of development, the change was immense.

Life expectancy at birth rose from 64.7 years in 1991 to 73.9 in 2010, which means that, on average, a Brazilian gained an extra 9 years of life. By including 2012, we can say that they gained 10 more years to complain about our bad development processes. Gaining so many years of life in such a short time is highly significant as it involves a complex set of factors, such as children who eat better, families living in more decent homes, and so on. That is what the economy is for, not just to count the percentage of the GDP.

In terms of education, we went from 30.1% of adults over 18 years of age with primary education to 54.9%. In terms of young peoples' school enrollment, according to the indicator of the item, we moved from 0.268 in 1991 to 0.666 in 2010, which represents an increase of 128%. This area of education advanced the most, yet it continues to be the most backwards, due to its particularly low starting level. Also, in terms of monthly income per capita, we went from 0.647 to 0.739 in the period, which represents an increase of 346 reais. It may seem little to those who earn a lot, but for a family of four people and at the grassroots of society, the extra 1384 reais

[91] On the deformation the GDP represents, see my technical note from 2009, *O debate sobre o PIB: estamos fazendo a conta errada*; this is a short note on the main references of the proposed changes, including the Stiglitz Commission, Amartya Sen and Jean Paul Fitoussi: http://dowbor.org

creates a revolution and helps explain the additional 10 years added to the average life span.

TABELA 1: IDHM DO BRASIL – 1991, 2000 E 2010

DIMENSÃO	ÍNDICES E INDICADORES	1991	2000	2010
	IDHM	0,493	0,612	0,727
Longevidade	IDHM Longevidade	0,662	0,727	0,816
	Esperança de vida ao nascer (anos)	64,7	68,6	73,9
Educação	IDHM Educação	0,279	0,456	0,637
	Subíndice: Escolaridade da população adulta	0,301	0,398	0,549
	População com 18 anos de idade ou mais que concluiu o ensino fundamental (%)	30,1	39,8	54,9
	Subíndice: Fluxo escolar da população jovem	0,268	0,488	0,686
	População de 5 a 6 anos de idade frequentando a escola (%)	37,3	71,5	91,1
	População de 11 a 13 anos de idade frequentando os anos finais do ensino fundamental*(%)	36,8	59,1	84,9
	População de 15 a 17 anos de idade com o ensino fundamental completo (%)	20,0	39,7	57,2
	População de 18 a 20 anos de idade com o ensino médio completo (%)	13,0	24,8	41,0
Renda	IDHM Renda	0,647	0,692	0,739
	Renda mensal per capita (R$)	447,56	592,46	793,87

*Anos finais: 6º ao 9º ano do ensino fundamental Fonte: IPEA, PNUD e FJP

Source:
http://www.ipea.gov.br/portal/images/stories/PDFs/130729_AtlasPNUD_2013.pdf p. 41

These are extremely significant transformations, for the first time, Brazil had begun to systematically retrieve its immense social debt. Here, there was no “chicken flight” (an expression regarding the cycles of Brazilian capitalism) and it was, instead, an example of consistent and sustained progress. However, the same data also shows what a long way we have to go. Data on those who are aged 18 to 20 years of age with a high school education is characteristic: 13.0% in 1991; 41.0% in 2010. This demonstrates significant progress and the way ahead. To not see this progress is blindness, but to believe that the bottom-up economic dynamics have been exhausted is to fail to see the extensive pathway ahead that will enable us to build a decent society.

The evaluation of Brazil's performance by the World Bank is blunt: "Until the late-1990s, little progress was made in reducing income inequalities in Brazil, but in the past decade Brazil’s socioeconomic progress has been remarkable and internationally noted. From 2003, the country has become recognized for its success in reducing poverty and inequality and its ability to create jobs. Innovative and effective policies to reduce poverty and ensure the inclusion of previously excluded groups have lifted millions of people out of poverty. Nevertheless, even today, in Brazil 5% of the population receives 30% of the income generated (together with Colombia the highest proportion for any country in Latin America)" (World Bank, 2016, p. xv). Here, with the utmost clarity is evidence of our immense progress and, also, the long way we need to go in order to reduce inequality and escape our prehistorical structure.

The evaluation of the international role played by Brazil is also explicit: "Brazil has also been assuming global responsibilities. It has been successful in pursuing economic prosperity while protecting its unique natural patrimony. Brazil has become one of the most important emerging new donors, with extensive engagements particularly in Sub-Saharan Africa, and a leading player in international climate negotiations. Brazil’s development path over the past decade has shown that growth with shared prosperity, but balanced with respect for the environment, is possible. Brazilians are rightly proud of these internationally recognized achievements" (World Bank, 2016, p. xvi).

The World Bank report is from May 2016 and, therefore, assesses what blocked the success of what it qualifies the "Golden Decade" between 2003 and 2013. With the crisis and recession, the assessment is as follows: "Against this background, some Brazilians are now asking whether the gains of the past decade might have been an illusion, created by the commodity boom, but unsustainable in today's less forgiving international environment. The answer provided in this Systematic Country Diagnostic (SCD) is a qualified "no". There is no reason why the recent socioeconomic gains should be reversed; indeed, they might well be extended with the right policies" (World Bank, 2016, p. xvi).

These advances are based on a premise that works: money that goes to the base of society has a multiplying effect in terms of economic growth and to a much larger extent than money going to the top. People in the middle and bottom of the pyramid use their money to buy products they need, creating additional space for numerous small businesses which will, in turn, stimulate employment (a goal in itself) and with this, more demand: the result is a virtuous circle. Additionally, this generates sustainable development, as it improves the living conditions of those who need to have a better life. Today, the 1% or 10% of the richest tend to make financial investments, and what could become productive investment and capital accumulation is currently only equity in the form of more financial papers. The outcome is low growth or recession and the sterilization of savings. Finally, money going to the State through taxes can be exceptionally productive when transformed into social policies and infrastructures but, of course, not when it is turned into interest paid to bankers, which generates greater returns for rentiers. No one eats bonds; however, those who live on unearned income, to use Joseph Stiglitz' terms, are very strong and they have the power to disrupt the virtuous circle, and transform it into a cumulative process of political and economic disorganization.[92]

The golden decade policy, which is not only based on the much propagated Bolsa Família but also on 149 social and economic inclusion programs, clearly worked. However, it was interrupted by a parliamentary coup, as we have seen, in the middle of the road. The immense task we have ahead to reduce inequality is clearly presented in the 2017 study by Oxfam-Brazil, *A distância que nos une: um retrato das desigualddes brasileiras* (Oxfam, September 2017).

[92]An excellent statistical presentation of the social and economic transformation of Brazil during the 2002–2015 period can be found in *Faces da desigualdade no Brasil,* by Tereza Campello and Pablo Gentili:
http://209.177.156.169/libros/Faces_da_desigualdade_no_brasil.pdf

Breaking down the virtuous cycle I: public debt

In the last few decades, we made extremely positive structural advances that raised the Brazilian economy to a new level. As of 2008, with the global financial crisis, these advancements became more irregular. In 2013, the progressive trend was already reversed as it was brought to a halt by the financial system, which essentially intensified the diversion of resources from productive activities to speculative gains. This led to the peculiar situation where the GDP had stopped growing but financial intermediaries maintained and even increased profits, despite the deep recession. The fact that financial intermediaries have profits that grow at a rate of 20% per year while the GDP is stalled, clearly signals where the problems are.

At a political level, an alliance was formed between international interests (in particular those related to finance, oil, and large global construction corporations), the oligopoly of the mainstream media, segments of the judiciary and, of course, legislative power. The latter, as we have seen, came to be essentially elected with corporate money, thereby strengthening the already traditional systems of corruption. I leave it to political science experts to pinpoint who was bought in the immense bartering ground that the political-electoral system has become and will leave here my general recommendation that when we hear "stop thief" it is prudent to check who is shouting. The expressions of high ethical indignation that we see so often on television, do not affect me very much. Perhaps it is a question of experience or maybe age. Understanding the mechanisms is what really matters.

The economic policy of the current government (2018) is based upon an immense farce: that the redistributive policies of the progressive era broke the country, while the new power with bankers in control of money would rebuild it. According to the story, acting as a good housewife should, they would be responsible and spend only what is earned. The truth is that the interest extorted by the bankers is what generated the breakdown. The good 'housewife' that governs us has joined the bankers and is increasing the deficit. Here the calculations are explicit and there is no need to be an economist or a banker to understand this. In addition, we will use the original data from the Central Bank, because reliability, in this ideologically tricky era, is fundamental. To see the data in the Central Bank itself, just click on the link under the table, opening "Historical Series: new structure" and look for Table 4.1.

Tabela 4.1. Resultado Primário do Governo Central - Brasil - Anual

R$ Milhões - Valores Correntes e % PIB

Discriminação	2012		2013		2014		2015		2016		2017	
	R$ Milhões	% PIB	R$ Milhões	% PIB	R$ Milhões	% PIB	R$ Milhões	% PIB	R$ Milhões	% PIB	R$ Milhões	% PIB
I. RECEITA TOTAL	1.059.889,4	22,0%	1.178.983,2	22,1%	1.221.474,1	21,1%	1.247.789,3	20,8%	1.314.952,9	21,0%	1.383.081,6	21,1%
II. TRANSF. POR REPARTIÇÃO DE RECEITA	171.394,4	3,6%	181.895,0	3,4%	198.461,5	3,4%	204.684,3	3,4%	226.835,3	3,6%	228.335,3	3,5%
II.4 Compensações Financeiras	*22.614,6*	*0,5%*	*23.441,1*	*0,4%*	*25.151,0*	*0,4%*	*18.836,9*	*0,3%*	*15.240,7*	*0,2%*	*22.184,8*	*0,3%*
II.5 CIDE - Combustíveis	*1.117,9*	*0,0%*	*57,3*	*0,0%*	*116,1*	*0,0%*	*448,0*	*0,0%*	*1.239,3*	*0,0%*	*1.698,7*	*0,0%*
II.6 Demais	*672,6*	*0,0%*	*800,3*	*0,0%*	*1.014,9*	*0,0%*	*1.235,7*	*0,0%*	*1.290,7*	*0,0%*	*1.471,5*	*0,0%*
III. RECEITA LÍQUIDA (I-II)	888.495,0	18,5%	997.088,3	18,7%	1.023.012,6	17,7%	1.043.105,1	17,4%	1.088.117,6	17,4%	1.154.746,3	17,6%
IV. DESPESAS	815.907,0	16,9%	924.929,1	17,3%	1.046.495,0	18,1%	1.164.462,3	19,4%	1.249.393,2	20,0%	1.279.007,8	19,5%
IV.1 Benefícios Previdenciários	*316.589,5*	*6,6%*	*357.003,1*	*6,7%*	*394.201,2*	*6,8%*	*436.090,1*	*7,3%*	*507.871,3*	*8,1%*	*557.234,8*	*8,5%*
IV.2 Pessoal e Encargos Sociais	*188.394,5*	*3,9%*	*205.152,9*	*3,8%*	*222.375,4*	*3,8%*	*238.499,0*	*4,0%*	*257.871,8*	*4,1%*	*284.041,1*	*4,3%*
IV.3 Outras Despesas Obrigatórias	*105.868,1*	*2,2%*	*133.442,0*	*2,5%*	*160.358,0*	*2,8%*	*236.586,6*	*3,9%*	*199.949,6*	*3,2%*	*185.190,4*	*2,8%*
IV.4 Despesas Discricionárias - Todos os Poderes	*205.054,9*	*4,3%*	*229.331,1*	*4,3%*	*269.560,4*	*4,7%*	*253.286,5*	*4,2%*	*283.700,4*	*4,5%*	*252.541,4*	*3,8%*
V. FUNDO SOBERANO DO BRASIL	12.400,0	0,3%	0,0	0,0%	0,0	0,0%	855,0	0,0%	0,0	0,0%	0,0	0,0%
VI. PRIMÁRIO GOVERNO CENTRAL	84.988,0	1,8%	72.159,1	1,4%	-23.482,4	-0,4%	-120.502,2	-2,0%	-161.275,6	-2,6%	-124.261,5	-1,9%
VII.1 AJUSTE METODOLÓGICO ITAIPU [11/]	1.313,8	0,0%	858,4	0,0%	0,0	0,0%	3.888,4	0,1%	3.721,9	0,1%	4.461,7	0,1%
VII.2 AJUSTE METODOLÓGICO CAIXA-COMPETÊNCIA	0,0	0,0%	0,0	0,0%	0,0	0,0%	0,0	0,0%	161,7	0,0%	3.115,6	0,0%
VIII. DISCREPÂNCIA ESTATÍSTICA	-215,7	0,0%	2.273,1	0,0%	3.010,7	0,1%	-41,8	0,0%	-2.081,4	0,0%	-1.758,1	0,0%
IX. RESULTADO PRIMÁRIO DO GOVERNO CENTRAL (VI + VII + VIII) [12/]	86.086,0	1,8%	75.290,7	1,4%	-20.471,7	-0,4%	-116.655,6	-1,9%	-159.473,4	-2,5%	-118.442,2	-1,8%
X. JUROS NOMINAIS [12/]	-147.267,6	-3,1%	-185.845,7	-3,5%	-251.070,2	-4,3%	-397.240,4	-6,6%	-318.362,1	-5,1%	-340.907,3	-5,2%
XI. RESULTADO NOMINAL DO GOVERNO CENTRAL (IX + X) [12/]	-61.181,7	-1,3%	-110.554,9	-2,1%	-271.541,9	-4,7%	-513.896,0	-8,6%	-477.835,5	-7,6%	-459.349,5	-7,0%
Memorando												
PIB Nominal [13] /	4.814.760,0	-	5.331.619,0	-	5.778.953,0	-	5.995.787,0	-	6.259.227,8	-	6.559.940,3	-

Source: Banco Central do Brasil, Resultado Fiscal do Governo Central—Estrutura nova (Jan/1997–Apr/2018), Table 4.1: http://www.tesouro.fazenda.gov.br/pt_PT/resultado-do-tesouro-nacional

The table, as it is shown on the Central Bank's website, seems complex but it is simple to read. In line IX, "Primary result of the central government", it is possible to follow the evolution of these figures. The primary result is the basic account of how much the government collected from taxes and then ended up spending in its actual government activities through investments in education, health, security, and so on: i.e., public policies.

When it is said that the government should be responsible by not spending more than it earns, this is what we are talking about. The numbers concerning Line IX are simply exported from the table above, here magnified for legilbility purpose:

Line IX: The primary results from central government

2010	2011	2012	2013	2014	2015	2016	2017
78,723.3	93,035.5	86,086.0	75,290.7	-20,471.7	-116,655.6	-159,473.4	-118,442.2
2.0%	2.1%	1.%	1.4%	- 0.4	- 1.9%	-2.5%	-1.8%

In this case, there was a surplus in the years 2010 to 2013 (less was spent than collected). In addition, there was an insignificant deficit of 20 billion in 2014 and a moderate one in 2015 (116 billion reais; 2% of the GDP) which was perfectly normal. In the European Union, for example, a deficit of up to 3% of the GDP is considered normal, with variations between one year and another. As such, it is clear that, contrary to what is commonly said, public policy expenditures had not caused any "breakdown". In political terms, it is important to emphasize that in 2013, when the major accusations against the "spending spree" and the war against the government begins, we still have a good surplus of 75 billion, which was little over 1% of the GDP.

In 2016, with the bankers in power, the deficit they said they intended to squash reached 159 billion, which returned to1.8% of the GDP in 2017. In any case, the reality is that with bankers in power the deficit was not reduced, and that the deficit under Dilma (0.4% of the GDP) was much lower. The economic justification for the coup, repeated ad nauseam in the press conglomerate, was that Dilma had broken the economy by spending on the poor money that she did not have. This was a farce or, as it is now called, a narrative.

The next line of the table, “X: Nominal Interest Paid", gives the key to the breakdown and recession. Nominal interest represents the amount of resources the government spent on the interest on public debt. This is a black box that blocks the economy in its public sector dimensions.

Line X: Nominal interest paid

2010	2011	2012	2013	2014	2015	2016	2017
- 124,508.7	- 180,533.1	- 147,267.6	- 185,845.7	- 251,070.2	- 397,240.4	- 318,362.1	- 340,907.3
-3.2%	-4.1%	-3.1%	-3.5%	- 4.3%	- 6.6%	-5.1%	-5.2%

This is the part of our taxes that, instead of serving social infrastructures and social policies, is transferred to banks and other financial intermediaries. Politically important is also the fact that a good part of the upper middle class profited from the scheme as individual investors in the "Tesouro Direto". With a good profitability assured without effort, the financial groups that handle the bulk of this debt reinvest the interest they earn into more public debt papers; thereby increasing the flow and the size of the public debt itself. It is the traditional snow-ball effect which is paid for by our taxes.

With the high Selic rate in 2010, the government transferred, according to the calculation of the Central Bank, 125 billion reais on the public debt. In 2011, this amount rose to 181 billion, dropping to 147 billion in 2012 with the reduction of Selic interest (to 7.5%) by the Dilma government. The drama begins in 2013; under pressure from the banks, interest rates rise again on the public debt, and the money transferred or re-invested by the rentiers generates 186 billion in 2013. During the Joaquim Levy phase (a banker placed in the ministry of finance to placate financial interests), with a banker handling the cashbook, this figure explodes to 251 billion in 2014 and then to 397 billion in 2015. The figures here presented by the Central Bank clearly show that the deficit created by the high interest rates on the public debt is outstandingly greater than the deficit of public policies *per se,* as seen in line IX "Primary result of the central government" above. In 2016, transfers were reduced to 318 billion, which was still more than double what was transferred in 2012: the last year or normality in the Dilma government. In 2017, it reached 341 billion. It should be stressed that the Bolsa Família, which had caused such hatred from the rich but took 50 million out of poverty, while being presented as the cause of the disaster, cost a mere 30 billion reais a year (about 0.5% of the GDP): 10 times less than what Brazilians came to call the "Bolsa Banco".

In 2015 almost 400 billion reais (500 billion if swaps are included) that could develop into investments in infrastructure and social policies, essentially became appropriated by financial intermediaries, such as banks, funds and even foreign investors. This generated the recession we now live with, which is still increasing in 2018 as we continue with more bankers in control of the system. A financial speculator, co-founder of Banco Pactual, (a relatively small bank with 31 affiliates in tax havens), Paulo Guedes, is expected to take over in 2019.

In a broader perspective, public debt is normal in a number of countries, ensuring zero-risk financial investment, as well as total liquidity and, therefore, paying in the range of 0.5% to 1.5% a year; this is the case in most countries, including, of course, the USA and EU. It is not designed for people to invest in and get rich, but for them to keep the money safe while deciding where they want to invest their money.

In Brazil, the system was created in July 1996 and it paid a fantastic Selic rate of more than 15%, already discounting inflation. A system that transfers public resources to banks and other financial investors was thus established by law. With interest rates of this size, the government barely managed to roll over its debt and paid only what it could, while the remainder increased the debt stock. This is a familiar process to any Brazilian family that takes on a debt to pay off another one.

In 2003, Lula took office with a Selic rate that paid 24.5% and when inflation was at 6%. It is important to note that these are huge profits for banks and rentiers in general, without any corresponding productive activity. They are also of no benefit to the government or the population, because the government, with this level of interest, just rolls the debt.

This system is absolutely unsustainable in the long term. It is illegitimate, because those are earnings without a productive counterpart, which generate economic entrenchment. In the transition from 2012 to 2013 and aware of the deadlock, the Dilma government began to gradually reduce the interest rate on public debt, from 14% to 7.5% per annum and inflation around 5.5%. This approached the rates practiced in other countries and generated immediate revolt by the banks and rentiers in general.

Why do so many countries maintain an interest rate on public debt of around 1% or less? Due to the fact that a low interest rate on public debt encourages the owners of financial resources to pursue other more profitable investments, in particular productive investments, which generate earnings while boosting the economy. In Brazil, the opposite was stimulated: why should a businessman risk his money in productive investments, if the public debt yields more?

The uprising by bankers and other rentiers, particularly the higher middle-classes, opened the way for hysterical reactions and to political opportunism. This provoked the great demonstrations of 2013. In addition, with a legislative power elected by corporate money, the attempt to reduce interest rates and rescue the government's economic policy was attacked by Congress. The mass media, who were controlled by four major groups (particularly the Globo empire), unleashed a general attack on the Dilma presidency. Rightwing political candidates also saw an opportunity for a political overthrow. Pressured from all sides at the top, Dilma retreated, initiating a new cycle of high interest rate on the public debt, hoping she would regain political terrain by reestablishing financial profit for banks and rentiers.

It is difficult to say what caused the government to retreat. The fact is that since the middle of 2013 the political war and the boycott had settled in. There has hardly been a day of government since 2013. Dilma won a new term in the election at the end of 2013, but this was now in a country in turmoil. There was no political space for any public policy.

The essential thing for us is that there was no fiscal crisis in terms of expenditures on public policies, because on this level the balance was maintained. What blocked the system and is, essentially, worsening the crisis, is the volume of transfers of public resources to banks and other financial intermediaries that are mainly unproductive. The correct attempt to restore the equilibrium by reducing the interest was precisely what led to the war, boycott, and the re-establishment of interest rates to maintain the interests of financial intermediaries.

Let us now examine the line "XI: Nominal Result of the Central Government", which will show the growing overall deficit. This includes expenditure on public policy and interest on the public debt (Lines IX and X).

Line XI: The central government's nominal results

2010	2011	2012	2013	2014	2015	2016	2017
-45,785.5	-87,517.6	-61,181.7	-110,554.9	-271,541.9	-513,896.0	-477,835.5	-459,349.5
-1.2%	-2.0%	-1.3%	-2.1%	- 4.7%	- 8.6%	-7.6%	-7.0%

Overall deficit jumps from 46 billion in 2010 to 272 billion in 2014, where we are already under the economic policy of bankers, and reaches an astronomical 514 billion by 2015, where the policies are comfortably oriented to divert public resources to financial intermediaries. In 2016, it reached 478 billion and 459 billion in 2017. The public deficit soared under the bankers' administration and instead of fixing the economy they brought it down. The GDP growth in 2017 was 0, and 1% expected in 2018.

These three lines of the Central Bank table show the misconception of the so-called "fiscal adjustment" of the government. They also allow us to clearly understand that it was, by no means, a government that spent too much on public policies, but was indeed a government in which resources were diverted from public policies to suit the financial system.

The percentage of the GDP spent on interest on the public debt, which means the volume of public money transferred to financial groups, represented 3.2% of the GDP in 2010, 4.1% in 2011, 3.1% in 2012 and, when it expanded under the bankers' administration, it reached 5.1% in 2016 and 5.2% in 2017. The bill is still growing, since the volume of public debt is now much greater.

Those who generated the crisis are the ones who are in power today. In the name of austerity and "of responsible spending of what was earned", they raised the primary deficit by transferring money to representatives and senators (parliamentary amendments) and increasing the salaries of judges and civil servants (reducing expenditures), while the population still endured the explosion of interest rates for private individuals and legal entities.

A key point is that the constitutional amendment, EC 95/2016, blocks expenditures on public policies. These are expenditures that affect the primary result, that is, where the deficit is very limited and the usefulness and multiplier effect of public investment is large in both economic and social terms. However, this EC 95 does not limit expenditures on public debt, which is where the real and immense drain occurs. The new government simply expanded the transfer of resources from society to financial groups. Inflation has undoubtedly decreased, not because the Selic rate is high, but because the economy is at a standstill. Additionally, with the decrease of inflation, the significant reduction in the Selic rate to 7.5% at the end of 2017, and 4.5% in real terms, does not solve the problem.

Here the issue is not to reduce State expenditures, but to maintain interest expenditures, which fuel financial investments, to the detriment of public investment and social expenditures. This is nothing more than extending the very mechanisms that have led us into this crisis.[93]

Seriousness? Responsible management? The image of the housewife who spends only what she has? A farce was set up. The figures are there. Paying for the crisis they generated has been transferred to the general population through traditional austerity measures similar to the ones applied in so many countries. This reduces demand and private sector activity and, consequently the volume of tax collection which increases the deficit. This policy does not add up either in terms of elementary accounting nor in political terms.[94]

Breaking down the virtuous cycle II: debt of families and private companies

The stranglehold on household consumption and business activities by exorbitant interest played a decisive role in the crisis after 2013, but was already visible before. Debt to income ratio grew during the preceding years, as installment sales and credit interests were rising. This data belongs to the same report from the Central Bank, "Credit operations of the financial system" (March 26, 2018). To rely on the primary source is not a minor precaution, we know how important it is to be careful in this era of number manipulations and general circumspection.[95]

The amount of credit in the hands of private individuals and legal entities––i.e., the stock of debts of families and companies—reached 3,062 billion reais in February 2018: representing a credit to GDP ratio of 46.47%. This was not particularly high. This debt is distributed basically half-way between families and legal persons: 1,404 and 1,658, respectively. Another breakdown is between free and targeted credit: 1,568 and 1,493

---

93 Bresser Pereira puts this bluntly: "There is no economic explanation; the fundamental cause of high interest rates in Brazil is the power of money lenders and financiers." Pereira, Luiz Carlos Bresser - *Juros e indignação cidadã*. Article published in *Valor Econômico*, March 6, 2017

94 For a broader view, there is an excellent document, *Austeridade e Retrocesso,* with a complete financial analysis. This document is from October 2016, 50p, and available at
http://brasildebate.com.br/wp-content/uploads/Austeridade-e-Retrocesso.pdf

95 BCB – *Operações de crédito do sistema financeiro* – March 26, 2018:
http://www.bcb.gov.br/htms/notecon2-p.asp

billion, respectively. Targeted credit is concerned with cheaper credit through Caixa Econômica Federal and other official institutions and aims to fund long term housing purchases by low income families.

The amount of debt is not particularly high compared to other countries where it often exceeds 100% of the GDP; the scandal is the interest rate. By averaging free and targeted credit for families and business, the Central Bank presents an overall average interest rate of 26.9% (for an inflation rate of 3%). That is, the interest extracted from the stock of 3.062 billion debt is 823 billion reais per year. This is the amount that families and companies pay for interest, and which is no longer transformed into consumption or investment by the private sector of the economy. This represents 12.5% of the GDP that has been appropriated by the financial intermediation system. Imagine that you have a loan on which you have to pay more than a quarter of the loan in interest each year. It does not work for families and obviously not for producers.

This average of 26.9% covers the huge difference between free credit, with an interest rate of 42.2%, and targeted credit with 9.7%. The interest rate for real estate lending in Canada, to give an example, is in the order of 2.27% per annum. In all cases, free or targeted, and taking inflation in account, the numbers are absurd.

For private individuals, interest rates on a debt of 1,658 billion, are on average 33.3%, of which 856 billion is in free resources, paying a rate of 57.7%, and 802 billion in targeted resources, paying 8.2% per year. Interest paid by households, therefore, runs to 494 billion reais in free credit, and 66 billion in targeted credit creating a total of 560 billion: around 8% of the GDP. Home financing, with relatively lower interest rates, can have a dynamic effect on the economy. Meanwhile, the 494 billion, 7.5% of the GDP, that burdens household consumption is a heavy load for a relatively small volume of purchases. Consumption credit should stimulate consumption, not reduce it. The obvious culprit is the usurious interest rate.

For legal entities, such as small and medium enterprise, interest rates on a debt of 1,404 billion average 17.9%, with 712 billion in free resources paying an average interest of 22.2%, and 691 billion in targeted resources, paying 12.2% interest. As such, the interest paid by companies is 158 billion on free credit, and 84 billion on targeted credit which is a total of 242 billion (4% of the GDP).

The banks' earnings, which are evident in the spread, reach an impressive 20.4%. In terms of targeted credit, it stands at 5.1%, perfectly respectable in international terms, while the true spending spree comes in free credit, where it reaches 34.1%. This kind of profit from other people's money is enviable.

Finally, the excuse that high interest is a result of the high delinquency drama is simply false. In the system, only 3.4% had delays of more than 90 days, with 3.7% for private individuals and 3.1% for companies. The delinquency rate does exist, of course, but it is essentially found in free credit set at 5.0%, while in targeted credit it is only 1.8%. A saying among Brazilian bankers and credit providers sums it up: the poor keep their word; the rich turn to lawyers.

Overall, the credit system in Brazil offers a limited volume of credit with usury-level interest rates. It could eventually earn more by offering a bigger volume of cheaper credit, but this kind of economic and social inclusion through credit is not on the horizon. We are a divided society and inequality extracts its toll. As it stands, the system extracts instead of promoting. This extraction of social surplus through interest rates in the private sector is around 13% of the GDP. Add the flow of interest on the public debt that we have seen above, essentially paid by our taxes, represents around 6% of the GDP, and the recipe for recession is obvious. No economy can be drained this way by unproductive intermediaries and rentiers and still function; this is referring to roughly 20% of our financial resources. Accusing the progressive government of breaking the economy by aiding the poor constitutes a farce.

***

Let us return to the general dynamics. The driving force of exports is undermined by transformations that are beyond our control. This makes internal economic dynamics much more important. At this level, the main engine—family demand—was blocked by the high interest rates, not because of the volume of purchases and credit, but due to the interest rates that are usurious by any definition that you can find. As of mid 2018, 63.3 million adults (almost half the adult population) were unable to pay their debts. They are vilified by the official Credit Protection Service and Serasa-Experian, but none of the financial intermediaries are denounced. The third engine—production and business investment—is blocked for three reasons: fragility of demand, high interest rates, and the alternative of making money without risk by investing in public debt, instead of investing in production. And the fourth engine—public investment in social policies and infrastructures—is hampered by the diversion of resources to debt services. With a tax system that does not redress but, instead, creates a greater imbalance, the whole economy becomes dysfunctional. No economy can work with this perverse articulation of interests.

Is corruption important? Unquestionably, but to find out that there is corruption in large infrastructure contracts and the oil sector is, frankly, not very innovative. Today, with my thirty plus years of experience in planning and contracts in many countries as part of the United Nations, I have never seen a country that does not have this problem on a large scale. How contracts of this type are negotiated has been widely described in the excellent and very reliable report by John Perkins, a contract negotiator, in *Confessions of an economic hit man.* This is a book with a great international impact because it was written by someone at the top of the proceedings: the chief economist of large construction corporations.[96] It was a confession with no counterpart: a curious and rare burst of ethics.

"As I carried on with my work," Perkins writes, "I began to put together two lists for each of the projects I envisioned: one for design and construction contracts, the other for long-term service and management agreements. MAIN, Bechtel, Brown & Root, Halliburton, Stone & Webster, and many other USA engineering and construction companies would have generous profits for the following decades. The expansion of the firms was accompanied by the negotiation of their military protection, evidently presented as security for the country, conveniently threatened by regional tensions. Their presence (defense industry) would require another phase of engineering and construction projects, including airports, missile sites, military personnel base, and all the infrastructure associated with these facilities." One of Perkins's chiefs referred to the kingdom of Saudi Arabia as "the cow we will milk until the sun sets over our retirement" (p. 87). Does this sound familiar? Another vortex of corruption is the area of energy, particularly petroleum and today one of the powerful bosses, Exxon's Rex Tillerman, has been appointed to direct USA foreign policy. Well, he did not last, as these are Trump times.

---

[96] John Perkins, *Confessions of an economic hit man,* Berrett Koehler, San Francisco, 2004. See a summary of the book at http://dowbor.org/2005/01/confessions-of-an-economic-hit-man-confissoes-de-um-agressor-economico-250-p.html/ published in Brazil by Boitempo.

The battle against corruption will not succeed with theatrical measures and soap opera announcements of "we found the thief". TV has made a daily entertainment out of it. The so popular "gotch'a", which leads to a general catharsis that focuses the accumulated hatred on a few people. The solution lies in setting and enforcing transparent laws. What makes it a parallel coup is the paralysis of national companies that exercised strong competition with other transnational corporations in the area, while none of the transnationals present in Brazil, who negotiate contracts and bribes using the same procedures, have been denounced. Apart from the duly buried case of the São Paulo subway because the governor of São Paulo State belongs to the right-wing elite. The fact is that the dismantling of these national companies costs far more to our economy than the volume of diverted resources. Proclaiming the arrest of some corrupt individuals does not change anything in the system. For those who know how large-scale contracts are negotiated, there is little doubt that it is a legal show which only makes connoisseurs smile and shake their heads.[97]

Here we have addressed the central issue of interest on public debt, aiming to show the absurdity of the arguments that the Lula and Dilma governments "broke" the economy. However, it is essential to see the integrated financial flow, because interest rates also drain the consumption capacity of the families, as well as production and business investments. The systemic crisis by means of financial processes does not even make us original. Financialization and its ravages have become a worldwide problem. It is noteworthy that the volume (stock) of public debt, in the order of 70% of the GDP (much less for net debt), is not particularly larger than that of other countries, and much smaller than, for example, that of the USA or Japan.

Financial investments can be very profitable, but they generate profits by transfer, not by creating additional wealth. If I buy dollars estimating that the currency will rise, and I win the bet, I can sell them profitably, and buy

---

[97] In my book *A reprodução social* (1999), I explained the design of the major corruption schemes by the contractors in Brazil, but also how Brazil follows the practices of other countries. In the planning ministries where I worked, only the degree, not the substance, varied. The solution lies in the regulation and the commitment to open accounts, the transparency that new technologies allow. Not in the show. See L. Dowbor, *A reprodução social*, 1st edition, Vozes, Petrópolis 1999, p. 171. On Brazil's own corruption mechanisms, see Dowbor, *Os estranhos caminhos do nosso dinheiro*, Perseu Abramo Foundation, São Paulo, 2015, full book free online: http://www.fpabramo.org.br/forum2013/wp-content/uploads/2013/12/colecaooquesaber-01.pdf

more things. Contrary to this, the purchasing capacity of the person who sold them will decrease in the same proportion: the person now has reais and the dollar is more expensive. Inside the country not a single additional pair of shoes was made and not one more house was built, therefore, the accumulated wealth of the country remains identical, even though we have made frantic financial transactions. They are transfer earnings, concerning rights on products that already exist, or in the case of speculative processes like the futures market, on products that have not yet been produced but already have owners.[98]

Nevertheless, if I really make what may be qualified as investment, which can be either through setting up a shoe factory, or by organizing a technological training course for small and medium-sized enterprises, I am creating wealth and increasing the country's capital. In the case of productive investment, even if I build houses that later I have to sell at a loss, the country has gained houses where people can live, even if I lost money. This is real economy and real risk. The country's stock of wealth has increased. If I productively invest my assets, I am turning them into capital that generates more wealth. If I make financial transactions, I might be increasing my assets but not creating capital in the productive sense; this is literally, unearned income, or rent.

Anyone who saw *Pretty Woman* will remember how the financial investor, when asked by the prostitute what he did for a living, replies: "I do the same as you, I screw people for money". He knows perfectly well that he is not creating any wealth and he is, instead, taking over what has been created by others. David Ruccio, for *Real World Economics*, makes this clear: "Finance can be very profitable, both for banking institutions and for Harvard students, but the only thing they do is capture part of the value created elsewhere in the economy. Instead of creating wealth, the rentiers simply transfer it— from the others to themselves." Today, among the great fortunes, very few are those who create wealth, for it tends to be much more profitable to take over the wealth produced by others. For capitalism, whose basic justification for existence was that it may be unfair but would, in the long term, be productive and positive for society, the time to seek new pathways, and not only new justifications, has come.

---

[98] Michael Hudson: "A century of classical economists has defined economic rent as an extractive means of increasing wealth [...] Today they use jargon with expressions like 'zero-sum activities' or 'transfer payments' to differentiate rent seeking and real wealth based on the production of tangible consumer goods and capital goods" Hudson, *J for Junk Economics,* 2017, p. 8.

14 - OVERVIEW: RECOVERING SYSTEM PRODUCTIVITY

No matter how you look at the numbers, the fact is that the Brazilian economy is being bled by intermediaries who produce little or nothing, and corroded by scandalous illegalities. If we add the interest rates for private individuals, the cost of installment plans, credit card interest and fees, interest on producers, the drain through public debt and tax evasion, and the volume of assets in tax havens and illegal transfers, in addition to taxation that not only does not reestablish the balance, but worsens the inequality, we have a structural deformation of the economy.

This account is not complicated, just remember that instead of the numbers we count at home to make the ends meet, using a thousand reais as unit, in the country we are talking about billions. The GDP of Brazil, rounded up, is 6.6 trillion, that is, 6,600 billion in 2018. The interest extracted by financial intermediaries from private individuals and legal entities has reached 840 billion. This represents around 13% of the GDP. The interest extracted through the public debt, about 400 billion reais, represents 6% of the GDP. Tax evasion, estimated at 570 billion in 2016, represents 9% of the GDP. This taxation is already unequal for the rich and the poor, and quite clearly, the rich and, in particular, those who control the financial systems, are precisely those who can easily achieve tax evasion. Furthermore, these groups have about 520 billion dollars abroad in tax havens (a stock of resources, not what goes out every year), which amounts to about 1,700 billion reais, some 26% of the GDP. Here we can discuss whether any figure is higher or lower, or add tariffs and other trinkets, which bankers kindly call “reciprocities”. However, on the whole, with these figures, it is not difficult to perceive that the country's economic system has been invaded and paralyzed by financial dynamics that have little to do with the traditional capitalist producer of goods and services. The economy is being drained by parasites.

Trying to energize the economy becomes rather difficult when we are dragging this speculative rubble that clings to our feet. There are more hurdles in our economy, but here we are talking about a gigantic mass of resources that are needed by the country. It is time for the business world itself—the one that effectively produces wealth, especially small and medium-sized enterprises—to recognize the imbalances and set the responsibilities where they really belong. The organized retrieval of the productive use of our financial resources is essential.

It is time for unions and social movements to reinforce the understanding that the traditional form of surplus value—such as the employer who produces but pays poorly, triggering struggles for better wages—while albeit still surviving, has been brutally worsened by a broader system of extracting the surplus produced by society. In this way, we are all exploited via every purchase or transaction, whether by installment plans, credit cards, charges and abusive interest rates, or in the unfair structure of taxation. Today, rentierism is systemically more exploitative and an obstacle to productive processes and public policies. Its power is impressive, as it is the most pervasive power structure in the public and private decision-making processes; however, its great vulnerability lies in the fact that it is unproductive and creates a dynamic of mostly extraction without any contribution to society.

The central guideline is the search for productivity in the financial system: the so-called social return on investment (SROI). It is surprising that we have so many studies on the evolution or regression of the productivity of each industrial or agricultural sector, but we have no study on the productivity of the financial system. Ipea's interesting initiative, already mentioned, to estimate the yielding from each real invested in "Bolsa Família" (positive) and each real invested in public debt (negative) is a starting point, but it has to be extended in order to promote the understanding and monitoring of the various financial subsystems. Furthermore, the regulation of the system must be centered on the economic and social multiplication effect of each real invested. The more roughly 1 trillion reais in private pension funds, for example, can be induced to make productive investments. The same goes for the roughly 1 trillion reais of the insurance system, which survives by milking the public debt instead of stimulating productive activities. It is absurd that the Monetary Council has authorized these funds to invest up to 100% of the stock of resources it controls in public debt securities. Money out of our pockets to finance third-party retirement and the insurance giants, which has a negative economic impact.

The proposals, from the point of view of good functioning, can be seen as more or less realistic according to our outlook on the power relations that exist in society. People may feel more to the left or right than what we propose here, but it all depends on the time horizon we consider and on how we see what is feasible. Piketty, Stiglitz, and others may be seen as theorists who only seek a more civilized capitalism. However, it is not a question of leftist "legitimacy", rather of seeing what can be done. In particular, we are interested in measures that, when introducing transformations, generate space for further transformations—structuring measures, so to speak—or, in the interesting expression of Gar Alperovitz, measures that open space for a progressive revolution.[99]

Paying attention to what works in different countries and systems

We have to look, in particular, at examples that work in our own and other countries. There are specific conditions, no doubt, but the financial world is basically one. Not trying to learn from others, in this age of seeking new ways, would be unintelligent. Additionally, the basic criterion is that the financial resource must be productive and, therefore, a vector of increasing social wealth. The basic principle of interest is simple: the financial cost must be less than the increased productivity it permits. Anything above this is negative net productivity and economic parasitism.

It is no longer possible to keep up our lack of knowledge about how China works; a country which, with 20% of the world's population, by far presents the most efficient system of economic and social management, which is now strongly investing in the environmental dimension. The Chinese financial system is dominated by the Bank of China, with a powerful guidance tool for large flows, while the public funding system is radically decentralized, allowing for flexible and efficient local management. Arthur Kroeber, editor of China Economic Quarterly and author of *China's Economy*, is not just another person who spent some time in China and wrote a book.[100]

---

[99]Gar Alperovitz and Lew Daly, *Unjust Deserts: ow the rich are taking over our common inheritance*, National Center of Economic and Security Alternatives, The New Press, New York 2008. According to Kenneth Arrow, "Nobel" prize winner of economics in 1972, the authors "rely on impeccable sources and use them with considerable mastery. Everyone will learn by reading this book." See the review at http://dowbor.org/2010/11/apropriacao-indebita-como-os-ricos-estaindo-a-ossa-heranca-comum.html/

[100] Kroeber, Arthur, *China's Economy*, Oxford University Press, 2016. See a summary in Portuguese at http://dowbor.org/2016/11/arthur-r-kroeber-chinas-economy-oxford-oxford-university-press-2016-isbn-978-0-19-023903-9-320-p.html/

Living in Beijing and New York, Kroeber may have a point of view somewhat skewed by the “a priori” that privatization is the saving grace but, overall, he proves that the balance built by China between public policies, public business sector, private business interests, and international groups ultimately ensured the success of the whole. It is a different architecture of power and management, apparently much more balanced than our so-called "Western" economies. In fact, Kroeber, shows impressive good sense: "In any country, the real enemies in the battle for broad-based prosperity are not international competitors, but domestic elites who constantly struggle to preserve their own privileges at the expense of all others. Innovation, education, openness, and a redistributive State are reliable weapons in this battle" (p. 256).

Particularly interesting is the management aspect. We all try to mentally draw the kind of organizational architecture that China has created and the kind of tiger it has become. “China is formally centralized, but in practice it is highly decentralized [...] In the quantitative dimension, because of the proportion of revenues and fiscal expenditures handled by local governments, China is by far the most decentralized country on earth, with the participation of local governments in earnings and expenditures more than double those typical in developed OECD countries, which in turn tend to be more decentralized than developing nations" (p. 111). This point is absolutely central, as it has blended strong central political guidance with a radical local flexibility in the application of the guidelines, thereby combining systemic coherence and administrative agility. It is an essential lesson, even for Brazil, which has a very centralized government and fragile local finances that have become even more reduced in recent years, if not plundered.

Inheriting an essentially rural world, Deng Xiaoping promoted an economic and social dynamism that focuses on improving the economic conditions of family farming: supporting local production, marketing, financing, access to land, and expansion of access to social policies. It was, therefore, building the country from the base by increasing the production surplus that was essential for the second mainstay of expansion in the cities. The whole system is essentially driven by a broad base of popular consumption. Thus, the expansion of production ensured its symmetrical complement of demand expansion. As we have seen, according to the World Bank, of the nearly one billion people brought out of poverty in the world in recent decades, 700 million are Chinese.

A second mainstay is the significant investment in infrastructure, in particular connecting rural areas in an electric power and transport network that tends to increase overall productivity. Thus, a still relatively poor and low-wage country would have "a probably unmatched combination of low labor costs with good infrastructures, almost like those of a rich country" (p. 45). A second generation of infrastructures, in particular with high speed trains, would come in this millennium, but on the whole, essentially, this part of the development was rigorously planned, in order to ensure the synergy between networks and make the enterprises and regions more productive (p. 83). Today, China is expanding its infrastructures to make connections with the rest of Asia and Europe; this is in line with what it has called "infrastructure diplomacy" and includes the establishment of the Asian Infrastructure Investment Bank (AIIB), which 60 countries have already joined (p. 245).

The financial bases and macroeconomic balances of these efforts were ensured by a highly controlled financial system, and guided by public interest: "Those who guided economic policy believed that direct government control over the banking system was crucial for macroeconomic policy to be effective" (p. 93). Here, we also note a search for balance, with large state-owned companies able to manage resources in a flexible way through in-house finance institutions, but with the government avoiding the loss of "control over the financial system if corporate financial companies were allowed to become fully-fledged banks" (p. 98). Overall, access to finance, particularly for local governments, was based upon ultralow interest rates (p. 84).

Good infrastructures, a large domestic market, and cheap labor were irresistible to international corporations, which were allowed to set up within special economic zones with the terms of reference largely defined by the Chinese. Similar to the experience of South Korea, in China the financial, organizational, and technological capabilities of international corporations were used to gradually build their own capabilities and in particular to serve as an export base, which would generate complementary trade surpluses and import capability for the internal productive matrix. By using the external inputs to dynamize their own capabilities, it was possible to create a process of restoration of balances and not of dependence. In 2014 direct foreign investment was limited to 3% of the total investment (p. 55).

Finally, the process of urbanization played a major role as a gigantic movement that has led hundreds of millions of people to the cities; this then required a larger production of cement, steel, and other basic materials, which was essentially in the hands of large state-owned enterprises. Also required was a capability to build local infrastructures, gradually leading to the growth of production of basic household appliances, and the transition to mass consumption by the urban population. According to the author, the growth rate reduction of more than 10% over several decades to the current 6–7% characterizes this last transition, with a gradual reduction of the gross growth rate of house building and corresponding infrastructures.

This book is pleasant reading because of the seriousness with which Kroeber expresses the futility of simplifying ideological arguments about China, even pointing to foreign research showing that suggestions about the country scamming its statistics were false. These claims, such as the claim that it is a dictatorship, simply do not hold and usually result only from ignorance. It is different, it has many defects, and it works. It is not a matter of being against it or in favor, or of being satisfied merely with ideological reactions and it is, instead, about understanding how it works. A financial policy that works for decades and for more than a billion people is interesting.

But what about the general political overview? "Politically, China is a resilient authoritarian system whose legitimacy is based upon effective governance rather than democratic elections. This system has strengthened substantially since the political crisis of 1989, achieved three peaceful transitions of leadership, responded competently to changing circumstances and, apparently, enjoys a high level of citizen support or at least acceptance" (p. 253).

It is not just China, of course. Ellen Brown wrote an exquisite book, *The Public Bank Solution*, which begins from the obvious idea that the resources, which are ours and not the bank's, must be productive for society. It is worth recalling once again, that Article 192 of the Brazilian Constitution stated that the national financial system would be "structured in such a way as to promote the balanced development of the country and serve the interests of the community." This initial part of the article, which survived and which defines the general direction and principle that should govern the financial system, simply means that the entire current system of usury is unconstitutional.

Ellen Brown gets straight to the point: "Banks are privately owned and controlled, mandated to serve the limited interests of their shareholders;

and these interests and the public interest often conflict. What is good for Wall Street is not necessarily good for the economy [...] The private banking framework is a massive machine whose main purpose is to uphold itself. What is being preserved is an extractive form of banking activity that is proving unsustainable, and which has reached its mathematical limits. It is a parasite that devours its source of supply and will perish along with its source of supply" (p. 419). Here we have a very close standpoint, which also uses the image of the parasite, to Michael Hudson's work, *Killing the Host*, as seen above.

What is particularly interesting for us is that Brown brings countless examples of how financial systems are organized. The first part is a recollection of the historical process, from Wall Street to Beijing, which helps us to understand how institutions and large interest groups are articulated. The numerous examples of both the regulatory initiatives as well as the different forms of organization in each country—Germany with its Sparkassen, Poland with its credit cooperatives, China with its decentralized financial management systems, France with its system of local financial intermediation NGOs (Placements Ethiques), even the role of our "Caixa Econômica Federal" (now in danger), and many others—help us to understand that this universe can be redeemed by applying proven solutions. The study closes with proposals for a new monetary theory which is very helpful. A glossary of technical terms and an excellent bibliography make this book a first-rate tool.

The German example has been extensively studied:[101] "In Germany, large national banks account for only 13% of the banking system, which is overwhelmingly based on localities, supporting small and medium-sized enterprises that generate 80% of employment in any economy. Seventy percent of the banks are owned and controlled locally (42.9% saving banks and 26.6% cooperative banks). These banks and saving banks have a legal commitment to invest locally; they do not make speculative loans, but rather loans to productive enterprises that increase real GDP. To grow and thrive, they must do so in partnership with the local productive economy. It is a system that does not extract, but supports and is sustainable" (p. 269). Germany has faced the 2008 crisis well, not only because it has a solid production base, but because this productive base is heavily financed

[101] Ellen Brown – *The Public Bank solution: from austerity to prosperity* – Third Millenium Press, Louisiana, 2013 - http://dowbor.org/2015/08/ellen-brown-the-public-bank-solution-from-austerity-to-prosperity-third-millenium-press-baton-rouge-2013-471p-isbn-978-0-9833308-6-8.html/

by the public funding network. Deutsche Bank's speculation and its successive fraud convictions found a stabilizing counterbalance in the local banking network. Savings belong to the population and, therefore, local banks have to account for what it intends to do with them.

The municipal saving banks, Sparkassen, have a strong tradition in Germany. There were already 2,834 in 1903, and today there are over 15 thousand, distributed throughout the territory and employing 250 thousand people. In each region, as if they were state banks, there are 7 public banks, the Landesbanken, which function as universal banks and also need to report to the local banks. These public banks even operate in a network, which allowed them to withstand the attack of liberalization and financial globalization. The essential fact is that German banks serve the community, ensuring both savings and the useful distribution of money. Examples such as this one from Germany, the *Cajas de Ahorro* of Spain, the 470 credit cooperatives in Poland, or China as we have just mentioned, point out that the appropriation or re-appropriation of the use of our financial resources by society is essential.

Additionally, we obviously have to refer to some quite successful experiences in Brazil. Here we have impressive examples of the effectiveness of productive microcredit developed by the Banco do Nordeste, showing how the small resources that reach the small producer with low interest rates, can have impressive effects of multiplication. The experience of the Caixa Econômica Federal in the area of housing, or that of the Banco do Brasil in the rural credit area, have formed an accumulation of practical knowledge that is precious and can be retrieved. Initiatives such as the Community Development Banks, now numbering more than 100, have shown impressive results in terms of the social return on small investments. They also present precious innovative experiences, even if on a very limited scale, which, in particular, have the flexibility that virtual currencies can offer today.[102] The knowledge and systematization of successful experiences in the crucial area of access to financial resources has become essential; this extends to well beyond fiscal balance, as the goal is to channel financial resources to where they are useful and increase their stimulating effects on the economy.

[102] *Banco Palmas 15 Anos* – Inst. Palmas and NESOL-USP (Orgs.) – A9 Editora, São Paulo, 2013, 178 p.

The Brazilian proposals

The alternatives for Brazil are pretty obvious. They consist in intensifying what has already proved to be successful in terms of economic and social inclusion: strengthening the model centered on the internal market, expanding mass consumption, and productive inclusion. The guiding idea is to reduce the shocking inequality, which was only partially reduced during the "golden decade", through inclusive and sustainable development. In very broad terms, this means basing the economic dynamics of the country on the opportunity offered by the huge internal market of individual and social consumption. Politically and socially, this represents an immense effort to create a new set of fair ground rules, in particular through tax reform and by redirecting the national financial system. With regard to the environmental front, we have to remember again that the country does not belong only to our generation. The resumption of Amazon deforestation and the liberation of land sale to international groups are crimes against the future.

The attack that has blocked our progress, since 2013, does not present a coherent alternative program but does, on the contrary, strengthen privileges and inequality. We face an alliance of the financial system (national and international) with the oligopoly of mainstream media, segments of the judiciary, and much of the legislative power. The current legislative power, elected on the basis of the already unconstitutional (since the end of 2015) corporate financing of campaigns, grossly deformed the system of representation. We have had the powerful representation of agribusiness, the automotive industry, the strong mainstream media oligopoly, and the banking oligopoly and now we are left searching for who effectively represents citizens and the nation's interests. Here, and regrettably in other countries too, it is democracy itself that is under threat.

It is not my aim here to evaluate the initiatives of the illegitimate government that took over in Brazil. Nevertheless, as a contrast, let us remember what must be fixed. I refer here to the useful and eloquent summary that Roberto Malvezzi sent to me: "Most of the proposals [of the Temer government] we already know: dismantling SUS (public health system) in favor of private medicine; draconian modifications of social security in favor of private pension; modifications in labor legislation resembling the times of industrial revolution, in favor of private capital; handing over the Pre-Sal [oil reserves]; dismantling public education—including universities—in favor of private education; handing over public lands to foreigners; repression of social movements; suppression of funding for scientific research; growth of fascist intolerance; and so forth to infinity. Social policies will remain only as marketing, no longer with the intent of social inclusion. The end of 15 years of development of the policy of Coexistence with the Semiarid." Behind each of these dismantling initiatives, we have clearly identified corporate national and international interests, which equates to widespread plunder. The newly elected far-right president, in the name of change ("mudança") only added more repression to the list.

Proposals from the point of view of good functioning can be seen as more or less realistic according to the power relations that exist within society. In particular, it is essential to construct an explanatory discourse to enlarge the circle of people who understand what is happening, and who can support the necessary transformations and reconstruction.

It is important to remember that this study is not against banks and the credit system, but it is against the deformation of its use by national and international groups that have turned our savings potential into drainage, rather than using it for development. It is a system based on short-term profit that radically violates the legal bases ruling its functions, and it also fuels an international casino whose illegalities are widespread. We must keep in mind that a bank, even a private one, operates on the basis of a charter, delivered by the Central Bank, which authorizes it to work with society's money, thereby generating profit which is legitimate when it performs its social systemic function of promoting development. This point is essential, because if a bank gets its profit by appropriating a portion of the social surplus generated in society by productive financing that it helped organize, it is perfectly legitimate and positive for society. However, if you get your profit from speculative moves and high interest rates that block investment and demand, or via collecting tolls and making access more difficult, the result is crisis, recession, or simply slow growth that is hampered by financial drains.

In fact, in Brazil today we have an impressive installed capacity in terms of financial management infrastructure, with a high density of branches across the country, a large computer network, excellent technicians, as well as a trained and experienced workforce. We also have a great potential for regulation by the Central Bank, as well as top-tier economists to help with its redesign. The use of this knowledge, infrastructure, and organizational capital must be reoriented. In this sense, it is a financial reform, which does not require large investments since the apparatus is already established; however, it does require a major structural transformation with regard to its use, and this implies deep political change.

Operating with decent interest rates, but with a much larger volume of credit, banks and other financial intermediaries could have legitimate profits. Truly reinvesting in goods and services in the country, instead of multiplying financial products, they will achieve their economic viability in the long run and in a sustainable way. By financing productive activities in Brazil, and thus boosting the economy, they should undoubtedly pay taxes, but in the long run, the current option for tax havens, illicit if not illegal, is not sustainable, and the "everybody does it" argument is slippery. Indeed, honest profit is healthy for everyone. This is not about making gigantic innovative investments, but about intelligently using what we already have.

We have presented below some proposals that seem the most obvious and which are in line with the general standpoint of this study. We will leave here the set of broader structural reforms that Brazil always postpones. Our conviction is that any government that intends to work for the country, and not just for elites, will have to repeal the whole legal rubbish that has been building up since the coup in 2016.

Overall reduction of interest rates

On a domestic level, measures cannot be direct. ANEFAC, as we have seen above, stresses the limitations of a system that is formally ruled by private law: "We emphasize that interest rates are free and are set by the financial institution itself, so there is no price or ceilings control over the sums charged. The only commitment that the financial institution has is to inform the client what fees will be charged if he uses any type of credit." Naturally, since it is a cartel, the borrower has no choice. ANEFAC's recommendations are very simple: "If possible, postpone your purchases to have the money and buy in cash, avoiding interest." That is, do not use credit. For the "Associação dos Executivas de Finanças, Administração e Contabilidade" (Association of Executives of Finance, Administration and Accounting) to give out this recommendation is impressive.

However, the government has powerful weapons. The first one is to resume the progressive reduction of the Selic rate, which would oblige banks to look for alternative investments, irrigate entrepreneurial initiatives, and obviously curtail the scandalous transfer of public resources to banks.

The second is to reduce interest rates to the final borrower through the network of public banks, as tried in 2013, but this time it is imperative that we persist in this action. This is the best way to introduce market mechanisms into the financial intermediation system, which will help to weaken the cartel and compel it to reduce stratospheric interest rates. This would mean that the final borrower would have options once again. The technical procedure to complete this is perfectly clear, what we lack is the organized political strength that might counterbalance the country's speculators and rentiers, who in 2013, with the support of the media cartel were able to block and reverse the process. *Pecunia pecuniam parit*: money begets money, will not work. We must migrate to a system where productive contribution begets money.

The reconversion of speculation to economic development

In a broader perspective, it is essential to understand that financial intermediation is not productive as an activity, since it is a means-activity: its productivity is indirect, when it invests the funds raised from the economy to finance productive activities thereby stimulating the real economy and the so-called end-activities. By using our savings to boost the economy, it plays a positive role. If it drains them for speculative purposes, weakening demand and investment, it is being counterproductive because it assumes the role of what we call in Brazil an *atravessador*: a useless, or a nocive intermediary. In fact, a parasite. As the major banks are few and large, cartelization becomes natural and the fact that the Central Bank, which should act as a regulator, was co-opted and placed in the hands of bankers closes the circle. The capacity to generate systemic crises, in the line of the "too big to fail" argument used in the USA, Europe, and other regions, may be slightly different in Brazil, but it is basically similar in that it resulted in political blackmail. Simply put, this system is powerful and not only useless but also counterproductive. This represents a huge systemic weakness.

Reduced tax evasion

It is important to consider the international context and the limits it imposes on government action. As long as there is a *de facto* tolerance of tax havens by American and European elites, including in the USA itself (such as in Delaware), and in Europe (e.g. in Luxembourg and Switzerland), there is hardly any possibility of control. Tax evasion becomes too simple and the possibility of identifying illegal or illegitimate financial flows is greatly reduced. In any case, the gigantic volume of tax evasion—in the order of 10% of the GDP—is unsustainable, particularly because it is generally a matter of who can better afford it: the big fortunes and corporations which have more political power and more capacity to resort to this "fiscal optimization". The BEPS we have seen above, with an international agreement on flow control which has not yet been enforced, has already been weakened by the populist election in the United States.

Tax reform

It is vital to redeem a minimum of tax balance: it is not about raising taxes, but about rationalizing their incidence and overseeing payment. Taxing unproductive financial capital, in particular, would be an excellent incentive to invest and boost the economy. Odilon Guedes and others have organized the well-known main lines: to seek social justice by establishing tax progressiveness rather than the current regressiveness (the poor pay proportionately more), raising direct taxes and lowering indirect taxes, and introducing decent taxes on wealth and inheritance. It should be about favoring those who produce and taxing those who simply accumulate. [103]

Local financial systems

It is a matter of extending, in terms of scale as well as capability, the whole of the local financial systems: the so-called proximity finances. Going back to the example seen briefly above, the German credit system, which is highly decentralized and forms a powerful vehicle for supporting small and medium-sized enterprises, is an interesting reference point. We have already seen the importance of local financing systems in China and other countries.

Brazil already has 114 community development banks and interesting microcredit programs, but it is essential to understand that the banking and financial intermediation system itself, which today comprises a limited number of economic giants and behaves like an oligopoly, has to start

[103] Odilon Guedes (and others). *Reforma Tributária com Transparência das Contas Públicas: a sociedade e o Estado*: http://dowbor.org/2015/04/a-reforma-tributaria-abril-2014-7p.html/ See a complete overview of the necessary tax reform in ANFIP/FENAFISCO – *A Reforma Tributária Necessária* – Brasilia 2018, 804 p. http://plataformapoliticasocial.com.br/wp-content/uploads/2018/05/REFORMA-TRIBUTARIA-SOLIDARIA.pdf

contributing to the productive dynamism of the country. Local and regional systems are simply deprived of their capacity to finance, as public and private debt unbalances the system. Marcio Pochmann presents the figures: in 1997 the states owed 111 billion reais and in 2016 this amount reached 476 billion, which involved high payments for debt service that were "sterilized in the primary surplus."[104]

Reorient pension fund investments

Roughly 1 trillion reais are invested by private pension funds. These funds can either pursue financial transactions, for example through public debt bonds, or could contribute to economic development by investing in the real economy. How do these funds impact the economy, as a drain or as development, and what are the amounts? In 2015, the figures we have stood at R$733 billion (12% of the GDP), 65% invested in financial papers, of which 78% in public debt. Only 3% can be considered as fostering the real economy. Absurdly, the CMN (National Monetary Council) authorizes the funds to invest up to 100% of the resources in public debt. Changing these rules could stimulate funds to invest in productive activities (see CMN Resolution 3792, article 35, September 24, 2009). A similar reasoning has to preside over the analysis of insurers and para-financial systems, such as health plans and other systems of private appropriation of collective consumer goods and services.

Transparency of financial flows

Given the importance of financial intermediation, research on internal financial flows needs to be stimulated and made widely available in order to generate greater transparency in this area. People in general are simply confused. In order to create the political power capable of reducing the degree of cartelization, reintroducing market mechanisms, and transforming the system of financial intermediation, an informed population is mandatory. One of the most striking things in this vital area for the country's development is the profound silence, not only by the media but also from academia and research institutes, on the scandalous process of deformation of the economy by the financial system. The fact that financial groups are big advertisers in the media, obviously does not help with transparency. Additionally, the fact that we have a national economy

---

[104] Marcio Pochmann, interview, Carta Capital, February 18, 2017

whose financial dynamics are deeply intertwined with the international financial system does not help either.

A good system of financial intermediation is one that promotes the economic health of those who use it. It is from this point of view that financial statistics and measures of the productivity of the national financial system should be organized. A structured instrument to monitor the country's integrated financial flow must be generated, which no longer looks only at the equilibrium of the main financial institutions themselves; it is more important to assess, in a coherent way, the impact of the financial flow on household demand, private investment, public investment, and export activities: the four engines of the economy. The overall approach we must develop should no longer aim only at measuring the productivity of a financial intermediation activity for the institutions themselves, but also at disclosing how it truly contributes to the economy in its various sectors.[105]

Coping with corruption

High-scale corruption is part of the power capture system that we have seen above. The basic principles of corruption, however, need to be understood for the fight it to be successful. The basic principle is that the politician who accepts corruption money and the corporation that finances him are both part of the same system: one hand holds the other. Focusing only on the dimension of politicians and not on the corporate culture will just replace one corruption with another. Secondly, in the area of accountability, corrupt people should be punished directly, without disrupting the entities to which they belong: attacking and disorganizing companies to facilitate their acquisition by other groups is just another degree of corruption. In 2016, Germany punished directors at Volkswagen without destroying the company or liquidating jobs. However, the main line of action is to rethink the management system that allows corruption to become widespread: here, the effective enforcement of the 2012

---

[105] An interesting comment from Stiglitz and Pieth on transparency: "In Norway, Sweden and Finland, income tax returns are posted on the Internet. Their attitude is: what do people have to hide? If they earn their income honestly, why not publicize it? [...] For a society to function well, everyone must contribute their fair share. However, some individuals like a free ride, to take advantage of the supply of public goods and not to pay. If we allow this to happen, the whole social contract may collapse" (p. 8). Globalization has resulted in a global economy, but not in a global government. Joseph E. Stiglitz and Mark Pieth - *Superando a economia paralela* - Friedrich Ebert Stiftung - Feb. 2017

Transparency Law could be quite useful. The great show of imprisoning corrupt people, undoubtedly creates ample social catharsis and allows the emergence of a new power nucleus, but does not change anything if the accounts are not disclosed: one corrupt person is arrested but the system will carry on, to the great satisfaction of the newcomers.[106]

In broader terms, it is essential to understand that large-scale corruption generates its own legality by allowing banks to charge extorsive interest rates, while paying absurdly low taxes. Privatizations that distribute public assets at scandalously low prices are legal, as well as the corporate financing of campaigns, which took place between 1997 and 2015. Finally, on a broader level, it is noteworthy that as long as there is free access to around 60 tax havens in the world, which most major corporations use to conceal financial flows, supervisory bodies will not be able to carry out their functions with a minimum of efficiency. Rather than creating a media show with corrupt prisoners and destroying companies, we must reconsider the accountability system. Of particular concern is the fact that multinational companies based in the country use strictly the same methods of corruption as the large domestic companies; however, none of them appears on the radar. It is essential that the legal system itself regains respect for the law.

***

It is not a matter of being against banks but an endeavor to reconvert them, so that they may become vectors of development. In this sense, the set of technological advances, infrastructures, and knowledge acquired in the financial mechanisms that are available to the national financial system today may all be used in a reconversion; this would make them a powerful lever for development.

The proposals above are not very profound, we are not discussing the changes that await us at a structural level, and they range from the land and political reforms to the redefinition of the federative covenant and the resumption of a sovereign national policy. We have been working on these questions in other studies: particularly on the concept of balance between the State, the private sector, and civil society; the potential for radical political decentralization at the base of society; the new opportunities for

[106] We have presented the mechanisms of corruption from a small book edited by the Perseu Abramo Foundation, *Os estranhos caminhos do nosso dinheiro,* FPA, São Paulo, 2013, 70p.: http://www.fpabramo.org.br/forum2013/wp-content/uploads/2013/12/colecaooquesaber-01.pdf

structural change opened by information and communication technologies; and the potential for collaborative economics in this era of connectivity. Here, we have focused on the dilemma of the draining of our resources, and the mechanisms that generated unproductive capital. The reality is that regaining control of the financial system is a necessary condition for any broader option we want to assume, since the crux of the matter is to recover the means that will rescue the productivity of the whole economic and social system.

CONCLUSION

The fact that the traditional exploitation of workers through low wages has been magnified and radically reinforced through the financial appropriation of what society produces has strong political implications and requires a change of discourse. The struggle against the financial constrictions of families but also of small and medium-sized enterprises is central, not only to give people room to breathe but also to recover the domestic market and employment. This is a major source of anguish for the bulk of the population. The strategic nature of this dimension of the struggle is brought about by the fact that this latest form of exploitation is carried out by financial groups and rentiers who do not invest, do not produce, and make lots of money. As we have seen above, unproductive rentierism is more complex to denounce, but also politically more vulnerable. No wonder banks have begun to advertise that you can "renegotiate your debt". This absurd system is certainly feeling the heat, as more people are starting to understand the systemic deformation.

It is important to view all the flows that make up the national financial system in an integrated way. Financial resources are just virtual information on computers, but they can play a role in paralyzing economic activities if the real economy is appropriated by unproductive financial intermediaries or rentiers; they can also have a powerful effect when they provide cheap and decentralized credit to millions of families, as well as small and medium-sized enterprises, as well as expanding universal access to healthcare and education, and so on.

The institutional nature of the financial system is essential here. It is not just about the banks as it is also about the tax system that has to favor the producer and charge the rentier who gains without producing; it is about ensuring that pension funds invest the resources we pay in productive activities; and it is about allowing local authorities, particularly at the municipal level, to invest locally the savings, which are currently drained to large centers and abroad. The basic criterion for change is that money must become a vector for increased sustainable production, as well as economic and social balance, and not a vector for exploitation and appropriation by non-producing minorities.

This approach is strengthened by the fact that today's dominant form of exploitation has become a worldwide process. The new and utterly outrageous fact that 8 families have more than the poorer half of the world's population and 1% of the richest families have more assets than the other 99% is no longer known only by informed minorities as it is becoming general knowledge. This dimension of the fight allows for important international articulations. Part of this aberration is the fact that, for example, in the United States over the course of a few decades, the financial system has gone from 10% to 42% of corporate profits, and that Brazil has experienced a brutal recession while banking profits simultaneously soared. The system that has taken over our resources is not only scandalously unfair, it is economically counterproductive.

We are destroying the environment, which the natural basis upon which humanity will have to survive, by depleting resources, polluting the waters, generating climate chaos, in an unbridled race of production and absurd consumerism. At the same time, an abyss of inequalities has been created that can only lead to political chaos, which in turn blocks economic dynamics. We are systemically dysfunctional.

One basic finding is that making financial transactions, speculating over future markets, enforcing abusive interest rates, and other practices continue to yield more than making productive investments, meaning that money will tend to target more financial transactions instead of productive investment. Essentially, money goes to where it generates more money.

The direct implication of this dynamic is that while financial earnings are higher than the increase in production, in net terms the financial system will have a negative impact on the economy: it will become a parasite of the productive process. So, for example, if the money lent to a seamstress to buy a good sewing machine costs more than the corresponding productivity increase, it is no longer an investment process but will, instead, be a financial capture. The seamstress will be as stuck in debt in the same way the farmworker was in the "shed" system, where he was always in debt to the farm's grocery store.

The parasitic character of the financial system has as its only possible counterbalance the public capability for control and regulation that limits interest and directs capital to productive investments, as well as charging taxes on unproductive financial assets. The capture of political power by the financial giants, which was particularly evident in the crisis of 2008, and the impressive transfer of public resources to private groups, renders the State's ability to regulate particularly precarious. This is the political dimension of the economic distortion.

A functioning system must remunerate the economic agents with a minimum of proportionality between the remuneration and the contributions. Here, it can be seen that the current remuneration of these efforts is not in accordance with the productive contribution, but is rather aligned with the degree of financial control over the productive systems themselves, which includes workers, companies, and governments. This affects both household consumption and the economic engine, as well as business investments, government social policies, and public investments. The prevailing remuneration logic is a systemic aberration.

It is not the lack of economic capacity that blocks progress—i.e., the lack of resources in the broad sense, including technological and educational advances as well as financial resources—but the logic of the decision-making process. Particularly, the type of "mono-phase" capitalism that considers any activity to be positive and legitimate when it generates profit, even if it is an obstacle in economic, social, and environmental terms.

Private property and freedom of initiative, which form the basic pillars of our economic and social organization, can no longer be dissociated from the responsibility for the use of property. Freedom cannot be separated from economic, social, and environmental impacts. So many speeches and regulations like the various "ISOs", corporate governance statements, and codes of ethics will continue to have no impact as long as the remuneration of economic agents does not incorporate the costs generated by their decisions. Externalities must be internalized. The very concept of commercial law, which sets shareholder's and other financial investor's remuneration as exclusive in corporate decisions, must evidently be amended.

The attempt to incorporate the outlook of balanced development—economically viable, socially just and environmentally sustainable—into the decision-making process of corporations is also paralyzed by the macroeconomic accounting that favors gross domestic product, rather than adopting full accounting that considers economic, environmental, and human costs. Therefore, both at the level of corporate and government decisions, there is a profound mismatch between what is intended and what is done. The quality of human life and the enrichment of our planetary natural heritage are undoubtedly part of the UN documents and the Sustainable Development Objectives, but the mechanisms and decision-making processes of corporations and governments have not been adjusted accordingly.

The planetary chaos in which we are gradually sinking occurs, strangely, in the context of an explosion of scientific capabilities, technological innovations, global connectivity, and the immense potentials of network collaboration. The dramatic gap that has been created between potentials and achievements is essentially due to the fact that governance systems in the public sector and in private corporations have not kept pace with the technological revolution and do not allow them to be leveraged for real systemic progress. The system is stuck in institutional frameworks from the last century and in economic theories from the century before that.

Economics is not a system of natural laws—a view that has spawned this strange creature we call "economic science", implying that we are forced to follow these laws—but a system of ground rules that have been negotiated and agreed upon by society. These ground rules need to be reviewed. We only have this planet and as the world's population increases by 80 million a year, and the very outlook of a "West" that protects itself by surrounding itself with walls so that the rich can use the rest of the world as a source of resources, leads us all to an impasse. The rest of the world is impatient and agitated. When even the World Economic Forum states that inequality is the main challenge, it means that the elites themselves are feeling the heat getting closer and closer. The UNCTAD *Trade and Development Report 2017* hits the nail on the head by stating that we need a "global new deal".[107]

The fact that real economic processes function in terms of the ground rules agreed upon in society, rather than mysterious natural laws leads us, evidently, back to the classics and the concept of political economy: the so-called common welfare will no longer be the natural result of an individual quest for advantages, but the collaborative construction of a future that humanity knows well today. It is perfectly described in the 17 goals and 169 objectives of the SDGs, which are legally binding for Brazil. What we have found in the present study, however, is the profound dissonance between the objectives and the logic of decision-making and remuneration of factors in the modern economy.

---

[107] Unctad, *Trade and Development report 2017—Beyond austerity: a logical new deal*:
https://mail.google.com/mail/u/0/?zx=iymwzkbf36ps#search/unc/15e87e3e586c15d0

The immense question that remains is: which social actors will be the ones to bring about change? Parties, governments—including those democratically elected—and even trade unions are weak and unreliable. What was a relatively homogeneous working class, capable of organizing around wages, has become extremely diversified through the multiplicity and complexity of the productive processes. Those affected by the system are in the vast majority and it does not make sense that 1% weigh more than 99%. Particularly, when that 1% has a negative net weight on the economic and social development of the whole. However, the organized capacity of the 1% remains stronger than the diffuse and disorganized interests of the vast majority. Furthermore, this 1% no longer needs democracy and has begun to show it in an increasingly aggressive way.

The subjective relationship of debt is particularly important. When it comes to negotiating wage increases in a company, one can count on the unions, for better or for worse, and on the strength of all workers to defend common goals and even to paralyze a company; this will, in turn, strengthen the organization. In the case of credit, each person faces the strangling noose of cumulative debt alone, and we seldom see any demonstration by those in debt in front of banks, because there are thousands of branches, scattered points of reference, and mysterious electronic flows and regulations. The victim of usury finds himself alone, shamed by the pressure mechanisms if he does not pay, and feeling disoriented, because he does not understand the calculations of either the store or the bank, and feels responsible because somehow it was he who contracted the debt. It is a paradox that the ethical argument "if you owe, you must pay" serves the banks so perfectly. The immense financial cheat that Greece has suffered is seen in the rest of Europe with high moral judgment: you were the ones who borrowed and now you must pay!

Interest that accumulates and the inability to pay off debt are part of the history of humanity and can be found in the oldest codes, religions, and different cultures. The year of "jubilee" was the year in which all debts were canceled in order to break the general paralysis of indebtedness that was harming even creditors. Recently, at an international level, "debt relief" was adopted for the least developed countries, whose debt hindered development and, therefore, reduced their capacity to pay. Debt write-downs or renegotiation are now part of the banking culture, as financial institutions realize that killing the host does not help.

A study published in Poland in 2016, *Dyktadura Dlugu*, (debt dictatorship), shows an interesting connotation with regard to the very concept of debt:

you *owe*, so you *must* pay. Debt is linked to the idea of duty, of doing what you have to do (pay what you owe), and to moral obligations, *debito.* Do we have moral obligations to loan sharks? Rafal Wos recalls that "even in economic debates debt is treated as a moral problem, not so much as an economic one. In German, the same word, *Schuld*, means debt and sin." There is no sin here, for those who offer credit have to deal with the risks, and if there is a moral problem it is not for those who cannot pay interest to a loan shark, but for those who profit from this type of credit. The basic principle here is that to pay what you owe is right, but to pay a loan shark interest on what is owed rewards a criminal activity. However, those who are in debt inevitably remain, particularly in Brazilian culture, with feelings of guilt and enter the renegotiation already feeling defeated. Capitalism has found the ideal form of extortion and criminality has built its own ethics.

Are there changes on the horizon? From the conversations I have had with researchers and ordinary people, a general idea emerges: only the growth of tensions will generate political power that is capable of reversing trends. It was the widespread upheaval and indignation of the European populations with the massacres and atrocities of World War II that generated political power for the creation of the European Union, democratic policies of social and productive inclusion, the UN itself, and the Bretton Woods agreement. These are rules for civilized conviviality. Crisis can be a source of change. How long should we wait?

The indifference with which we watch people drowning in the Mediterranean, and the children who are cold and hungry in the numerous refugee camps on television does not lead to optimism. Billions of people still do not have access to electricity, they cook with firewood and die of ridiculous causes. Impotent, they despair and find the difference between voting in one candidate or another increasingly ridiculous. Meanwhile, television entertains us with soap operas, the possible discovery of life on other planets, and what the financial market thinks of the GDP or the dollar exchange rate. The erosion of governance is planetary and we are losing control.

We are losing control in the United States, Brazil, Turkey, France, the Philippines, Argentina, Venezuela, Hungary, Poland, Nigeria, Arab countries, and many others. In this study we have favored an awareness of financial exploitation as the mainstay for articulating powers for political change. The reason is simple: control of financial resources is not just control over money as it is control over the transformative potential offered by the access to resources. Moreover, it also allows the retrieval of democratic processes, which is possible when resources are directed towards the requirements of balanced development. Political democracy has lost its link with its economic dimension.

To battle for decent interest rates and for the rationality of the financial system in its various dimensions has become as strategic as to battle for decent wages. For Brazil, facing the loan-sharking system that took over the country is a basic condition for the recovery of the development process.

ANNEX: AGENDA OUTLINE[108]

The text we have seen above, about unproductive capital and new architectures of power, shows that we are facing a systemically dysfunctional planetary system. A strange mixture of abundance of means and fragility of goals. We are technologically powerful, but politically unable to generate a civilized society. A few years ago, we met with Ignacy Sachs, a world-renowned researcher now living in France, and Carlos Lopes, until recently UN Under Secretary-General and the executive secretary of the Economic Commission for Africa, and now professor at the University of Cape Town, to design what would be the major outlines of a functioning society. Not the ideals of the countless utopias that fill our dreams, but a kind of common denominator, which is essential for this society not to fall apart.

A few years ago, in Salvador, during a meeting of the World Social Forum, we spent days discussing these "major outlines" with researchers from diverse origins and orientations, and found that this was a good starting point. If there is a philosophy beneath these ideas, it is that this poor *homo sapiens* tends to glorify himself and to be glorified by how much he manages to amass on this unfortunate planet, showing off his fortunes as if they were so many banners he would have taken from the enemy. The reality is that there are no enemies on this planet, so we had better just look after a better future for all. In a minimally realistic outlook, the measure of success shifts from how much we manage to extract for personal wealth to how much we manage to contribute to the common good, for example, leaving behind us a planet in a better condition and a less conflicted society for our children and grandchildren. Pasteur did not have to be rich to be a man of success and today, he is remembered and respected for his contributions, not for the size of his fortune. This is because vaccines are useful and fortunes per se are not.

---

[108] The proposals below are part of the text *Crises e Oportunidades em Tempos de Mudança*, published by several editing houses and in several languages. The full text in Portuguese can be found in Ignacy Sachs, *Desenvolvimento, inovação e sustentabilidade: contribuições de Ignacy Sachs,* from Garamond, Rio de Janeiro, 2014.

However, the materialization of a less destructive social universe demands institutional solutions. If another world is possible, we must show that another form of realistic social organization will allow its emergence. The dichotomous view that gave us the bureaucratic state of Eastern Europe on the one hand, and the corporate arrogance exemplified by Wall Street, on the other, is what is in crisis. The modern complex society no longer bears this type of simplification. We must develop more flexible and differentiated processes of regulation, not by strangling decision-making processes, but by bringing them closer to the real needs of society, with more transparency and democracy. As a society, we wish not only to survive, but to have a good quality of life. For that to happen, we need an orderly presentation of the challenges and answers. These are the minimum results to be achieved, alongside the corresponding decision processes.

The proposals or guidelines suggested below have a common denominator: they have already been tested and are being employed in various regions of the world, sectors, or jurisdictions of activity. These are initiatives that have worked, and whose generalization, with the due adjustment and flexibility in view of planetary diversity, are now viable. We have no illusions about the distance between today's political reality and the measures systematized below. However, it seemed essential, in any case, to list the necessary measures in an organized way, since having a clearer goal helps to design another planetary governance. They are not ordered by objectives, because most have simultaneous implications and interactive dimensions. They are points of reference.

1: Retrieving the public dimension of the State

How can we have regulatory mechanisms that work, if the money that elects regulators comes from the corporations that must be regulated? If the agencies that evaluate risk are paid by those who create the risk? Is it acceptable for the heads of a central bank to come from companies that will be regulated and then later return there for a job?

One of the most evident proposals resulting from the last financial crisis, which is mentioned in almost the entire political spectrum, is the need to reduce the capacity of private corporations to dictate the ground rules. The number of laws passed to reduce taxes on financial transactions, to reduce central bank regulation, to authorize banks to make any and all transactions without due oversight, as well as the power of financial lobbies all stress the need to regain the regulatory power of the state. This is why politicians must be elected by real people, not by corporations, which are fictions in terms of human rights. If we do not have political control over the financing of campaigns and policies that stand for the citizen's interests, short-term economic interests and corruption will prevail. The capture of political power must be reversed.

A widely underestimated dimension of this retrieval is the potential for the decentralization of decision-making and the movement of resources to a local level. The generalized urbanization of the planet brings the possibility for politics to move to cities, where the smaller scale economies of proximity and direct contact between stakeholders allow incomparably greater rationality, and much more democratic procedures, as can be seen in many developed countries and countless cities across the globe. Here, retrieval of the public dimension of the state evolves in the same proportion as politics are appropriated by the citizens.

2: Rethink our accounts

Accounts must reflect the objectives. The GDP indicates how intensively the productive apparatus is being used, but does not indicate the usefulness of what is produced, who it is for, or at what cost to the stock of natural goods. Environmental disasters, the increase of diseases, and the restriction of access to free goods all count as an increase in the GDP. The HDI has already been a huge step forward, but we need to move towards an integrated accounting of the actual results of our efforts, and particularly the allocation of financial resources for development that is not only economically viable but also socially fair and environmentally sustainable.

The methodologies exist and have already been partially used in several countries, sectors, or studies. The expansion of international indicators such as the HDI, the generalization of national indicators such as the Calvert-Henderson Quality of Life Indicators in the United States, the proposals by the Stiglitz/Sen/Fitoussi Commission, the GNH movement (Gross National Happiness) all point to a reformulation of accounts. The adoption in all cities of local indicators of quality of life—see, for example the Jacksonville Quality of Life Progress Indicators, or the IRBEM indicators of the "Nossa Sao Paulo" movement—has become crucial today to assess what really matters: sustainable development and the result in terms of the population's quality of life. Much more important than measuring the *output*, is measuring the *outcome*.[109]

3: Ensure basic income

Critical poverty is the greater drama, both for the suffering it causes in itself and for its articulation with the environmental dramas, the lack of access to knowledge, and the deformation of the production profile in a system not interested in the needs of those who have no purchasing power. The amount necessary to take the poor out of misery is ridiculous when considering the trillions transferred to financial economic groups in the context of the last financial crisis. The ethical benefit is immense because it is unacceptable that millions of children die of preposterous causes each year. The short- and medium-term benefit is great, as the resources directed towards the base of the pyramid immediately stimulate micro and small productions, thereby acting as a countercyclical process, as observed in the social policies of many countries. By expanding demand from the mass of the population, the transfers will generate economic dynamics that end up covering their costs. It will be a win-win situation.

In the longer term, there will be a generation of children who have been fed decently, which will translate into better school achievement and greater productivity in adult life. In terms of political stability and overall security, the impacts are obvious. This is the best-invested money one can conceive, and the experiences of Brazil, and other countries have provided us with all the relevant know-how. The common theory that the poor will cross their arms in idleness if they receive some help is simply not supported by the facts and the notion is deeply rooted in prejudice. In fact, getting people out of poverty stimulates them, and it is, in fact, great poverty and the corresponding lack of opportunities that holds people back.

4: Ensure the right to earn a living

Anyone who wishes to earn their family's bread should have access to work. On a planet where there is an endless number of things to do—including rescuing the environment—the number of people without access

---

[109] An excellent guide can be found in *Doughnut Economics: 7 ways to think like a 21st century economist* by Kate Raworth. Chelsea Green Publishing, White River Junction, 2017: www.chelsea green.com

to organized ways of producing and generating income is absurd. We have the resources and the technical and organizational knowledge to ensure that in each village or city there is access to decent and socially useful work. The experiences in the state of Maharashtra in India have proven their viability, as well as the many Brazilian experiments, not to mention the New Deal during the 1930 crisis. These are options where everyone wins: the municipality improves basic sanitation, housing, urban maintenance, food production, and so forth; families will be able to live decently; unemployment insurance expenses will diminish; and society will become better structured and less strained. In the Indian experiment, each village or town is required to have a register of labor-intensive initiatives.

Money borrowed or created in this way represents investment, improved quality of life, and gives excellent returns. The fundamental argument is that it ensures that everyone has his place to participate in the construction of sustainable development. In economic organization, it is essential to think not only about the volume of the resulting product, but also about the social structuring process generated. Industrial ocean fishing may be more productive in terms of the volume of fish, but the process is disastrous for both sea life and the hundreds of millions of people making a living by traditional fishing. The focus on the creation of jobs, in all economic initiatives, has to become central. To have a job is more than putting money in your pocket, it is to have a place in society.

5: Reducing working hours

Under-utilization of the workforce is a planetary problem, albeit uneven in its severity. In Brazil, with 100 million people in the economically active population (EAP), we have less than 50 million formally employed in the private sector, and 9 million public employees. What about the others? The figures do not add up. The informal sector is in the order of 40% of the EAP. Despite the great advances in 2003/2013, a huge part of the nation just "make do" in order to survive. However, when people have high-end jobs they do not have a life because the workload is too heavy. This is not a luxury because there are countless suicides in companies where the race for efficiency has simply become inhumane. Occupational stress is becoming a planetary disease, and the issue of quality of life at work occupies a central space. The social redistribution of the workload has now become a necessity.

The resistance to all of this is understandable, but the truth is that with advances in technology, particularly robotics, production processes have become less and less labor-intensive, and the reduction of the working day is just a matter of time. We cannot continue to set our development on ultra-modern technological islands, while generating a mass of outcasts, because it is about balancing access to income and, consequently, balancing demand. Shortening the working day will not reduce the well-being or the wealth of the population, but will shift it to new sectors. It is important that we become more focused on the use of free time, with more cultural, creative economy, and leisure activities in our lives. We do not necessarily need more cars and more Barbie dolls, what we need is a greater quality of life.

6: A change in individual behavior

In this planet of 7.5 billion inhabitants, with an annual increase of around 80 million, every policy also involves a change in individual behavior and consumption habits. There are a number of ways to organize our daily life that require a change of values and attitudes towards economic, social and environmental challenges: such as respect for environmental standards, moderation in consumption, attention to indebtedness, intelligent use of transportation means, generalization of recycling, and reduction of waste. This dimension of problem solving is essential; it involves appropriate legislation and, above all, active participation by the media.

Today, 95% of homes in Brazil have a television, and the intelligent use of this for information has become fundamental. Faced with the efforts needed to rebalance the planet, it is not enough to reduce advertising that calls for unbridled consumerism. The information dimensions of the media must be generalized. Scientific media has virtually disappeared and the news dwells on the attractiveness of crime and Hollywood/Bollywood, when actually we vitally need a population informed about the real challenges it faces. Much of the change in individual behavior also depends upon public actions: people will not leave the car at home (or give up on having one altogether) if there is no adequate public transport, they will not recycle if there are no corresponding systems for collection, and so on. We need public policies to change individual behavior.

7: Rationalize financial intermediation systems

The final allocation of financial resources is no longer organized according to the end- uses—to spur and guide economic and social activities—but instead suits the purpose of financial intermediaries themselves. This is financialization. Credit activity is always a public activity, whether within the framework of public institutions or within that of private banks that work with money from the public and, therefore, need a charter that authorizes them to make money from other's money. The financial crisis of 2008 has clearly shown the chaos generated by the absence of reliable regulatory mechanisms in this sector. In the last two decades, we have jumped from bubble to bubble, from crisis to crisis, without a balance of power allowing the reformulation of the regulatory system in accordance with the systemic productivity of resources. As long as a more favorable balance of power is not generated, we must battle for effective financial regulation. Money is not more productive where it yields more to the intermediary and we must seek the systemic productivity of a resource that is public.

South Korea has opened a $36 billion plan to finance public transportation and energy alternatives, generating 960,000 jobs. The positive impact is environmental by reducing emissions, it is anti-cyclical by stimulating demand, it is social by reducing unemployment and generating income, and it is technological by innovations it implements in search of cleaner production processes. It even has an impact that is seldom considered, which is the reduction of the time that people waste in transportation. This is, of course, a matter of public funding, since commercial banks would not have this concern or systemic outlook. Ultimately, resources must be made more accessible so that the objectives of their use are more systemically productive and aim for a more inclusive and sustainable development. Financial intermediation is a means, not an end. In the Brazilian case, this takes the form of a legalized loan-sharking system.

8: Taxation of speculative transactions

One of the most frequently suggested alternatives is the taxation of speculative transactions. In line with James Tobin's old proposal, a rate of, for example, 0.20% on each transaction would drastically reduce the profitability of those who are engaged in the constant movement of capital. This is an action presented by speculators as increasing market fluidity, when in reality it generates herd behavior that throws stock and commodity prices up and down, while disrupting any organized production planning and productive investment activities. A second important effect of such a rate is that all transactions would be recorded, which would drastically reduce the immense volumes of illegal movements: in particular tax evasion and the use of tax havens. This is a necessary, if not sufficient, measure for the disintermediation of transactions. It would also reduce the various types of leveraged activities that, today, are the main engine of financial institutions. Generating transparency is essential because there is no reason to hide honest earnings.

Among other intermediaries, special attention needs to be paid to those who earn only in the flows via securities that represent rights over other securities and who profits the most from maximizing flows because they are paid by commissions on the volume of transactions. They generate, therefore, volatility and instability, with the monumental volumes that leads, for example, to derivative values in the order of hundreds of trillions of dollars, for a world GDP of 80 trillion. Speculative intermediation—unlike the intermediation of purchases and sales between producers and end users—only worsens inequality and insecurity, while disrupting markets and economic policies.

9: Rethinking the logic of tax systems

A tax policy with balanced collection and which redirects the investment of resources is one of the fundamental instruments available, especially since it can be promoted by democratic mechanisms. The central point is not to reduce taxes, but to charge in a socially fair manner and guarantee an environmentally productive allocation. The taxation of speculative transactions (national or international) should generate funds to ensure funding for essential social and environmental investments. The tax on large fortunes is now crucial in order to reduce the political power of economic dynasties (1% of the world's families own more assets than the remaining 99%). The inheritance tax is fundamental to allow a more balanced sharing for successive generations. Income tax must gain more weight in relation to indirect taxes, with rates that effectively allow the redistribution of income. In particular, we must tax unproductive capital, because as long as financial transactions yield more than investing in production, the system will remain blocked: money, naturally goes to where it earns the most.

It is important to remember that, in general, the great fortunes of the globe are not tied to the planet's increase of productive capacities, but to the greater acquisition of companies by a single group. This generates an increasingly unstable and less governable pyramid of crossed properties and empires where the major struggle is for control of financial, political, and media power. The tax system must be reformulated in an anti-cyclical direction, so that it favors productive activities and penalizes the speculative ones. It must also be directed towards greater social balance by being strongly progressive and center on environmental protection by taxing toxic emissions that bring about climate change and other disruptions.

Particular attention should be paid to greenhouse gas emission rates, which should play an important role in fund-raising, and may provide resources of prime importance to creating environmental balance. It is becoming clear that the carbon market is simply not sufficient as an emission deterrent mechanism. To establish rates on emissions— already enforced in Sweden, Norway, and Italy—is technically simple, and their widespread use allows private or industrial users to incorporate into their economic decisions the actual indirect costs generated for the entire society, including future generations.

10: Rethinking budget logic

The redistributive power of the State is great and this is evidence through the policies it implements: for example, investments in infrastructure and social policies such as health, education, sanitation, and others that enhance the level of collective consumptions, well as those it can foster, such as energy options, digital inclusion, and so forth. Redistributive policies that involve wages, pensions, credit, pricing, exchange rates, and employment are also fundamental.

The strong presence of corporations alongside political power is one of the main obstacles to balance the allocation of resources. The key is to ensure that all proposals for allocating resources are analyzed under a triple economic, social, and environmental approach. In the Brazilian case, social policies ("Bolsa Família", social security policies, etc.) have shown that relatively limited amounts of resources are incomparably more productive when they reach the "base of the pyramid". They reduce critical situations and consequently increase quality of life, while stimulating economic activities induced by local demand. Here, economic democratization is essential. The appropriation of decision-making mechanisms for allocating public resources is at the core of corruption processes, involving large corporate caucuses of representatives that are, in turn, anchored in the private financing of electoral campaigns.

11: Facilitate access to sustainable knowledge and technology

The effective participation of the population in the transition to sustainable development involves a dense system of free and public access to the necessary information. The planetary connectivity provided by new technologies enables a broad direct access route. The cost-benefit of generalized digital inclusion is simply awesome because it lightens the load for higher administrative jurisdictions, as communities with access to information become subjects of their own development. The speed of appropriation of this type of technology, even in the poorest regions, can be seen in the propagation of cell phones. The productive impact is immense for small producers who have direct access to markets both with regard to supplies and consumption; thereby escaping the various systems of commercial and financial intermediaries. Generalized digital inclusion is a powerful vector of a process of change that is indispensable today.

The world often forgets that two billion people still cook with firewood; this is an area where there are significant innovations in caloric utilization through improved stoves. Technologies such as the cistern system from the Northeast of Brazil, the use of biomass, less aggressive crop protection systems, and so on are all vectors for changing the culture of production processes. The creation of networks of online technological development centers, with ample capacities, can be found in India, where nuclei were created in practically all the villages of the country. We need to make patent systems more flexible. Access to information is mandatory for the technological changes required by sustainable development. The main factor of production today is knowledge. And knowledge, contrary to physical supplies, is a factor of production where consumption does not reduce an inventory but rather grows it. We are entering a new logic of economic organization: the knowledge economy, where collaborative logic is more powerful and productive than sheer competition.

12: Democratizing communication

Communication is one of the areas that has shown the greatest advances, in terms of its relative weight in the transformation of society. We are permanently surrounded by messages. Our children spend hours exposed to ostensible or disguised advertising. The communication industry, with its fantastic international and national concentration—and its growing interaction between the two levels—has generated a lifestyle shaping machine: an obsessive consumerism that strengthens elitism, inequalities, and waste of resources as a symbol of success. The circular system allows costs to be embedded in the prices of products we buy, and we are surrounded by a permanent flood of silly messages paid for from our pockets. More recently, corporations use this approach to create a good image of themselves, to present themselves as sustainable and, more broadly, as good people.

The electromagnetic spectrum in which messages navigate is public, and access to intelligent, free information for the entire planet is quite viable. Gradually expanding the myriad alternative forms of media that pop up everywhere, there is a way to introduce a new culture, other outlooks on the world, diverse and non-pasteurized culture, and pluralism rather than religious or commercial fundamentalisms. The corporate giants of communication are producing an uninformed and insecure society, which is a sure formula for political chaos. The radical decentralization and democratization of the media will liberate the vast regional and local potential for creativity, thereby reversing the widespread pasteurization that prevails today.

13: Redeem the public planning capabilities

A population of 7.5 billion, which increases by 80 million each year, creates pressure on natural resources, explosive inequalities, and a chaotic financial system; this means that we must go back to planning as a necessary governance tool. It is no longer a question of the eternal ideological dispute over the dominance of the State or the private realm, but an understanding that in the mixed society that actually exists, the business, public, and civil society spheres must build a new social context for common welfare. Centralized and state-controlled planning has shown its shortcomings, but without democratic planning, which creates consensus and synergies between the different agents involved, there is no perspective for the governance we need. In the context of the current challenges, we do not lack resources but rather the instruments to use them in a more organized way. Economic, social, and environmental planning is a necessary condition for a more democratic decision-making process, by publicizing the development options beforehand and allowing them to be discussed. The tremendous progress that has already been achieved regarding the technical ability to organize information and to make it available to all levels of society opens up a wide range of opportunities for a system of resource allocation that is simultaneously centered on common welfare, economic democracy, and management efficiency.

The list of proposals and suggestions can, of course, be expanded. The most encouraging is the impressive multiplication of initiatives in the areas of technology, local management systems, the expansion of organized social movements, solidarity economy initiatives, the use of the Internet to democratize knowledge, the discovery of new forms of less aggressive production, and more balanced forms of access to resources. As such, Brazil has shown that to build a more dignified life for the "grassroots" and the two-thirds of the population relegated to the fringe of society, does not entail any tragedies for the rich. On the contrary, in a more balanced society, everyone will live better. The battle of the elite to block redistribution and to concentrate more privileges only causes chaos for all.

***

Carlos Lopes is a former UN Under-Secretary General, in charge of UNITAR in Geneva (www.unitar.org) and the UN Leadership School in Turin (www.unssc.org). He is a specialist in development in the Institute of Higher International Studies and Development at the University of Geneva, and a PhD in History from the University of Paris 1, Panthéon-Sorbonne. He has an extensive published bibliography and belongs to 12 academic councils. Currently, a university professor in South Africa. The opinions expressed here are personal.

Ignacy Sachs is an eco-socio-economist born in Poland in 1927, with higher education in Brazil, India, and Poland. In 1968, he became Professor of the Ècole des Hautes Etudes en Scinces Sociales in Paris (E.H.E.S.S.), where he successfully created and directed the Centre International de Recherches sur l'Environnement et le Développement (C.I.R.E.D.) and the Centre de Recherches sur le Brésil Contemporain (C.R.B.C.). Consultant on several occasions to the United Nations, he has participated in the preparations for the Stockholm Conference on the Environment (1972), and the Rio de Janeiro Earth Summit (1992). His bibliography can be accessed at: http://bit.ly/4AYaHu. His most recent book was published in Brazil: *A terceira margem - em busca do ecodesenvolvimento*, Companhia das Letras, São Paulo, 2009.

Ladislau Dowbor is a full professor in the postgraduate department of the Pontificia Universidade Católica of São Paulo. He is a consultant to several United Nations agencies, governments and municipalities, as well as Sebrae and other institutions. His books and articles can be accessed in full at http://dowbor.org under the Creative Commons copyright system (free non-commercial access). Contact: ladislau@dowbor.org

GLOSSARY

Surplus value and appropriation of the social product: The exploitation of workers and of the "99%" generally takes place by means of three basic mechanisms: the payment of low wages, the reduction of access to public goods and services, and exploitation through high interest rates. The payment of low wages is familiar to us, it generates surplus value in the hands of the owners of production means. Reducing access to public goods and services, indirectly affects the income of the population: salaries in Sweden or Canada may be lower than in the USA, but indirect wages in the form of education, health, public leisure infrastructure, and others, with free universal access, more than make up the difference. This is because privatized education and private health plans, for example, drains family income. Exploitation through high interest rates, in turn, drains the household's purchasing power, companies' investment and production capacity, as well as investments in infrastructure and the provision of public goods and services by the state. If the interest is higher than the productive impact generated, the real economy is being drained of the benefit to financial intermediaries.

Capital, assets, and wealth: it is agreed that it is appropriate to use the concept of capital as the set of resources involved in the process of producing goods and services; therefore, the financial resources invested in machines constitute capital, as do the machines and facilities themselves, and the inventories of raw material or products—in short, the set of factors that enter the productive process. This allows so-called capital accumulation. Assets are individually appropriated wealth that are generally evaluated as family assets, which, for example, is studied by Crédit Suisse when evaluating the inequality of family assets accumulated on the planet. The basic concept here is Net Household Wealth, (houses, stocks, bank accounts etc., minus debts). Wealth, in a general concept, is what distinguishes rich and poor people, but also rich and poor countries. In individual terms, wealth refers to the same family assets we have seen above. Since in English both assets and wealth are included in the same concept of wealth, the concepts mostly encompass one another.

Finance and financialization: Amyra el-Khalili has an interesting definition: "Financing is to provide a loan for the seamstress to buy a sewing machine ion such conditions that her added productivity allows her to pay for the loan. Financializing, on the other hand, means lending money to the seamstress to buy the machine with high interest, causing her to become indebted and consequently causing her to fail to fulfill her commitment, making her a debt slave." The difference is, of course, in the interest rate: if the burden on interest exceeds what the seamstress can earn from the investment, debt increases. The distinction, in other words, is very old: it is the difference between the credit that finances production, and the usury or loan-shark that exploits. Marx presents the example of "manual weavers to whom the capitalist lends raw material and tools. It is found that the rate of interest is so high that after having completely settled the accounts, after having repaid the advances and added his own work for free, the worker is still in debt with the capitalist." Financial exploitation gets lost in the night of times. Today, with virtual money and new technological systems, it has taken control (K. Marx, Principles of a Critique p. 246).

Asset allocation and investment: If you decide to invest your savings in the bank, your manager will ask you which product you want to invest in. Of course, this is not about any actual *product*, but the creation of the right of appropriation of goods and services that someone else will produce. It is also not an *investment,* but rather a *financial allocation.* You grant the bank the right to use your money in financial transactions, so it is not an investment. In French, the distinction is very clear: an *investissement* is different from *placement financier*, literally financial allocation. It is also clear (but only to specialists) in Portuguese, with the distinction between *investimento* and *aplicação financeira.* Your financial or asset allocation may eventually allow a private individual or legal entity to use these resources to set up a business to generate products and jobs; this would, in fact, constitute an investment, but you were not the one to generate them. The bank will decide what to do with your money. So much so that it can put your savings to earn in government bonds, whose remuneration will come out of your own pocket in the form of taxes you pay to the government. In other words, no extra molecule of economic wealth has been created in the country through this financial allocation.

Governance: The concept of governance is quite helpful in order to understand our challenges. The United Nations World Development Report 2017, provides a useful insight: "Governance is the process through which state and nonstate actors interact to design and implement policies within a given set of formal and informal rules that shape and are shaped by power [...] Depending on the context, state actors will play a more or less important role with respect to nonstate actors such as civil society organizations and business lobbies. In addition, governance takes place at different levels, from international bodies, to national state institutions, to local government agencies, to community and business associations. These dimensions often overlap, creating a complex network of actors and interests" (World Devt. Report 2017, p. 2). The concept is very useful. We know what government is, it is the public administrative machine. Governance is the ability of government, along with other actors in society, to generate a balanced management capability for the whole.

Income and rent: Brazilian economic literature has not appropriated the difference between income, which results from productive contributions, and rent, which is a transfer earning that gains through another person's losses: so-called *zero-sum* earning. No matter how many financial securities I buy and sell, even if I make money in the operations, the country did not register one more house, or even one extra pair of shoes. I can get rich being a good speculator and even call the securities I buy and sell "financial products", but they are not products because they are not consumed and do not generate social utility. In English, the distinction is easy to the extent that "income" is a clearly distinct concept from "rent", which is earning without the corresponding productive contribution. It is also clear in French, with the concept of *revenu* corresponding to income and *rente* corresponding to rent. To make it clearer, Michael Hudson, Joseph Stiglitz, Gerald Epstein, and so many others—and, if we want to go back to the classics to Adam Smith and Ricardo—use the concept of *unearned income*: an earning that was not "earned" in a biblical sense via the sweat of your brow. In a more popular way, this would be the case for free-riders of the economy. It was commonly said of aristocrats who did not have to bother to earn a living that they "lived upon their revenues" or "rents". Current rentiers live on interest and other forms of rent. Living on "rents" is the wildest dream of our elites, but they do not like to be considered unproductive. The concept of financial aristocracy would not be displaced.

Income and Wealth (or Assets): Income is what I earn each year with my work as a teacher, for example. It is calculated as annual flow. Wealth, in turn, represents the assets that I may have accumulated by using my income to acquire goods or to put money into asset allocation. The distinction has gained more importance since the latest research on inequality. Income inequality, calculated with the Gini coefficient, shows a very high rate of inequality in South Africa (around 0.60) or Brazil (around 0.50) and more recently in the USA (around 0.45). For comparison purposes, the Gini of the much more balanced Scandinavian countries is in the range of 0.25 to 0.30. On the other hand, the inequality of wealth is radically greater, reaching something in the order of 0.85. This because the poor consume and do not accumulate. They live in rented housing, for example, and at the end of the month there is nothing left. The rich, after meeting their basic needs and comfort requirements, still have ample leftovers to make financial allocations that yield even more. A billionaire who allocates one billion at 5% a year in any financial security is increasing his assets by 137 thousand a day. Note that inequality becomes a cumulative process, which generates the current surreal situation: 1% of the planet has accumulated more wealth than the remaining 99%, without having to produce it.

Individual wealth and wealth of the country: The distinction is important. If I have millions in the bank, I am rich and I can buy what I want. However, a country can issue rivers of money and there will be no more housing, so the country will remain poor. The real economy requires investment, production of goods and services, infrastructure, and social policies for collective consumption. If the rich only earn money with securities, they are accumulating rights over the products of others, yet producing nothing. As we have seen, this is the main mechanism for intensifying inequality today. However, for example, if a government issues money in the form of credit in order to raise the technological level of family farming or small and medium-sized enterprises, the money issued will be transformed not only into product, but into taxes that will repay the loan. The housewife's tale is an old wives' tale. Here, it is not a matter of spending less, but of spending well.

Leverage: The basic logic of credit, as it is presented and perceived, is that banks lend to third parties the money you have deposited. The difference between the interest they pay you on your deposit, and how much they charge when lending to a third party, covers brokerage costs and profits. However, in reality, banks lend much more money than deposited, and this money, without coverage, has a zero cost. This is, literally, the creation of currency. The German central bank, the Bundesbank, considered it wise to tell the citizens how it works: "This means that banks can create book money just by making an accounting entry. This refutes a popular misconception that banks act simply as intermediaries at the time of lending: i.e., that banks can only grant credit using funds placed with them previously as deposits by other customers".[110] The fact that banks can create currency in the form of credit, often in much larger sums than the deposits, grants the power to leverage. They lend, at high interest rates, money that they do not have and that, therefore, costs them nothing. Lehman Brothers, when it broke, had provided loans 27 times higher than it had available in deposit. They literally issued money.

Surplus: Surplus appears when productivity exceeds that which is required for simple reproduction. A farmer who sold part of his crop, kept what was necessary for consumption and seed, covered his family's living expenses and the wear of his equipment, and found some leftover, has generated a surplus. If reinvested in production, for example, with the purchase of more equipment, this surplus will lead to increased productivity, expanded reproduction, and capital accumulation. However, this surplus can also be appropriated by third parties, giving rise to a set of operating mechanisms by non-producers. A feudal lord appropriates in the name of his right to the soil, thereby generating a rent on the soil. Using a modern phase, what we have is an explosion of the mechanisms to appropriate the surplus, not only in the productive unit through low wages, but also through increasingly complex financial mechanisms. Inflation is a typically broader mechanism as it affects the entire population with a fixed remuneration (salary, pension, etc.), which means they cannot purchase as much, whereas the big producers, commercial, and financial intermediaries may raise prices when their costs rise; in practice, this creates a transfer to the richer members of society. High interest rates are, of course, a similar mechanism, that reduces the real consumption capacity of those who pay high interest rates on what they purchase. The rich buy cash and they use their own money.

The high interest rates for legal entities transfer the profits of the productive entrepreneur to financial intermediaries. Insurance, health insurance, supplementary pensions, oligopolies (think about what you pay for your cell phone), demand monopolies (you have to use Microsoft Word as others do, because you need to communicate), abusive patent systems (in particular in the pharmaceutical area), the appropriation of natural resources (see the role of traders), fiscal evasion (the wage earner is discounted at source, while fiscal evasion is essentially for the rich), ultra high executive remunerations, and extortion bonuses in large

---

[110] Bundesbank, *How money is created* April 25, 2017: https://www.bundesbank.de/Redaktion/EN/Topics/2017/2017_04_25_how_money_is_created.html

economic groups are all mechanisms that largely navigate the erosion of competition, misinformation of the population, and laws that protect the intermediary more than the producer. Understanding who appropriates the social surplus, with what mechanisms, to what amount, and with what impact on the economy, society, and the environment, has become essential. We must ensure a reasonable proportionality between who produces the surplus and who appropriates it. Social productivity results from the productive allocation of resources. The rentierism today penetrates in the most varied dimensions of our daily life, and sucks up our resources.

Unearned income (rent): A concept that, similar to the term *renta,* in Portuguese, defines earnings without a productive counterpart, but even more explicitly. In English, the unearned income concept is quite clear in that "unearned" implies a lack of merit. In reality, it is a matter of obtaining earnings and, therefore, rights over products. Products, incidentally, that are the result of other's work. This type of earning characterizes rent (unlike income, see above). Income comes from the productive contribution of the economic agent. This distinction is fundamental in order to understand the main deformation factor in today's economy, which is financialization. There are researchers in Brazil who use the concept of "*rentismo*" that result from gains without a productive counterpart to differentiate it from "*renda*", meaning income. Joseph Stiglitz proposes a definition of Rent-Seeking: "The practice of obtaining wealth not through economically valid activity but by extracting it from others, often by exploitation. Examples include a monopoly that overcharges for its products (monopoly revenues) or pharmaceutical companies that get Congress to pass a law that allows them to charge very high prices, as well as to provide less goods, services and effective innovation in the market" (Stiglitz, *Rewriting the Rules*, p. 14).

References

ABECS – Associação Brasileira de Empresas de Cartões de Crédito e Serviços - http://www.abecs.org.br/indicadores-de-mercado

Addis Ababa Action Agenda of the Third International Conference on Financing Development (AAAA) – UN – 2015 - https://sustainabledevelopment.un.org/frameworks/addisababaactionagenda

Alperovitz, Gar and Lew Daly, *Unjust deserts: How the Rich Are Taking Our Common Inheritance* – The New Press, New York, 2008

ANEFAC, Relatório sobre juros, tabelas das páginas 2, 3 e 5 http://www.anefac.com.br/uploads/arquivos/20147151531143 81.pdf ;

ANFIP/FENAFISCO – *A Reforma Tributária Necessária* – Brasilia 2018, 804 p. - http://plataformapoliticasocial.com.br/wp-content/uploads/2018/05/REFORMA-TRIBUTARIA-SOLIDARIA.pdf

Aron, Jacob - Capitalism's hidden web of power - *New Scientist, 23 May 2015* file:///C:/Users/Ladislau%20Dowbor/Downloads/Unravelling%20capitalism's%20hidden%20networks%20of%20power%20_%20New%20Scientist.pdf

Banco Central do Brasil – BCB/DEPEC - 2015 https://www3.bcb.gov.br/sgspub/localizarseries/localizarSeries.do?method=prepararTelaLocalizarSeries. Acesso em 03/06/2015.

Banco Central do Brasil – *Histórico da taxa de juros* – Selic - http://www.bcb.gov.br/?COPOMJUROS, 2014

BBC - *Deutsche Bank Reveals Radical Restructuring Plan* - 19 Oct. 2015 - http://www.bbc.com/news/business-34567868?ocid=global_bbccom_email_19102015_business

Bastos, Pedro Paulo Zahlut – *O que diz o PIB 2016* – Carta Capital, IHU – March 2017 - http://www.ihu.unisinos.br/565552-o-que-diz-o-pib-de-2016

Belluzzo, Luiz Gonzaga e Gabriel Galípoli – *Manda quem pode, obedece quem tem prejuízo* – FACAMP, Contracorrrente, São Paulo 2017

Belluzzo, Luiz Gonzaga de Mello, e Pedro Zahlut Bastos (Orgs.) – *Austeridade para quem?* Carta Maior e Friedrich Ebert Stiftung, São Paulo 2016, 352 p. http://cartamaior.com/_a/docs/2016/02/15.pdf

BIS Quarterly Review, June 2013, p.3 - http://www.bis.org/publ/qtrpdf/r_qt1306.pdf

Bradshaw, Samantha and Philip N. Howard – *A Global Inventory of Organized Social Media Manipulation,* University of Oxford, 2018 http://comprop.oii.ox.ac.uk/wp-content/uploads/sites/93/2018/07/ct2018.pdf

Brown, Ellen – *The Public Bank solution* – Third Millenium Press, Louisiana, 2013

Bundesbank – *How money is created* - April 25, 2017 - https://www.bundesbank.de/Redaktion/EN/Topics/2017/2017_04_25_how_money_is_created.html

Campello, Teresa, e Pablo Gentili - *Faces da desigualdade no Brasil,* novembro 2017 - http://209.177.156.169/libros/Faces_da_desigualdade_no_brasil.pdf

Castro, Jorge Abrahão de, - *Política social no Brasil: direito social, distribuição de renda e crescimento econômico* – Ipea, Brasilia 2013

Coletivo de economistas - *Austeridade e Retrocesso,* October 2016, 50p, available at http://brasildebate.com.br/wp-content/uploads/Austeridade-e-Retrocesso.pdf

Corporate Research Project – *Corporate Rap Sheet* - http://www.corp-research.org/credit-suisse (database on corporate criminality)

Costas, Ruth - *Porque os bancos brasileiros lucram tanto* - BBC Brasil in São Paulo – March 23, 2015 http://www.bbc.co.uk/portuguese/noticias/2015/03/150323_bancos_lucros_ru

Crédit Suisse – *Global Wealth Report 2016* - https://www.credit-suisse.com/us/en/about-us/research/research-institute/news-and-videos/articles/news-and-expertise/2016/11/en/the-global-wealth-report-2016.html

Cruz, Elaine Patricia da - *Entenda o financiamento de campanha no Brasil* - Revista Exame, June 8, 2010

DCI – *Metade do consumo é financiada por cartões* – August 20, 2014, p. B1 - https://www.google.com.br/search?q=metade+do+consumo+%C3%A9+financiada+por+cart%C3%B5es&ie=utf-8&oe=utf-8&client=firefox-b&gws_rd=cr&ei=dFaCWIaMF8aYwgSywZbwBw

Dowbor, Ladislau – *A captura do poder pelo sistema corporativo,* 2016, http://dowbor.org/2016/06/a-captura-do-poder-pelo-sistema-corporativo.html/

Dowbor, Ladislau – *Economic Democracy: a Brazilian Perspective* – Lambert Academic Publishing, Saarbrucken, 2014

Dowbor, Ladislau – *Os estranhos caminhos do nosso dinheiro* - Fundação Perseu Abramo, São Paulo 2015 - http://dowbor.org/blog/wp-content/uploads/2012/06/13-Descaminhos-do-dinheiro-público-16-julho.doc

Dowbor, Ladislau – *Os irresponsáveis no poder: desmontando o conto da dona de casa* - Nov. 2016, 4 p., - http://dowbor.org/2016/11/dowbor-os-irresponsaveis-no-poder-desmontando-o-conto-da-dona-de-casa-novembro-2016.html/

Dowbor, Ladislau – *Resgatando o potencial do sistema financeiro no país* – outubro 2015, 39p. - http://dowbor.org/2015/10/ladislau-dowbor-resgatando-o-potencial-financeiro-do-pais-31p-junho-2015-texto-provisorio-em-construcao-ampliacao-do-artigo-sobre-o-sistema-financeiro-julho-2015-31p.html/

Dowbor, Ladislau - *Os estranhos caminhos do nosso dinheiro,* FPA, São Paulo, 2013, 70p. - http://www.fpabramo.org.br/forum2013/wp-content/uploads/2013/12/colecaooquesaber-01.pdf

Economist – Giants of global finance are in trouble – *The Economist,* March 7th 2015 http://www.economist.com/news/finance-and-economics/21645807-giants-global-finance-are-trouble-world-pain

Economist, Dec. 7th 2013 – *The rise of BlackRock*, http://www.economist.com/news/leaders/21591174-25-years-blackrock-has-become-worlds-biggest-investor-its-dominance-problem

Economist, Feb. 16th, 2013 - The missing $20 trillion, *Special Report on Offshore Finance*

Epstein, Gerald and Juan Antonio Montecino – *Overcharged: the high cost of high finance* – The Roosevelt Institute, July 2016 – http://rooseveltinstitute.org/overcharged-high-cost-of-high-finance/

Fagnani, Eduardo – *Previdência* – Interview in Carta Capital – March 17, 2017 https://www.cartacapital.com.br/politica/eduardo-fagnani-o-deficit-da-previdencia-e-uma-pos-verdade

Farias, Lindbergh – *Imposto sobre lucros e dividendos* – Notícias do Senado, 2015 - https://www12.senado.leg.br/noticias/materias/2015/09/14/imposto-sobre-lucros-e-dividendos-geraria-r-43-bi-ao-ano-diz-estudo

Furtado, Celso – *Para onde caminhamos?* – article published in JB Nov.14, 2004 http://www.centrocelsofurtado.org.br/arquivos/image/201411191728100.Dossier%20CF%2020%20nov%202014%20ArtigoJBNovembro2004.pdf

Khalili, el-, Amyra - IHU/Unisinos Feb.11, 2107 http://www.ihu.unisinos.br/564769-a-construcao-de-outro-modelo-de-financas-depende-de-uma-estrategia-socioambiental-artigo-de-amyra-el-khalili

Global Environment Facility (GEF) – *Global Commons: the opportunity of the commons* – Washington, 2017 https://www.thegef.org/sites/default/files/publications/GEF_GlobalCommonArticles_CRA_web.pdf

GFI - *Brasil: fuga de capitais* - Global Financial Integrity, Sept. 2014 - http://www.gfintegrity.org/wp-content/uploads/2014/09/Brasil-Fuga-de-Capitais-os-Fluxos-Il%C3%ADcitos-e-as-Crises-Macroecon%C3%B4micas-1960-2012.pdf ;

GPF - Global Policy Forum – *Fit for whose purpose?* - New York, Sept. 2015 -

https://www.globalpolicy.org/images/pdfs/images/pdfs/Fit_for_whose_purpose_online.pdf

Greenwald, Glenn – *No place to hide,* Picador, 2015

Guardian – January 14, 2017 - https://www.theguardian.com/business/2017/jan/14/moodys-864m-penalty-for-ratings-in-run-up-to-2008-financial-crisis?CMP=share_btn_fb

Guardian – Dossier on HSBC - http://www.theguardian.com/business/hsbcholdings

Odilon Guedes (et al.) - *Reforma Tributária com Transparência das Contas Públicas: a sociedade e o Estado* - http://dowbor.org/2015/04/a-reforma-tributaria-abril-2014-7p.html/

Haldane, Andy - *The Money Forecast,* New Scientist, December 10, 2012

Hanauer, Nick – *Beware, fellow plutocrats* - https://youtu.be/q2gO4DKVpa8 (TED Talks, 20 min., 2014)

Hennessy, Kathryn (Senior Editor) – *How money works: The facts visually explained* - Penguin Random House, London 2017

Hinton, Elizabeth – *From the War on Poverty to the War on crime: mass incarceration in America* – Harvard University Press, 2016

Hudson, Michael – *Killing the Host: how financial parasites and debt destroy the global economy* - Islet, Baskerville, 2015 – www.michael-hudson.com

ICIJ - *International Consortium of Investigative Journalists, 2013-* www.icij.org/offshore/how-icijs-project-team-analyzed-offshore-files

ICIJ – *Luxemburg Tax Files* - November 2014 - http://www.theguardian.com/business/2014/nov/05/-sp-luxembourg-tax-files-tax-avoidance-industrial-scale (for data in Portuguese on |Itaú and Bradesco, see article by Fernando Rodrigues, Folha de São Paulo Nov. 5, 2014) http://www1.folha.uol.com.br/mercado/2014/11/1543572-itau-e-bradesco-economizam-r-200-mi-em-impostos-com-operacoes-em-luxemburgo.shtml)

IEA – International Energy Agency – *The mechanics of the derivatives markets* – 2011, IEA – p. 9

file:///C:/Users/Ladislau%20Dowbor/Downloads/The_Mechanics_of_the_Derivatives_Markets.pdf

INESC - *As implicações do sistema tributário brasileiro na desigualdade de renda* – September 2014, http://www.inesc.org.br/biblioteca/textos/as-implicacoes-do-sistema-tributario-nas-desigualdades-de-renda/publicacao/

IPEA – *Transformações na indústria bancária brasileira e o cenário de crise* – Comunicado da Presidência, April 2009, p. 15 http://www.ipea.gov.br/sites/000/2/pdf/09_04_07_ComunicaPresi_20_Bancos.pdf

IPS – *Indicadores de Progresso Social* 2014 – Summary in Press Release: http://www.deloitte.com/view/pt_BR/br/imprensa/532aa1d16d825410VgnVCM1000003256f70aRCRD.htm; Main report: http://www.socialprogressimperative.org/system/resources/W1siZiIsIjIwMTQvMDQvMDMvMTcvMzEvNTQvNzcyL1NvY2lhbF9Qcm9ncmVzc19JbmRleF8yMDE0X1JlcG9ydF9lXy5wZGYiXV0/Social%20Progress%20Index%202014%20Report_e%20.pdf

Kelly, Marjorie – *Owning our future: The Emerging Ownership Revolution* – BK Publishers, Oakland, 2012

KHAIR, Amir – *A borda da cachoeira* – OESP, FEB. 1,2015 - http://economia.estadao.com.br/noticias/geral,a-borda-da-cachoeira-imp-,1627819

Korten, David – *When corporations run the world* - Berrett-Koehler Publishers, San Francisco, 1995

Kroeber, Arthur - *China's Economy* – Oxford University Press, 2016 http://dowbor.org/2016/11/arthur-r-kroeber-chinas-economy-oxford-oxford-university-press-2016-isbn-978-0-19-023903-9-320-p.html/

Kurtzman, Joel - *The Death of Money: how the electronic economy has destabilized the world's markets and created a financial chaos* - Simon & Schuster, New York 1993

Lacerda, Antonio Correia de, - *Políticas macroeconômicas para o desenvolvimento brasileiro* – 2016 - p. 15 - Artigo apresentado no seminário o Futuro do Desenvolvimento Brasileiro no BNDES, May 3, 2016

Lumsdaine, R. L., D.N. Rockmore, N. Foti, G. Leibon, J.D. Farmer - *The Intrafirm Complexity of Systemically Important Financial Institutions* – May 8, 2015 – full article available at http://arxiv.org/ftp/arxiv/papers/1505/1505.02305.pdf

Luyendijk, Joris – *Swimming with sharks: my journey into the world of the bankers* – Guardian Books, London, 2015

Mattera, Philip – *Crédit Suisse: Corporate Rap sheet* – CRP (Corporate Research Project) - http://www.corp-research.org/credit-suisse

Michel, Anne – Le Monde – *SwissLeaks: HSBC – 2015* http://cartamaior.com.br/?/Editoria/Economia/SwissLeaks-HSBC-o-banco-de-todos-os-escandalos/7/32913

Ministério da Fazenda, Tesouro Nacional – *Resultado primário do governo central* - http://www.tesouro.fazenda.gov.br/pt_PT/resultado-do-tesouro-nacional - Tabela 4.1 - Resultado primário do governo central, série anual.

Morin, François – *L'hydre mondiale: L'oligopole bancaire* – Lux Editeur, Québec, 2015, 165p. – ISBN 978-2-89596-199-4 - http://dowbor.org/2015/09/francoismorin-lhydre-mondiale-loligopole-bancaire-lux-editeur-quebec-2015-165p-isbn-978-2-89596-199-4.html/

New Scientist – *The Capitalist Network that runs the World* – October 19, 2011- http://www.newscientist.com/article/mg21228354.500-revealed--the-capitalist-network-that-runs-the-world.html?DCMP=OTC-rss&nsref=online-news

OECD – ICIJ - *BEPS: Base Erosion and Profit Shifting* – 2014 http://publicintegrity.us4.list-manage1.com/track/click?u=8dc6eceed67f7f012462d0b12&id=f388dc1436&e=d256201ac5

OXFAM – *Uma economia para os 99%* - resumo executivo em português, janeiro de 2017, https://www.oxfam.org.br/sites/default/files/economia_para_99-sumario_executivo.pdf http://dowbor.org/2017/01/oxfam-uma-economia-para-os-99-2016-relatorio-10p.html/

OXFAM - *A distância que nos une: um retrato da desigualdade brasileira* - Oxfam Brasil, September 2017 – www.oxfam.org.br

Pereira, Luis Carlos Bresser - *Juros e indignação cidadã* - Artigo publicado no *Valor Econômico*, March 6, 2017

Perkins, John – *Confessions of an economic hitman* – Berrett-Koehler, San Francisco, 2004, http://dowbor.org/2005/01/confessions-of-an-economic-hit-man-confissoes-de-um-agressor-economico-250-p.html/

Piketty, Thomas – *Le capital au XXI° siècle* - Seuil, Paris, 2013

Piketty, Thomas; Emmanuel Saez and Gabriel Zucman – *Economic Growth in the United States: a Tale of two Countries* - December 6, 2016 – Washington Center for Economic Growth (3p) http://equitablegrowth.org/research-analysis/economic-growth-in-the-united-states-a-tale-of-two-countries/

Pochmann, Marcio, interview, Carta Capital, February 18, 2017

Provost, Claire and Matt Kennard – *The obscure legal system that lets corporations sue countries* – The Guardian, June 2015 http://www.theguardian.com/business/2015/jun/10/obscure-legal-system-lets-corporations-sue-states-ttip-icsid#_=_ In Portuguese http://cartamaior.com.br/?/Especial/O-golpe-fiscal-e-o-impeachment-do-Brasil/Assim-funcionam-as-cortes-de-excecao-do-capital/209/34806

Raworth, Kate – *Doughnut Economics: 7 ways to think like a 21st century economist* – Chelsea Green Publishing, White River Junction, 2017 – http://www.chelseagreen.com

Ruggie, John Gerard – *Just Business: multinational corporations and human rights* – Norton, New York, 2013 - http://dowbor.org/2013/10/john-gerard-ruggie-just-business-multinational-corporations-and-human-rights-w-w-norton-new-york-ouctober-2013-3p.html/

Sachs, Ignacy – D*esenvolvimento, inovação e sustentabilidade: contribuições de Ignacy Sachs* – Collection organized by Editora Garamond Universitária, Rio de Janeiro, 2014

Safatle, Vladimir - *Quem nos governa?* Carta Capital April 3, 2017 http://www.cartacapital.com.br/revista/837/quem-nos-governa-9428.html

Sassen, Saskia - *Territory, Authority, Rights: from medieval to global assemblies* – Princeton University Press, 2006

Schneyer, Joshua - *Commodity Traders: the Trillion Dollars Club* – http://dowbor.org/2013/09/joshua-schneyer-corrected-commodity-traders-the-trillion-dollar-club-setembro-201319p.html/ ou www.reuters.com/assets/print?aid=USTRE79R4S320111028

Shaxson, Nicholas – *Treasure Islands: uncovering the damage of offshore banking and tax havens* - St. Martin's Press, New York, 2011 - http://dowbor.org/2015/10/nicholas-shaxson-treasure-islands-uncovering-the-damage-of-offshore-banking-and-tax-havens-st-martins-press-new-york-2011.html/

Sicsú, João – *O que é e o que produz o ajuste fiscal* – May 19, 2015 (mailing sgeral May 19, 2016)

SINPROFAZ - Sindicato Nacional dos Procuradores da Fazenda Nacional - *Sonegação no Brasil – Uma Estimativa do Desvio da Arrecadação do Exercício de 2016* Brasília/DF, March 2017 - http://www.quantocustaobrasil.com.br/artigos-pdf/sonegacao-no-brasil%E2%80%93uma-estimativa-do-desvio-da-arrecadacao-do-exercicio-de-2016.pdf

SPC – Serviço de Proteção ao Crédito - https://www.spcbrasil.org.br/imprensa/noticia/2415, January10, 2017

Stiglitz, Joseph – *Rewriting the rules of the American economy: an agenda for shared prosperity* – New York, London, W. W. Norton &Company – 2015, 237 p. – ISBN 978-0-393 -25405-1 - http://dowbor.org/2016/09/stiglitz-rewriting-the-rules-of-the-american-economy-an-agenda-for-shared-prosperity-new-york-london-w-w-norton-company-2015-237-p-isbn-978-0-393-25405-1.html/

Stiglitz, Joseph and Mark Pieth – *Superando a economia paralela* – Friedrich Ebert Stiftung – February 2017 - http://dowbor.org/2017/04/joseph-e-stiglitz-e-mark-pieth-superando-a-economia-paralela-friedrich-ebert-stiftung-fev-de-2017-36-p.html/

Tax Justice Network – James Henry, *The Price of off-shore revisited* – http://www.taxjustice.net/cms/front_content.php?idcat=148; Data on Brazil is in Appendix III, (1) pg. 23 http://www.taxjustice.net/cms/upload/pdf/Appendix%203%20-%202012%20Price%20of%20Offshore%20pt%201%20-%20pp%201-59.pdf See also the site of TJN updated in June 2014, http://www.taxjustice.net/wp-content/uploads/2014/06/The-Price-of-

Offshore-Revisited-notes-2014.pdf as well as *The cost of Tax Abuse: the Cost of Tax Evasion Worldwide,* 2011, http://www.taxjustice.net/2014/04/01/cost-tax-abuse-2011/

Time Magazine – Alexandra Sifferlin – *Breaking down GlaxoSmithKline's billion dollar wrongdoing* - July 5, 2012, http://healthland.time.com/2012/07/05/breaking-down-glaxosmithklines-billion-dollar-wrongdoing/ Wikipedia in English is updated for the recent evolution at GSK.

Toussaint, Eric – *Bankocracy* – Resistance Books, UK, 2015

UN – *World Economic Situation and Prospects 2017* – New York, 2017 http://www.un.org/en/development/desa/policy/wesp/

UNEP - *Aligning the financial system with sustainable development* – 2015 file:///C:/Users/Ladislau%20Dowbor/Downloads/Inquiry%20-%20Pathways%20to%20Scale%20FINAL%2020150119.pdf

Valor – *Grandes Grupos: 200 maiores com organogramas e participações acionárias* – São Paulo, December 2014

Vitali, S., J.B Glattfelder and S. Battiston – ETH, *The Network, of Global Corporate Control.* http://arxiv.org/pdf/1107.5728.pdf

Vitali,S., J.B Glattfelder e S. Battiston – *The Network, of Global Corporate Control* –Chair of Systems Design, ETH Zurich – corresponding author sbattiston@ethz.ch ; http://j-node.blogspot.com/2011/10/network-of-global-corporate-control.html ; see review in http://dowbor.org/2012/02/a-rede-do-poder-corporativo-mundial-7.html/

Warren, Elizabeth – *Rigged Justice* - New York Times Jan. 29, 2016. http://www.warren.senate.gov/files/documents/Rigged_Justice_2016.pdf

Wolf, Martin – *Financial Times* – In: Real World Economics Review, September 8, 2016 - https://rwer.wordpress.com/2016/09/08/capitalism-vs-democracy/

World Bank, *Illicit Financial Flows,* April 2016 http://www.worldbank.org/en/topic/financialmarketintegrity/brief/illicit-financial-flows-iffs

World Bank – *World Development Report 2017: Governance and the Law* – Washington, 2017 - http://www.worldbank.org/en/publication/wdr2017.

World Bank – *Brazil Systematic Country Diagnostic – Retaking the path to inclusion, growth and sustainability* - May 2016 http://documents.worldbank.org/curated/en/180351467995438283/pdf/101431-REVISED-SCD-Brazil-SCD-Final-version-May-6-2016.pdf

World Economic Forum - *The Inclusive Growth and Development report 2017*, https://www.weforum.org/reports/the-inclusive-growth-and-development-report-2017